Hands in the Till

Hands in the Till

Embezzlement of Public Monies in Mississippi

James R. Crockett

University Press of Mississippi   Jackson

This volume is supported in part by the University of Southern Mississippi and its College of Business Administration and School of Accounting and Information Systems.

www.upress.state.ms.us

The University Press of Mississippi is a member of the Association of American University Presses.
We are grateful to the following publications for permission to reprint excerpts:
Associated Press
Jackson Clarion-Ledger
Madison County Journal
Meridian Star
Pontotoc Star
Kosciusko Star-Herald

First edition 2007

∞

Library of Congress Cataloging-in-Publication Data
Crockett, James R.
    Hands in the till : embezzlement of public monies in Mississippi / James R. Crockett. — 1st ed.
        p. cm.
    Includes bibliographical references and index.
    ISBN-13: 978-1-57806-935-4 (cloth : alk. paper)
    ISBN-10: 1-57806-935-1 (cloth : alk. paper)   1. Embezzlement—Mississippi—Case studies.   2. Misconduct in office—Mississippi—Case studies.   3. Political corruption—Mississippi—Case studies.   4. Local government—Mississippi—Corrupt practices—Case studies.   I. Title.
    HV6684.M7C76 2007
    364.16′2—dc22   2006027660

British Library Cataloging-in-Publication Data available

I am often asked to speak at continuing professional education programs for accountants and to civic clubs and other such groups. During my talks, I delight in asserting that the best money the state spends is on the Mississippi Office of the State Auditor. It is hoped that this book fully supports that assertion. Often the people who protect the public's interest never get the recognition they deserve. This book is dedicated to State Auditor Phil Bryant and all the men and women of the Department of Audit. They have earned the respect and gratitude of the honest citizens of Mississippi.

Contents

Preface

Phil Bryant became state auditor November 1, 1996, after he was appointed by Governor Kirk Fordice to complete the remaining term of Steve Patterson. Patterson had resigned his elected office after pleading guilty to a misdemeanor charge involving a false affidavit used to purchase license plates for a vehicle. Bryant was elected to a full term in 1999 and reelected in 2003. He is the only state auditor to have been appointed and elected to that office.

Bryant, who is an alumnus of Hinds Community College, the University of Southern Mississippi, and Mississippi College, brought to the Office of the State Auditor (OSA) a rich background in law enforcement, private investigation, and lawmaking. Prior to being appointed state auditor, Bryant served five years in the Mississippi House of Representatives as an elected representative from Rankin County.

The OSA employs approximately 170 people, and many of its auditors and investigators hold professional certifications such as certified public accountant (CPA), certified internal auditor (CIA), and certified fraud examiner (CFE).

The office has eight divisions. Administrative Services provides administrative support to all of the other divisions. Financial and Compliance Audit has three sections, the titles of which explain their responsibilities: agency audit, education audit, and county audit. Average Daily Attendance ensures the accuracy of public school attendance reports. Information Technologies supports the other divisions' electronic data processing requirements. Performance Audit evaluates the effectiveness and efficiency of state entities. Property Audit is charged with verifying the fixed assets of state agencies, universities, counties, and school districts. Technical Assistance provides accounting and legal compliance advice to state and local officials and their employees. Investigations investigates alleged violations of state laws by public officials and their employees.

As stated on the OSA's Web site, the office's mission is "to serve its customers and protect the public's trust by independently assessing state and local governmental and other entities to ensure that public funds are properly received, are legally, effectively, and efficiently spent, and are accounted for and reported accurately." The OSA motto, which also appears on one of its Web sites, reads: "In God we trust, all others we audit." Under Bryant's leadership, by the end of July 2005, the OSA had recovered more than $7,100,00 of embezzled or misspent public funds.

During a question-and-answer session with the Jackson *Clarion-Ledger* in October 2001, Bryant discussed his goal of preventing public fraud. Among the points made in the interview were the following:

There is a need for a law mandating jail time for those who are convicted of embezzling public funds. Bryant noted that during the past five years his office had completed investigations that led to arrest and indictments of seventy-three public officials and government employees relating to fraud or embezzlement of public funds. Prosecutors often plea-bargain these white-collar cases because they are usually based on circumstantial evidence. A mandatory jail sentence of not less than one year would send a message that these crimes will not go unpunished. A realistic threshold would be appropriate in such a law, but limiting jail time to one year would not be appropriate. Any such law should apply only when a public official pleads guilty or is convicted of a felony. Passage of such a law might result in more trials rather than plea bargains because the accused might be willing to take their chances with juries. Also, innocent verdicts in trials would limit the chances of recovering stolen funds.

Mississippi public officials are not generally corrupt. Most of them are good, hardworking public servants. "For those few who would break our laws, we must assure fair and equal punishment, plus deter all others who may be tempted. I want to prevent public fraud, not just keep investigating embezzlement after the fact."

Those who could conceivably oppose the proposed legislation include people who might be planning to commit a public fraud or embezzlement, defense attorneys who do not want their clients to face jail, and judges who might see loss of control in the strict sentencing guidelines.

The following editorial appeared in the December 18, 2001, *Clarion-Ledger:*

CORRUPTION
Officials who steal should do time

Mandatory jail sentences are not always the best approach to justice or public policy. But when public officials steal taxpayers' money, they should go to jail—

no probation, no parole, no suspended sentences. That may sound drastic but it appears necessary in Mississippi.

State Auditor Phil Bryant is proposing legislation that would require jail time for public officials who take public money. The law would require that any public official convicted of converting public money to his or her use in the amount of $10,000 or more would be required to go to prison for at least one year. The law would not allow suspended or reduced sentences, nor would it allow probation or parole.

Even though the Department of Audit may uncover embezzlement of public money, the matter must be prosecuted by district attorneys. Sentencing is done by local judges. For whatever reason, some district attorneys and judges have been reluctant to pursue jail time in cases of public official corruption.

Some district attorneys might argue that they would not treat those accused of property crimes so harshly and are treating the cases as any other. But a public official is not just any offender. A public official who embezzles public money not only is a thief, but also has broken the public trust given by the people to conduct the public's business.

Citizens should be able to have the upmost trust in the honesty of those chosen to lead. When that trust is broken, there should be more than just a slap on the hand. A public official who steals public money should go to jail—period.

In a January 30, 2002, OSA media release, Bryant explained his support for a mandatory prison sentence for persons convicted of embezzling $10,000 or more of public money.

First let's us get one thing straight. I cannot abide a thief. I have put a lot of them in jail with the help of prosecutors like Attorney General Mike Moore. Our agency has been responsible for the indictment and conviction of over seventy government employees and officials. I'll put that record against anyone. There has been one problem with our success. In some instances, corrupt public officials repay the stolen money, plead guilty, receive a suspended sentence, and go free.

That practice must stop. Obviously, some cases are stronger than others. Plea bargains often benefit the prosecutor and the people as much as the defendant, and, in some instances, we take our best avenue to make the entity whole. Others, however, are settlements of political expediency.

I have taken a bold step by asking the Legislature to pass a new law mandating at least one year in prison for anyone convicted of stealing $10,000 or more of taxpayers' money. Now, I know the cynical will ask why the high threshold. Let me explain. Mandatory sentencing for any offence is rare. District Attorneys and judges usually don't like it. Most mandatory sentences, such as for D.U.I.'s, require multiple offences as a threshold. Only the third conviction for D.U.I. mandates imprisonment for adults 21 or older.

Finally, I realize the Legislature is not going to force judges to imprison public officials for one year for giving away a truckload of gravel or stealing petty cash. I believe only a reasonable attempt to imprison the serious offenders without political grandstanding will have any chance of passing. My attempt is not to develop a political issue but an effective law that will guarantee punishment of corrupt officials that are now going free.

It is important to note that my proposal will be a new code section adding the mandatory sentencing to the current embezzlement statute. It does not prevent a judge from sentencing a corrupt official or anyone who embezzles tax dollars of eleven hundred dollars to twenty years if he so chooses. If someone embezzles eleven thousand dollars, a judge could sentence him to ten years to serve. This bill does not lessen current sentencing statutes in any shape or form.

In simple terms, I'm going after the serious offenders; the people who break their oath and steal thousands upon thousands of dollars. These thieves, whenever convicted should go to jail. This proposed new law would do just that. No one could interfere or plea bargain any prison time. That's what I want.

State Senator Charlie Ross introduced a bill in the 2002 term of the legislature that would require a sentence of at least one year in prison for anyone convicted of embezzling $10,000 or more of public money. The legislation was prompted by the case of Faye Moss, a former Rankin County justice court clerk (her story appears in chapter 3). Moss, who pleaded guilty to embezzling $110,000, was required to make restitution and given a ten-year suspended sentence and one year of supervised probation. Rankin County District Attorney Rick Mitchell, who prosecuted the Moss case, said, "In general, I will be in favor of the law." Mitchell noted, however, that a prosecutor with a weak case might want to plea-bargain with an option of an agreement that didn't include jail time. Bryant noted that the bill would not restrict judges from imposing sentences that do not include jail time on those who embezzle less than $10,000, and that it did not prevent judges from imposing longer jail sentences on those guilty of embezzling more than $10,000. Bryant also noted that both the Mississippi Association of Supervisors and the Mississippi Municipal Association supported the legislation.

The legislature passed the proposed bill in March of 2002. Phil Bryant responded, "No longer will persons convicted of embezzling public funds simply repay the money and walk away. Under the law as stated in Senate Bill 2419, they will have a mandatory one-year prison sentence. I would like to commend the legislature for passing this historic bill and taking measures to ensure that public officials, government employees, and any persons that deal with public funds will be held to a higher standard of accountability and honesty."

In a May 2002 interview conducted by the *Meridian Star*, Phil Bryant reflected on his job and the effects of recently passed legislation:

S T A R : How do you like being auditor?

B R Y A N T : I really love being state auditor. It is one of the jobs in state government that you can actually do something, you can actually have an effect. You can stop embezzlements. You can stop fraud. You can go out and find better ways to conduct business and government and make recommendations to agencies.

Last legislative session, we went to the Legislature and said, there's too many people who historically believe that if you are a public official and you get caught embezzling money you can just pay it back and go away.

We went in and said, "We want to make sure it has a mandatory sentence. We want to make sure if you embezzle more than $10,000 . . . in public money in the state of Mississippi and you are convicted, you must go to jail for at least one year." That will begin the first of July.

This means you can't be plea bargained. This means none of your friends in the political world can help you. This means it doesn't matter if you pay the money back. If you are convicted, you will go to jail. That's going to be a strong deterrent for anyone who wants to embezzle money in the state.

We are the only state in the nation that has a mandatory—think about this—a mandatory sentencing law for public corruption. Most mandatory laws deal with drug convictions or maybe DUI. But public corruption? We think that's important.

S T A R : What are your plans for the future?

B R Y A N T : I plan on staying here at the state auditor's office. One of the things I think has happened in the past is auditors have come into office and they'll spend four years or so and then they are off and running for something else. To really change this policy . . . you do so in the legislative process. It takes more than one term. I'm committed to change the way we've done business in the auditor's office.

Here's one more piece of legislation.

For years we've been a reporting agency. We'd go in and we will do our audit and will write a finding that says, "You should make sure you reconcile your accounts." Usually, boards will write, "We'll do that next year." Well, you go back and you have the same audit again for findings. We've had some seven years in a row with the same finding and the agency will say, "We are going to correct that next year."

We went to the legislature and said, "Give us an opportunity to have a pre-audit function." If I go in and the third finding is a substantial finding—by that we mean you can't reconcile your accounts, you don't know how much money you have in your bank accounts—we can go in that entity . . . seize those records and reconcile those accounts.

When we leave there the problem will be solved. What we are trying to do is prevent that train wreck that occurs when five or six years down the road we come in and find out someone has embezzled $200,000 and no one has known about it.

We have the authority—which we will have the first of July—to go in and seize those records. We will go in there and say, "We are going to seize your records. We are going to reconcile these accounts. We are going to make sure that the people's business is being taken care of. You are going to pay our audit fees for doing that. And when we leave here your books will be in order."

Bryant's expectations relating to the effects of the mandatory sentencing law may have been overly optimistic. Plea bargains have been structured in ways that were apparently designed to thwart the clear intention of the law. An individual may be indicted on several counts, one or more of which involve embezzlement of $10,000 or more, and one or more of which involve embezzlement of less than the threshold or other crimes that do not carry mandatory prison sentences. Plea bargains have been made that allowed individuals to plead guilty to the count or counts that do not require a mandatory sentence and for the count or counts that do require a mandatory sentence to be dropped. In several such cases, the individuals did not receive prison sentences. Also, judges have apparently construed a year of house arrest as satisfying the law's imprisonment requirement. In a few cases, individuals convicted of embezzling more than $10,000 have been sentenced to a year of house arrest rather than actual imprisonment.

Phil Bryant appointed Jesse Bingham director of investigations in June of 1998. Bingham, a graduate of the FBI National Academy, was retired from the Mississippi Highway Patrol, where he had served as Director of Special Operations in the Criminal Investigations Bureau. In September 2001, the

Clarion-Ledger ran an article about Bingham in a question-and-answer format. In the article, Bingham answered questions about the work of his office and discussed public corruption.

Responding to a question about the apparent increase of embezzlement cases, Bingham said, "Statistics confirm that to be true. Frankly the number one factor appears to be greed, but we also are seeing a trend in embezzlement cases where the subject has large losses at casinos. The majority of the cases can also be associated with a lack of internal controls and proper accounting systems within the organization. Many times the Audit Division of the State Auditor's Office has cited the lack of internal controls and discussed it in exit conferences with responsible officials. In one particular case the official was told on at least three occasions that internal controls were lacking and he failed to rectify the situation. In the near future, a former employee of that office will be indicted for embezzling $200,000."

Bingham explained how the Investigations Division gets cases and discussed the number of cases processed. "Any allegations of misuse or embezzlement of tax dollars must be investigated. Complaints come from concerned citizens, public officials and employees, audit referrals and the media. The identity of a complaint is strictly confidential . . . We receive an average of 300 complaints or referrals per year. While numerous complaints are determined to be unfounded, we must address each case in which we have jurisdiction."

Discussing legal protection of whistle-blowers, Bingham said, "The Whistle-Blowers Act was originally passed in 1991 and amended in 1999 with the help of Auditor Bryant. This act gives the employee extensive legal protection from retaliation by an employer."

In response to questions about decisions to prosecute, Bingham said, "The Office of the State Auditor has no prosecutorial authority. In the event an indictment is issued on a case we work, the attorney general of Mississippi or the local district attorney is responsible for prosecuting the case. In the event a federal indictment is returned, the U. S. Attorney's Office will handle the prosecution."

In May of 2002, Phil Bryant spoke to the Starkville Optimist Club about his agency's fight against public corruption. Bryant said, "The vast majority of public officials do their jobs well and do them honorably. But there are those who do not. I don't believe you should take an oath to serve and protect the public that elected you and then steal their money. That's just not right." Bryant noted that not only did his staff investigate allegations of corruption but that the Office of the State Auditor sponsored numerous programs designed to help public officials avoid problems. Also, a toll-free telephone line is maintained by the OSA to provide public officials with advice about spending practices and procedures required by law. "I'm here to keep public officials out of trouble," Bryant said. "We're saving taxpayers millions of dollars by preventing situations that may lead to an audit or investigation by our office."

While noting that accusations against public officials are sometimes politically motivated, Bryant said, "We have to weed those out. We have to understand when someone is trying to use us, and we're not going to be involved in someone's political game. That's why we are careful to work through every investigation. I'm not going to talk about the facts of any investigation publicly when those facts may prove erroneous." Bryant went on to say that his stance of "neither confirming nor denying an audit" sometimes caused problems with the media. "Sometimes the media gets angry because they think we're on a witch hunt and sweeping something under the rug. When we're in the middle of an investigation, we often take a lot of heat from supporters of the official in question who know we must be wrong. That's why we have to be careful and make sure we have all the facts."

The Investigations Division of the OSA employs about twenty professionals, all of whom are sworn law enforcement officers. This book deals primarily with the work of the division regarding embezzlement of public monies.

The book is designed to, as much as possible, let the story tell itself—thus the extensive use of materials taken directly from official documents and quotes from those involved in the cases. Materials attributed to specific documents have sometimes been edited slightly for readability.

Acknowledgments

I thank the University of Southern Mississippi for granting me a sabbatical leave in the fall of 2004 to jump-start this project.

While many people provided encouragement and support, the contributions of several in particular must be acknowledged.

Mississippi State Auditor Phil Bryant encouraged me to focus on the embezzlement of public monies and ensured the complete cooperation of his agency.

I am grateful to the men and women of the Investigations Division of the Office of the State Auditor and their director, Jesse Bingham. Without their commitment to public service, their attention to detail, and their dedication to the OAS and to the taxpayers of Mississippi, this book simply could not have been written.

My wife, Dorothy Crockett, served as the first reader and made numerous helpful suggestions and corrections. As always, she was understanding and supportive of my efforts, and I am more than blessed to have her.

Charles Jordan, professor of accountancy and valued colleague at the University of Southern Mississippi, was the second reader; he, too, made many corrections and useful recommendations.

Pamela Massey, who is an excellent copy reader (as well as being my cousin), also reviewed the manuscript and offered many helpful insights and suggestions.

Hands in the Till

Introduction

The demise of the USSR is a complex matter and not to be oversimplified. There were many factors, including a changing world-economic climate. But historians agree that one of the largest contributors to the toppling of Soviet Communism was the incredible personal corruption of government officials. They used their positions, not to serve the nation's starving farmers and factory workers, but to line their own pockets. They exploited the system, nibbling at its foundations until the whole edifice teetered and collapsed from the inside.

DAVID JEREMIAH

The *Random House College Dictionary* defines malfeasance as "the performance by a public official of an act that is legally unjustified, harmful, or contrary to law."

This book spotlights embezzlement of public funds in Mississippi and the involvement of the Office of the State Auditor in investigating such malfeasance and recovering public monies. Thirty-seven representative cases are examined in detail to illustrate how the embezzlements were perpetrated, what motivated them, and how they were detected. The scope of the problem is portrayed with the goal of raising public awareness and indignation concerning the theft of public funds. It is hoped that public awareness will lead to reforms necessary to reduce the embezzlement problem that continues to strain the financial resources of the Magnolia State.

Curtis Wilkie, a native Mississippian and former correspondent for the *Boston Globe*, wrote in his 2001 book *Dixie: A Personal Odyssey Through Events That Shaped the Modern South*: "We are a different people, with our odd customs and manner of speaking and our stubborn, stubborn pride. Perhaps we are no kinder than others, but it seems to me that we are. I would never claim superiority over the people of Washington or Boston or Jerusalem or the other places I've lived and traveled, but I found during my long exile that we are surely no worse."

On the other hand, a 2004 nationally publicized report indicated that Mississippi was worse than all the other states regarding malfeasance of public officials. *Corporate Crime Reporter* released a report entitled "Public Corruption in the United States" at the National Press Club in Washington, D.C.,

January 16, 2004. The report asserted that Mississippi was the most corrupt state in the country, even more so than states with reputations for corruption including Louisiana, Illinois, Rhode Island, and New Jersey. These conclusions were drawn from a report published by the federal government in 2002 that gave a compilation of all federal corruption convictions over the past decade and the 2002 population of each state. Authors of the report summed the total convictions for each state and used the 2002 populations to compute a "corruption rate" defined as the total number of corruption convictions from 1993 to 2002 per 100,000 residents.

The ten most corrupt states were:

1. Mississippi – 7.48
2. North Dakota – 7.09
3. Louisiana – 7.05
4. Alaska – 6.06
5. Illinois – 5.26
6. Montana – 4.95
7. South Dakota – 4.86
8. Kentucky – 4.59
9. Florida – 4.58
10. New York – 4.56

The report included three caveats that should be kept in mind when one considers the findings. First, only public corruption convictions that resulted from federal prosecution were included; about 80 percent of public corruption cases are brought by federal officials. Second, even though public officials in a state might be corrupt, if federal prosecutors did not have the resources, courage, or political will to prosecute cases, they were not reflected in the data. Third, much public corruption was revealed in 2003, but that year's information was not in the data set. A fourth caveat could be added, which is that authorities might be more aggressive and competent in investigating public corruption in some states than in others.

In 2002, the Better Government Association released a ranking of all fifty states based on the relative strength of laws that protect against corruption and promote integrity in the operations of state government. The association analyzed laws concerning freedom of information, whistle-blowers, campaign finance, gifts, trips, and honoraria. Executive Director Terrance A. Norton said, "We chose those laws because they reflect three principles that are central to open and honest government—transparency, accountability, and limits."

Mississippi ranked eighteenth (the higher the better) in that report, which claimed to be the first comprehensive report on integrity in all fifty states. The *Corporate Crime Reporter* study found little correlation between strong laws and integrity, and its authors concluded that "if a public official wants to violate his or her trust, the laws don't stand in the way."

The Mississippi Code on embezzlement reads:

> The state treasurer, auditor of public accounts, assessors and collectors of taxes, and all other state and county officers, and officers of cities, towns, and villages, shall make and keep in their offices, subject to inspection at all times, an accurate entry of each and every sum of public money, securities, stocks, or other public money whatever, by them received, transferred, or disbursed; and if any of said officers, either municipal, county or state, or a clerk, agent or employee of such officers, shall willfully and fraudulently make any false entry therein or make any certificate or endorsement of any warrant, or shall loan any portion of the public moneys, securities, stocks, or other public property entrusted to him, for any purpose whatever, or shall, by willful act of omission of duty whatever, defraud or attempt to defraud, the state, or any county, city, town or village, of any moneys, security, or property, he shall, on conviction thereof, be guilty of embezzlement, and be fined not less than double the amount or value of the moneys, security, stock or other property so embezzled, or committed to the department of corrections for not more than ten (10) years, or both.

According to WhiteCollarCrimeFYI.com, "Embezzlement is defined as the misappropriation of items with which a person has been entrusted. Embezzlement differs from larceny in that the perpetrator of embezzlement comes into possession of property legally, but fraudulently assumes rights to it. Charges of embezzlement can even be levied if the embezzler intended to return the property later."

Four points must be proved to support the case for embezzlement: (1) the relationship between the defendant and the aggrieved party was a fiduciary one; (2) the lost property came into the defendant's possession through that relationship; (3) the defendant fraudulently assumed ownership of the property or transferred it into the ownership of another; (4) the defendant's misappropriation of the property was intentional.

How does embezzlement relate to employee theft? One of the most common instances of embezzlement in today's society is employee theft. Employees have access to an organization's property, creating the potential for embezzlement. How can such theft be detected? There are a number of warning signs;

general indicators include missing documents, delayed bank deposits, holes in accounting records, a large drop in receipts, a jump in business with one particular customer, customers complaining about inaccurate accounts, repeated duplicate payments, numerous outstanding checks or bills, disparity between accounts payable and receivable, and disappearance of petty cash.

A particular employee may be embezzling if he or she goes out of his or her way to work overtime, begins spending more lavishly than salary might indicate, and/or has the same address as a vendor.

Employee schemes that involve misappropriation of cash require taking such money in some manner or tricking the employer into paying cash to the employee. Taking cash before it is recorded in the employer's accounting records is skimming; taking it after the recording has been done is larceny. Tricking the employer into paying the employee cash always involves fraudulent disbursement schemes such as paying fictitious vendors or fictitious employees, paying overstated expenses, tampering with checks, and disbursing money from cash registers.

Occupational fraud is another name given to employee embezzlement. In this type of fraud, employees deceive their employers by taking assets owned by the organization. The theft may be either direct or indirect. Direct embezzlement involves employees stealing the organization's cash, inventory, supplies, or other assets. When employees set up sham companies and have their employers pay for goods not delivered or for services not supplied, they engage in another form of direct embezzlement. The money thus acquired goes directly to the embezzler without involving a third party. In contrast, indirect embezzlement involves a third party dealing with the embezzler's employer and paying a bribe or kickback to the embezzler. Such bribes and kickbacks are associated with lower sales prices, higher purchase prices, nondelivery of goods or services, or delivery of inferior goods or services. The payment to the embezzler in such cases is usually made by the organization that deals with the employer rather than the employer of the embezzler.

The cases summarized in this book show that conditions in Mississippi, which have spawned an almost unbelievable number of embezzlements of public monies, reflect the accuracy of WhiteCollarCrimeFYI.com's points concerning embezzlements.

In his 2003 book *Fraud Examination*, W. Steve Albrecht cites a research study which concluded that those who commit fraud have characteristics very much like the ones that organizations look for when hiring employees, seeking customers, and selecting vendors. A study that compared the characteristics of incarcerated fraud perpetrators (including embezzlers) with persons incarcerated for other property offenses and with noncriminal college students found that the fraud perpetrators had little in common with those incarcerated for other property offenses and much in common with the students. Only 2 percent of the property violators were women, but 30 percent of the fraud perpetrators were women. The fraud perpetrators were better educated, more religious, less likely to have criminal records, and less likely to have abused alcohol and drugs than the other offenders; they were also more optimistic, had more self-esteem, were more motivated, and had better psychological health. On the other hand, fraud perpetrators differed only slightly from the college students. The fraud perpetrators were less honest, suffered more psychic pain, and were more independent than the students. But, overall, the fraud perpetrators were much more similar to college students than they were to property offenders. This explains why a lot of embezzlements, including a number of those documented in this book, are Jekyll and Hyde stories.

Statement on Auditing Standards No. 99, *Consideration of Fraud in a Financial Statement Audit,* was issued by the Auditing Standards Board of the American Institute of Certified Public Accountants. This document provides guidance that CPAs must follow when conducting an independent audit of an entity's financial statements. It outlines three conditions that are almost always present when fraudulent activity occurs. First, the person involved must be under some sort of perceived pressure or there must be some other incentive to commit fraud. Second, there must be a perceived opportunity to commit fraud because controls are lacking, ineffective, or outdated, or the person committing the fraud has the ability to override existing controls. Third, the person must be able to rationalize his or her fraudulent activity. Pressure/incentive, opportunity, and rationalization combine to form the fraud triangle.

In *Fraud Examination,* Albrecht compared the fraud triangle to the fire triangle, which consists of heat, oxygen, and fuel. When these three elements come together in the right combination, fire will result. Likewise, when the elements of the fraud triangle exist at the same time and place, fraud is almost inevitable.

Pressures build on the embezzler and put the first side of the triangle in place. Some of these that provide incentives for theft are personal financial problems, vice, and work-related matters. Examples of financial pressures are greed, money-related setbacks, unanticipated needs, high living, and debt. The vices of drug and alcohol addiction, gambling, and expensive extramarital relations sometimes bring pressures that lead to embezzlement. Employees who think that they are in danger of losing their jobs or who consider themselves overworked, unappreciated, underpaid, or unfairly passed over for promotion may feel the need to get even with their employers. Other factors that lead to embezzlement are a drive to achieve, a spouse who wants an improved lifestyle, and a desire to beat the system.

Opportunity, the second side of the triangle, must be provided by conditions within the employee's organization. Circumstances that provide opportunities for embezzlement include inadequate internal controls, inability to judge the quality of performance, failure to discipline those guilty of inappropriate activities, inadequate information, ignorance, incapacity, apathy, and the lack of an audit trail.

The final side of the fraud triangle is rationalization; there is simply no limit to the way people justify their embezzlements to themselves. Some common rationalizations include: I deserve more; I am only borrowing the money and will pay it back; the organization owes me; I had rather keep my reputation for paying my debts than protect my integrity; it will not hurt anybody; it is for a good cause.

The stories of individual embezzlements recorded in this book reflect the fact that the fraud triangle is a reality. While public officials can do little to alleviate most forms of pressure or prevent rationalizations, they can reduce opportunities for embezzlement. Inadequate internal controls provided the opportunity for most of the embezzlements described here. A brief review of some basic principles of internal control will facilitate the reader's understanding of the conditions that allowed the thefts to take place.

Internal control systems should be designed and implemented by management to protect an organization's assets, promote effective and efficient performance, and produce accurate accounting records and reports. Internal control structures consist of three parts: the control environment, the control procedures, and the accounting system. The control environment affects the overall quality of the system, and it involves management's philosophy and style, personnel policies, and the organizational structure. Control procedures involve proper segregation of duties so that one person does not control several facets of a transaction, authorization procedures, the use of adequate documents and records, physical control over assets, and independent checks on performance. The accounting system should ensure that only valid transactions that have been properly authorized and completed are recorded in a timely way in the proper amount, and that transactions are summarized and reported correctly.

1. Chancery and Circuit Clerks

In order to understand the eight embezzlements that have occurred in chancery and circuit clerks' offices that are chronicled in this section, it is helpful to review the fee system of compensation and the duties and requirements of the offices. The following is a brief summary of the fee system—how fees are earned, some duties of the clerks, how the clerks' operations are financed, and problems associated with the system.

Under Mississippi law, chancery clerks and circuit clerks are elected officials who are paid from the fees they collect for their services. Prior to 1996, clerks were allowed to retain, as their pay, all the monies left over from fees generated after paying the expenses of running their offices. The legislature imposed a fee cap of $75,600 beginning in 1996. The cap was increased to $83,160 beginning in 2000 and to $90,000 beginning in October 2004. After the law establishing the fee cap became effective, chancery and circuit clerks were required to remit to the county by April 15 each year all monies collected as fees during the previous calendar year in excess of their salaries and expenses of running their offices.

The Mississippi Code requires the following:

> After making deductions for employee salaries and related salary expenses, and expenses allowed as deductions by Schedule C of the Internal Revenue Code, no office of the chancery clerk or circuit clerk of any county in the state shall receive fees as compensation for the chancery clerk's or circuit clerk's services in excess of [now $90,000]. All such fees received by the office of the chancery or circuit clerks that are in excess of the salary limitation shall be deposited by such clerk into the county general fund on or before April 15 of the succeeding calendar year . . . There shall be exempted from this subsection any monies or commissions from private or governmental sources which: (a) are to be held by the chancery clerk in trust or custodial capacity (as prescribed by law); or (b) are received as compensation for services performed upon order of a court or board of supervisors which are not required of the chancery clerk or circuit clerk by statute.

The wording of this law has caused problems because expenses allowed as business deductions on Schedule C by the Internal Revenue Code are ill defined and vary by type of business. That is, they include all necessary and normal business expenses. Other Mississippi laws explicitly prohibit public funds from being spent on certain things, and all monies coming into the clerk's possession as fees are deemed at least potentially public funds. The OSA has worked with chancery and circuit clerks to produce lists of allowable and unallowable Schedule C–type expenses. These lists are modified as specific questions arise.

The reason clerks are allowed to receive compensation over and above the fee cap for services that are not required as a part of their duties as clerks is that small counties often cannot afford to pay other professionals to perform these needed services. For example, some boards of supervisors appoint the elected chancery clerk to serve as the county administrator. Such an appointment is specifically allowed by statute.

Monies received by chancery and circuit clerks from certain sources must be deposited to the "chancery (or circuit) court clerk clearing account." Included for chancery clerks are receipts for garnishments, attachments, child support, spousal support, judgments, certain fees in civil cases, and monies that are deposited with the court and held in a trust or custodial capacity in cases proceeding before the court. Included for circuit clerks are receipts for garnishments, attachments, marriage licenses, judgments, certain fees in civil cases, and monies that are deposited with the court and held in a trust or custodial capacity in cases proceeding before the court. The clerks are allowed to disburse monies from these accounts as prescribed by law and are charged with properly accounting for the monies flowing in and out of the accounts.

Monies received by the clerks from the following sources are subject to the fee cap restrictions.

For chancery clerks, monies include fees for filing, recording, or abstracting any bill, petition, or decree in any civil case in chancery; fees collected for land recordings, charters, notary bonds, certification of decrees, and copies of any documents; all land redemption and mineral documentary stamp commissions; any other monies or commissions from private or governmental sources for statutory functions that are not to be held by the court in a trust capacity.

When such fees exceed the salary limitation, they must be maintained in a county account and accounted for separately from those monies in the chancery clerk clearing account.

For circuit clerks, monies include fees for filing, recording or abstracting any bill, petition, pleading, or decree in any civil action in circuit court; monies received for copies of documents; any other monies or commissions from private or governmental sources for statutory functions that are not to be held by the court in a trust capacity.

All fees received by the clerks should be recorded in fee journals and deposited in the clerk's fee account. The OSA prescribed the forms of fee journals for both chancery and circuit clerks in 1996. The prescribed journals have several columns for various types of receipts and disbursements and changes to the cash balance. State law establishes standard fees for the various services rendered by the clerks. Chancery and circuit clerks must file financial reports by April 15 each year with the state auditor. The reports show revenues subject to the salary limitation by type, expenses, revenues not subject to the salary limitations by type, wages paid to family members (such wages are subject to strict requirements), retirement contributions—revenues subject to the salary limitation, retirement contributions—revenues not subject to the salary limitation.

Chancery and circuit clerks are also required to maintain a cash journal for recording cash receipts for furnishing copies of any materials on file, for rendering services as a notary public, and for receipt of any other fees where the total fee does not exceed ten dollars. The cash journal must include the date and the amount and type of transaction. The clerk is required to issue a receipt to the person rendering the payment. Clerks are permitted to furnish copies and render notary services free of charge.

County boards of supervisors provide chancery and circuit clerks fully functional offices and budgets for supplies and equipment. Out of fees earned, the clerks must pay their employees and themselves. The clerks may also buy supplies and equipment out of fees earned.

Fees earned by the chancery and circuit clerks and deposited to their clerk's fee accounts have the potential to become public monies if the fees collected in a calendar year exceed the statutory cap. If the amount spent for supplies and equipment plus nonexempt fees exceeds the statutory cap, such supplies and equipment are public property and belong to the county. If the combined amount does not exceed the statutory cap, then such supplies and equipment remain the property of the clerk. That is, any supplies and equipment bought by the clerks with fee monies become the personal property of the clerks if the fees earned (and not paid to the clerks' employees) do not exceed the salary cap. In such cases, the clerks, in effect, buy the supplies and equipment out of their salaries. On the other hand, if they pay their employees and receive the maximum salary allowed under the cap, any supplies and equipment purchased from fee monies become the property of the county.

The fee system for compensating chancery and circuit clerks almost invites abuse. The clerks have no incentive to manage their offices in a fashion that will result in their turning over to the counties any monies earned from fees. The clerks have incentives to hold expenses to a level that will allow them to receive the maximum salary allowed. But once they are assured of receiving the maximum salary, there are no incentives for operating efficiently. Once this point is reached, clerks can spend more on salaries for their employees and for supplies and equipment with impunity. Another potential problem with the system involves the annual settlement to the county. A large balance may build up in the fee accounts during a year, tempting clerks to take monies that should go into the accounts and use them for unauthorized purposes. On the other hand, a continuing large balance in the fee account can be advantageous to clerks since interest earned on the fee accounts is not subject to the fee cap. That is, the clerks can keep the interest on the fee accounts.

William M. (Mel) Williams, Greene County Chancery Clerk

OSA Investigations Division Special Agent Darrell Chance was honored by his law enforcement peers in 2002. The following is taken from an AP story that ran in several Mississippi newspapers in August 2002.

He's got a Smith & Wesson 9 mm pistol on his hip. He drives an unmarked state car for deep cover. And he takes down crooks that steal into the millions.

Impressed yet? If you're a crooked public servant, maybe you should be: Darrell Chance is an investigative auditor.

"I audit public officials. I spend my time at courthouses and at city hall," the quiet unassuming 43-year-old said.

Although trained for it, he's had relatively few car chases. Well, none actually. And, in truth, he has never pulled his gun from his holster—but he does wear it sometimes.

No, headline-grabbing James Bond antics are not what has gotten Chance public notice, but his diligence in tracking down funds stolen by public officials has. He was recently named law enforcement officer of the year by the Mississippi Law Enforcement Officers Association.

Chance works his magic by getting to the nitty gritty in public records. He spends hours studying payroll and bank records. The Hattiesburg resident could be a part-time librarian, given his frequent use of miniature microfilm checks that banks file away.

Other days he's in the field interviewing people or writing reports—his least favorite part of the job. What he really likes is authoring the story of corruption—putting all of the pieces together.

"I enjoy a good money trail. I enjoy the challenge of trying to find out what happened," he said. "You get excited when you're going through records and you know you're seeing things that that person didn't want you to see."

On a recent sweltering Tuesday, Chance strapped on his 9 mm and covered it with a blue blazer. Months of money trail hunting were about to pay off.

Chance traveled to George County to watch former Chancery Clerk Ricky Churchwell turn himself in. Churchwell was indicted on 15 counts of embezzlement totaling $65,400.

Chance has mixed feelings about seeing the men and women he's been hunting down come to trial. "It's a sad day, but there is some satisfaction," he said after watching Churchwell's bond hearing.

Chance joined the auditor's office in 1981, soon after graduating from the University of Southern Mississippi in accounting. For 16 years he did accounting [county] audits. In November 1997 [actually, January 1998] he became a special agent, joining the investigative arm of the auditor's office after [actually, two and one-half years later] graduating from a law enforcement academy.

His first case was a big one. He helped bring down former Jackson County Chancery Clerk Lynn Presley, who was indicted for stealing $1.2 million and eventually pleaded guilty to embezzling $300,000.

State Auditor Phil Bryant said Chance had an auditor's mentality. "Most people who are in accounting are somewhat introverted, quiet, serious, deliberate. But they're very determined," he said. "There's no stone unturned when Darrell is doing an investigation."

Chance's work on the Churchwell case helped him earn the law enforcement officers award. His job, like much work in the public sector, does not bring a lot of glory. "It's very humbling," Chance said of the award. "It's a team effort, but to be singled out is quite an honor."

Darrell Chance picked me up at my home about 9 A.M. on September 27, 2004. We headed south from Hattiesburg on U.S. 98 on our way to Leakesville, the county seat of Greene County. Having passed a rigorous national examination on fraud investigations, Chance is a certified fraud examiner as well as a sworn law enforcement officer. He was on his way to arrest William M. (Mel) Williams, chancery clerk of Greene County, and his wife, Tracy, who had worked in the clerk's office. Chance allowed me to go along to observe the arrests. It took us about an hour to drive to Leakesville, and on the way he graciously answered numerous questions about the work of the OSA's investigative division.

I inquired about the car he was driving and its license plate, because I knew that for security reasons state auditors had been concerned about protecting the identity of their investigators. Chance said the nondescript Ford was state owned and that if anyone tried to trace the license plate number they would get a reply stating "no record found." I asked Darrell if he was carrying a gun, and he said he was. He said he usually did not carry a gun when he was going to be in what he considered his own "turf," but that when he was on an investigative subject's "turf" he had one with him. I noted later that he had a badge clipped to his belt, but I never actually saw the gun. Chance said that the people he dealt with were usually nonviolent, and that they were usually well thought of in their communities.

I asked about the law enforcement role of the investigative audit division, and Chance said that former state auditor Steve Patterson secured the law enforcement power for the OSA in 1993. Even though they were law officers, OSA agents used to be able to make an arrest only after a subject of their investigation had been indicted. This changed when State Auditor Phil Bryant secured full arrest power for his agents from the state legislature in 2003. Not all investigative audit division agents were required to be sworn law enforcement officers until after Jesse Bingham became director of the division in 1998. Bingham insisted that agents undergo the required training and become certified law enforcement officers. Although the OSA agents' law enforcement powers are generally restricted to matters directly related to their investigations, they can arrest persons involved in any illegal activity that they observe in the course of their duties.

Chance outlined to me what usually takes place before and during an arrest. The suspect is generally not surprised. An extensive investigation is performed before anyone is arrested, and the suspect is usually interviewed and asked to produce documents during the investigation. Suspects have usually been indicted by a grand jury before the arrest. If the suspect has engaged an attorney, the attorney is informed about the plan and is asked to have the client report to a specified place to be arrested. The attorney is also invited to be present at that time. Those arrested are usually well-respected members of the community, are nonviolent, and are very likely to agree to show up at the appointed place. OSA investigators go out of their way to be respectful and courteous to all parties during an arrest. Once arrested and processed, the suspects usually bond out of jail immediately.

The story behind today's planned arrests was related to me by Chance as we drove to Leakesville. William M. (Mel) Williams was in his second term as chancery clerk of Greene County, having been reelected in 2003. Tracy E. Williams is Mel's wife, and she had served as bookkeeper for the chancery clerk's office. Mel Williams was often difficult to find because he had been in the habit of not showing up at the courthouse much since the beginning of 2004. Mel Williams was arrested June 15, 2004, on one charge of embezzlement. He had now been indicted on that charge, and he and Tracy had been indicted on an additional charge of making false entries in official records. Chance was going to rearrest Mel Williams on the embezzlement charge, and he was going to arrest both Mel and Tracy Williams on the false entries charge.

Arriving in Leakesville about 10 A.M., we went directly to Circuit Court Clerk Scharlotte Fortinberry's office, where Chance secured copies of the capias (authority to arrest) and the grand jury indictments. We went by the chancery clerk's office and found that Mel Williams was not there. Then we went to Greene County Sheriff Stanley McLeod's office, and Chance asked if he could arrange to make the arrests in the sheriff's office. The earlier arrest of Mel Williams had taken place in the sheriff's office. Chance explained to Sheriff McLeod that I was writing a book about activities of the OSA and asked if he minded my observing the arrest. The sheriff gladly consented to this request. Sheriff McLeod obtained three phone numbers where Mel Williams might be reached. Chance tried two of the numbers and found that they were no longer in service. Mel Williams answered the phone when the third number was called. Chance told Williams that he was there to arrest him again and that this time he was going to arrest Tracy also because both of them had been indicted. The sheriff said that 1 P.M. would be a good time to have the Williamses show up at his office for the arrests, and Chance asked Mel Williams to get Tracy and their lawyer, if they had one (they didn't), and come to the sheriff's office at that time. Williams indicated that his wife was not there and that it would probably be 1:30 P.M. before they could get to the sheriff's office. Chance agreed to wait for them. Had Mel and Tracy Williams been represented by a lawyer, Chance would have asked the attorney's permission for me to observe the arrest.

Mel and Tracy Williams arrived at the sheriff's office a little after 1:30, and the sheriff and I observed the ensuing events. Chance first read both suspects their rights, then presented them with copies of the indictments and asked if they wanted him to read the indictments. They declined to have the indict-ments read. Chance gave them the opportunity to sign a standard OSA form waiving their rights to have the indictments read. After assuring them that they had a right not to, Chance asked whether either wanted to make a state-ment or respond to questions that he might ask. Both said "no" and indicated they would do their talking in court. Mel Williams was informed that, because he was already out on a bond from his first arrest, he would not have to make bond again. Tracy was taken by the sheriff to be booked, photographed, and fingerprinted. After being processed, she was released on a recognizance bond. Neither Mel nor Tracy Williams demonstrated any emotion during the entire episode. Darrell Chance was very calm and professional as he performed his duties. It was obvious that he had done this before.

Chance secured copies of all documents related to the indictments and ar-rests, and we headed back to Hattiesburg. On the way, I was allowed to see the indictments for the first time. Indictments are not public information until they have been served on the suspects. Mel Williams had been indicted twice on September 9, 2004. One indictment involved two counts of embezzlement; the other, which named both Mel and Tracy Williams, alleged one count of making false entries in official records. Count one of the embezzlement in-dictment alleged that Mel Williams embezzled $4,977 that rightly belonged to Greene County. Count two of that indictment alleged that Mel Williams embezzled $28,244.13 that rightly belonged to Greene County. The only count of the second indictment alleged that both Mel and Tracy Williams were in-volved in making false entries on official records.

Because the indictments did not give details, I asked Chance for more in-formation on the charges. He indicated that the $4,977 embezzlement in-volved Mel Williams simply writing unauthorized checks to himself out of his court account. The $28,244.13 embezzlement involved Williams having the county pay the payroll for his chancery clerk's office, not reimbursing the county, and not intending to reimburse the county. In effect, this was an illegal loan from the county that the clerk had secured. The chancery clerk is the county treasurer and writes county checks with board of supervisors' approval. The activities of the chancery clerk's office are separate from other county operations, and the clerk must support his payroll with fees earned for services rendered.

The false entries story is convoluted. A check for $2,099.50 was written by Tracy Williams on the chancery clerk's court account. The check itself showed no payee and the check stub showed no payee. The check was actually de-posited into Mel and Tracy Williams's personal account. Tracy Williams was alleged to have changed the bank statement in an elaborate manner to hide what had happened. She was also alleged to have written a fake letter from the bank that explained the discrepancy in the bank statement. Mel Williams was alleged to have known all of this.

The fact that Mel Williams had now been arrested twice on the same embezzlement charges puzzled me. I asked Chance if suspects were often arrested for the same offense before and after indictment. He said that this was the first time he had ever been involved in arresting a suspect twice on the same charges. Chance said the reason they arrested Williams the first time was because they had enough evidence to do so, and they wanted to bring pressure on the chancery clerk to do the right thing and step aside. As of the date of the second arrest, Williams still had not resigned.

Special Agent Darrell Chance and I agreed that this whole affair, which resulted in a one-time respected public official and his wife being indicted and arrested, was simply sad. To me it was especially sad to learn that this couple, who were in their thirties, had five children. The only satisfaction either Chance or I could derive from this whole episode was the knowledge that the taxpayers of Greene County and the state of Mississippi would be better served when Mel Williams was no longer chancery clerk of Greene County.

Nearly a year later, Mel and Tracy Williams faced a scheduled September 6 trial in Greene County Circuit Court. On August 16, 2005, Mel Williams resigned from the position of chancery clerk of Greene County in a letter to William M. Hill, president of the Green County Board of Supervisors. New charges were pending against Mel Williams, and prosecutors and defense attorneys agreed to postpone the scheduled trial to allow a grand jury to hear evidence concerning those allegations. Mel Williams had continued as chancery clerk for a year and two months after he was first arrested and charged with embezzlement. Under Mississippi law no elected official or elected board can suspend or remove any elected official, except a tax collector, who has not been actually convicted of a felony.

Richard (Ricky) Earl Churchwell, George County Chancery Clerk

The Office of the State Auditor received a complaint on March 2, 2001, alleging that George County Chancery Clerk Richard Earl (Ricky) Churchwell was embezzling county money. The complaint dealt with Churchwell's handling of land redemption fees. The resulting investigation revealed a sordid tale of chicanery and duplicity that began long before Churchwell became chancery clerk and continued for nearly ten years. Churchwell resigned as chancery clerk in April 2001 soon after the investigation began.

Ricky Churchwell served George County as its bookkeeper from September 1992 through December 1999. As county bookkeeper, he had full responsibility for all aspects of accounting for revenues and expenses. Churchwell ran successfully for George County chancery clerk in 1999 and assumed that office in January 2000. The new chancery clerk began embezzling county funds handled by his office the very month he took the oath of public service. Over a fourteen-month period, this erstwhile public servant embezzled more than $65,000 of county money that came into his possession as chancery clerk. Churchwell had actually been stealing from the county when he was county bookkeeper, and his new position simply allowed him to steal larger amounts of money over a shorter time frame. Churchwell embezzled in excess of $48,000 when he served as bookkeeper and successfully covered his trail until his dealings as chancery clerk came into question.

According to a November 6, 2000, OSA memorandum, Ricky Churchwell used the following methods to steal county money and cover up his actions while he served as county bookkeeper:

> Beginning in January 1993 through July 1993, Ricky Churchwell paid his wife, Susan Churchwell, $2,460.00 from the George County payroll account. Supposedly, Susan Churchwell was being paid for serving as Secretary for the Public Defender. Mr. Bailey confirmed that he was solely responsible for paying his secretary from the monies provided to him by the George County Board of Supervisors for serving as Public Defender. When questioned, the Board of Supervisors and other officials had no knowledge of Susan Churchwell ever being on the County's payroll.
>
> During the years 1993 through 1999, Ricky Churchwell failed to properly withhold the insurance premiums from his pay checks. Mr. Churchwell then paid these amounts to the insurance companies for his (and his family's coverage) from George County funds. The loss to George County is undetermined at this point, but the amount would exceed $3,000.
>
> During the period September 1996 through August 1999, Churchwell failed to deposit at least $11,800 of cash collections for George County that came into his possession as Bookkeeper. Mr. Churchwell covered up his actions by infrequently depositing collections and using a single deposit ticket to deposit a

large amount of monies received on numerous warrants. It was observed that Mr. Churchwell would go for months at a time without depositing any of the cash (bills, coins) monies that came into his hands. Mr. Churchwell would often substitute (cover) the cash collections in bank deposits with checks received from other collections.

During the period October 1997 through August 1999, Ricky Churchwell issued himself at least twenty-three (23) extra paychecks totaling more than Twenty-Six Thousand Five Hundred Dollars ($26,500.00). During this time, Mr. Churchwell had also fully compensated himself for his normal salary. Mr. Churchwell covered up his actions by deleting the records of these extra checks from the computerized payroll system. After receiving the payroll bank statement, Mr. Churchwell removed the cancelled checks for this extra pay from the statement.

During the period January 1999 through November 1999, Ricky Churchwell used at least $4,700.00 ($5,500.00 - $800.00) of George County funds to make payments on four (4) of his personal loans at the First National Bank of Lucedale. Mr. Churchwell was supposedly withholding an amount for loan payments from his paychecks but the actual amount withheld was about Eight Hundred Dollars ($800.00) ($5,500.00 - $4,700.00).

When he became chancery clerk, Churchwell was able to embezzle monies that came into his possession from land redemptions. When landowners do not pay their taxes on time, the county "sells" the land to investors for the amount of the taxes due. However, there is a grace period within which the prior owners can redeem the land by paying the taxes and interest to the date of the redemption. Land is almost always redeemed, and the redemption payments are made to the chancery clerk. The chancery clerk is supposed to deposit the money in a land redemption account (an escrow account), pay himself appropriate fees, reimburse the investors for the amount of taxes they paid plus interest, and record the tax payments, thus clearing any tax lien on the land.

Churchwell would often not establish accountability properly for the redemption payments and then convert the money to his own use by writing checks to himself and to his chancery clerk fee account out of the land redemption account. Generic unnumbered receipts were often given to those making redemption payments. This facilitated the failure to establish accountability because it was not obvious that money was missing as would be the case if a numbered receipt were missing. But the clerk's scheme had two problems that led to his demise. The investors never got their money, and the tax liens were not canceled on the redeemed property. Investors and property owners eventually noted the discrepancies and registered complaints with the OSA.

Chancery clerks collect various fees from fines imposed by the chancery courts and for services the clerks' offices perform. These fees are supposed to be deposited into chancery court and chancery clerk fee accounts. The clerks pay their office expenses, including their salaries, out of their fee account and annually remit the balance to the county. Churchwell was able to embezzle money from his fee account by not properly establishing accountability for receipts and by paying himself more than his authorized salary. Churchwell also made unauthorized payments to himself out of the court account.

Ricky Churchwell was indicted on fifteen counts of embezzlement on July 22, 2002. He was later arrested and charged with embezzling more than $65,000. He faced up to twenty years in prison. Prosecutors alleged that Churchwell started stealing county money the very month he took office, January 2000. He was said to have embezzled funds during nine months of 2000 and two months of 2001. Bond was set at $25,000, and arraignment was scheduled for October 3.

The indictment listed Churchwell's alleged embezzlements during his term as chancery clerk as follows:

Count 1 – January 2000, $1,755
Count 2 – May 2000, $1,357
Count 3 – August 2000, $627.15
Count 4 – September 2000, $1,897
Count 5 – November 2000, $1,715
Count 6 – December 2000, $285
Count 7 – June 2000, $792.72
Count 8 – July 2000, $2,661.26
Count 9 – August 2000, $526.47
Count 10 – September 2000, $1,684.64
Count 11 – October 2000, $1,570.83
Count 12 – November 2000, $9,536.59
Count 13 – December 2000, $8,883.66
Count 14 – January 2001, $6,598.68
Count 15 – February 2001, $11,114.90

Total $65,389.90

Churchwell thus joined the former chancery clerks of Jackson, Union, and Madison counties, becoming the fourth chancery clerk to be indicted in four years, according to Phil Bryant, who found the trend disturbing. The state auditor said, "I think it's troubling, not only troubling to us but the other chancery clerks around the state." Bryant indicated that the fee system itself was part of the problem with chancery clerks. "It's very complex," he said. "It's easy for them to try to manipulate those funds. The system itself does afford some opportunities for an individual who has those [criminal] tendencies."

On October 24, 2002, the OSA issued a letter demanding that Churchwell pay $128,399.34, which included funds embezzled, interest, and the cost of the investigation. Churchwell was arraigned before Circuit Court Judge Kathy Jackson on November 2, 2002. He entered a not guilty plea, and bond was set at $25,000.

On January 9, 2003, circuit judges Kathy Jackson, Dale Harkey, and Robert Krebs recused themselves from the case because Churchwell had been chancery clerk of George County, and they had dealt with him in his official capacity. On January 24, 2003, Chief Justice Edwin Pittman of the Mississippi Supreme Court appointed former Circuit Court Judge Richard McKenzie of Hattiesburg as special judge to preside over the case.

Based on a plea agreement, Richard Earl Churchwell pled guilty May 15, 2003, to fifteen counts of embezzlement while he was chancery clerk. Churchwell also pled guilty to a bill of information charging him with embezzling $48,000 between September 1993 and December 1999 while he was bookkeeper for George County. Judge Richard McKenzie sentenced Churchwell to one year of house arrest and one year of postrelease supervision and ordered him to repay $48,000 within sixty days and to forfeit $100,000 from his bonding company. The bonding company's payment of $100,000 was paid to George County by Phil Bryant on the day of the guilty plea. Churchwell paid the $48,000 by cashier's check in July 2003. In September 2003, George County Chancery Clerk Clayton Howell indicated that Churchwell had complied with his plea agreement. "He's clear with the county," Clayton said.

At sentencing, Churchwell told the court, "I deeply regret the actions I took. Certainly, I don't want my life to reflect this type of character. I want the rest of my life to reflect truth, decency, and honor. I commit to make it up to George County and the taxpayers of George County." Judge McKenzie asked a simple question: "Why?" Churchwell replied, "I took a wrong first step. I have learned along the way that we are not perfect. What I did was wrong. It was something that I didn't premeditate."

The judge responded, "I wanted to know if there might be medical or financial problems or something other than outright greed." To this the former public official replied, "I've had financial problems [he had declared bankruptcy in 1992]. When you put a person having financial problems in a position of trust, the temptation is great. I deeply regret breaking the public's trust. It's certainly not something I'll ever forget. For the past two years since my resignation as chancery clerk, not a day has gone by that I haven't thought about what I did wrong."

Defense attorney Trey Bobinger had given McKenzie more than fifty letters from local citizens asking that Churchwell be put on probation rather than being sentenced to prison. The judge said, "I am most impressed with community support as evidenced by these letters by responsible citizens." Then McKenzie indicated that he considered the one-year house arrest term "a lean but fair sentence."

In a December 2002 letter, Churchwell solicited support from some of the citizens of George County.

Dear Friends:

My family and I would like to take this opportunity to wish you and your family a very Merry Christmas and a Blessed New Year.

As you know, I am facing a legal battle in the wake of my resignation as George County Chancery Clerk. I am sure by now you are aware of the charges pending against me. Circuit Judge Kathy King Jackson has set my trial for January 31, 2003.

My attorneys, Darryl A. Hurt, Jr. P. A. and Trey Bobinger, P. A. are now in the process of settling this matter in lieu of a court proceeding. We are very excited to report that much progress has been made, in that the monies in question will be fully repaid to George County prior to any court action.

Certainly my concern now is the freedom and ability to pay this money back and to continue being with my family as well. My attorneys and I felt it necessary to gather a show of support from a select group of George County residents. I chose a group of people whom I felt may be supportive of our efforts in bringing this matter to a close that would be suitable for all parties.

With that in mind, I respectfully ask that you read the letter prepared by my attorneys enclosed, sign above your name, and return in the self-addressed stamped envelope.

I want to thank you for your generosity during this time in my life. My family and I have continued to put our Faith and Trust in God regarding this matter. He has never failed us nor will He ever! I hope that this matter will soon be over. I hope that this lesson in life for me can result in something very positive in the future. My family and I will be forever grateful for your prayers and support in this matter.

May God Bless You

Ricky E. Churchwell

The following, signed by Rev. Dick Brown, is one of the form letters sent to the assistant district attorney Dustin Thomas and eventually seen by Judge McKenzie:

> This will advise that I am personally acquainted with Ricky Churchwell, and I am aware that he has been charged with fifteen (15) counts of embezzlement in the Circuit Court of George County, Mississippi.
>
> As a life long resident of George County, Mississippi, I do not believe that sentencing Mr. Ricky Churchwell to state prison benefits the county or its people. This is especially true if Mr. Churchwell admits the charge[s] against him and is willing to reimburse amounts claimed due and owing to George County, Mississippi.
>
> Ricky is gainfully employed at this time by PMT, Inc., in George County, Mississippi. He is supporting his wife of sixteen years and his three daughters, ages fourteen, ten, and five. Mr. Churchwell and his family have been faithful members of Agricola Baptist Church for many years.
>
> As you know, Ricky voluntarily resigned his position of Chancery Clerk upon notification of problems within his office by the State Audit Department. To my knowledge, Ricky has never been charged or convicted of another crime and has always enjoyed a good reputation in the community.
>
> I would sincerely appreciate your consideration of my request not to seek jail time for Ricky but rather consider some alternative form of sentencing such as House Arrest. If he pleads guilty or is convicted, he would certainly be considered a first time non violent offender. Ricky and his family have already suffered tremendously. Admitting the charge[s] against him and making restitution to the county should be enough punishment.

The Churchwell case gives a classic example of the fraud triangle mentioned in the introduction. Churchwell claimed to have financial problems that probably created a perceived need. OSA investigators found that his family had for a long time lived a lifestyle that appeared to be above their means, including the use of a limo for a birthday celebration. In 1999, $68,000 had been deposited in Churchwell's bank account when his salary was $28,000. During 2000, his first year as chancery clerk, more than $95,000 was deposited to his account. Churchwell had opportunities as both bookkeeper and chancery clerk to get his hands on cash and cover it up for a while. In fact, when he was the county's bookkeeper he stole *all* of the cash that came into his hands over a period of several months. Churchwell was obviously able to rationalize his actions in some way. Such rationalization should have been difficult for a man who taught Sunday school and served as the treasurer of the local Baptist Association. However, considering the amount of money involved (a total of more than $108,000), the number of individual embezzlements (dozens), and the length of time over which his embezzlements took place (1992–2001), it appears that Richard Earl Churchwell was nothing more than a common thief whose greed drove him to steal.

Steve Duncan, Madison County Chancery Clerk

Over about a four-year period beginning in 1998, Chancery Clerk Steve Duncan embezzled hundreds of thousands of dollars from Madison County. Inadequate controls and lack of oversight by the board of supervisors allowed Duncan to pay himself large salaries for four different jobs, write checks to himself from the Madison County Medical Center and from county funds, and to spend county money in unauthorized ways. Duncan's chicanery began to come to light when the board of supervisors requested that a CPA determine how much money the Madison County Medical Center had received from the county. Subsequent work by the OSA established the total amount stolen. Duncan, who had been indicted on state and federal embezzlement charges, committed suicide in March of 2002. Nearly $400,000 was recovered from the insurance company that bonded Duncan.

The former Madison County chancery clerk was found dead by the Lawrenceville Police Department in Gwinnett County, Georgia, on March 20, 2002. Duncan had served as chancery clerk from September 1993 through August 2001. Federal and state law enforcement agencies had been searching for Duncan for about a week because he had been indicted on both federal and state embezzlement charges. He was charged with embezzling money from Madison County from 1998 to 2002.

Gwinnett County public relations officer Ray Dunlap said preliminary results indicated that Duncan had taken his own life by consuming antifreeze. Duncan's body was found about 3 A.M. Wednesday, March 20, in the backseat of a vehicle where there were antifreeze containers. Dunlap indicated that because of unusual circumstances surrounding the death, including the fact that the body was in the backseat, the investigation was continuing. He said a toxicology report was needed to confirm the cause of death because Duncan had apparently used antifreeze in an earlier attempt to commit suicide. Back in Mississippi, Bill Banks, Madison County supervisor, said that Duncan's problems might have been caused by an addiction to prescription medication. The cause of Duncan's death was subsequently determined to be suicide.

A federal grand jury indicted Duncan on March 6, 2002, on two counts of embezzlement. Both counts charged that Duncan "did knowingly embezzle, obtain by fraud, otherwise, without authority, convert to his own use, and intentionally misapply, property that was valued at $5,000.00 or more and which was under care, custody, or control of Madison County, Mississippi, a local government." Because Madison County received benefits of at least $10,000 in a year from the United States government, embezzlement of county funds was subject to federal law. Duncan was alleged to have paid himself salaries for performance of various duties even though the board of supervisors had not approved such payments. Since each count carried a maximum sentence of twenty years in prison, Duncan faced a possible sentence of two hundred years.

An April 2000 editorial in the *Madison County Journal* shows how highly Steve Duncan was thought of and challenged the motives of his accusers.

D U N C A N : An injustice must be made right by providing details of his indictment

The suicide death of Steve Duncan, the embattled former Chancery Clerk of Madison County, has left an indelible mark on the collective conscience of this county in a twisted tale of corruption alleged but never proven.

For many who knew him and are familiar with his sudden resignation last August and the probe by local, state and federal authorities into alleged "widespread corruption in county government," plastered as it was regularly atop the state's largest newspaper, there is a deep, unsettled gnawing for answers, answers to how a man with an otherwise impeccable reputation could see such a catastrophic demise so quickly.

We contend that Steve Duncan was one of the good guys, somewhat of an insider in the back-slapping good-ole-boy politics of county government, but a man of high integrity who actually used his position as an instrument to thwart wrongdoing.

For example, when a brother-in-law at the time was involved with some questionable bidding practices of the Board of Supervisors, Duncan took the high road and exposed the issue, turning no favors for kin.

During his 14 years in the State Auditor's Office, holding just about every position except elected State Auditor, Duncan was known for his late-night telephone calls to members of the Capitol press corps and others. And that carried over to county government as well.

Duncan's reputation, of course, isn't enough to protect him from the facts; that is, proof of wrongdoing, but we think he was used as a scapegoat by some of the highest ranking officials in the state for their own personal gain. But why?

State Auditor Phil Bryant was determined to make an example of Duncan and his more than $300,000 salary for doing more than one job—which of course the Board of Supervisors authorized.

In a press release the day of Duncan's death, Bryant, Attorney General Mike Moore and others stated: "The embezzlement charges related to money Duncan received as County Administrator, Purchase Clerk, and Records Restoration Clerk for Madison County during the years 1998 through 2000."

Duncan was a scapegoat in a political shell game, we believe.

The actions of the State Auditor and Attorney General give the appearance that they are running to cover their political behinds. Bryant has in the past had a reputation of being an honorable man, but was he used in this instance?

Moore, on the other hand, is a political opportunist and will eat your lunch if he's against you, but having a charismatic personality and wherewithal obviously makes him a good advocate. At the very least, Moore, as the state's chief law enforcement officer, has an obligation to make public the charges against Duncan, since they seem so flimsy and unfounded.

Now few if any believe the indictment will ever be unsealed, but that doesn't mean that decent people can't insist that it happen.

Moore best make the charges public himself rather than, say, have a grand juror speak openly 18 months later, as one attorney and former legislator suggested could happen. Rest assured that this page will not, it will not rest until every single juror has been pressed for answers within the bounds of the law.

Steve Duncan was lily white when it came to right and wrong, and he was a servant of the people, a genius with numbers, someone who because of his personal financial position did not have to tolerate elected public life, although he did to serve.

The circumstances of Duncan's death only cast an ever deeper shadow over what was already largely a presumed guilt for the man on the street. But perhaps the character assassination and slanderous, unjust reporting was simply too much for a man who had some experience with depression as well as other medical problems that were only complicated by stress. We simply can't pronounce Duncan an innocent man and move on because we don't know all the facts, apparently.

But here's part of that press release:

"Attorney General Mike Moore, State Auditor Phil Bryant, Madison County District Attorney Rick Mitchell, United States Attorney Dunn Lampton, and Federal Bureau of Investigation Special Agent in Charge Edwin L. Worthington announced today that Steve Duncan, former Madison County Chancery Clerk, was found dead in Gwinnett County, Georgia. Steve Duncan's body was discovered early this morning by the Lawrenceville Police Department. Duncan, age 47, had served as Chancery Clerk for Madison County from September 1993 through August 2001. An autopsy is being performed."

Why not let the indictment die with Duncan? Why a press release on the day of his death that raises more questions than it answers?

Moore, Mitchell and Bryant et al. should right this horrible injustice and let Duncan rest in peace.

The writer of this editorial simply didn't know the facts. Investigators had unraveled Duncan's Jekyll and Hyde world. Moore, Mitchell, Bryant, et al., had solid evidence that the former chancery clerk had been a big-time thief. The federal indictments of Duncan had actually been part of the public record since the former public official's death was confirmed. The details of the state indictment had not been released because, under court rules, indictments are sealed until served, and authorities were attempting to serve papers on Duncan at the time of his death. The indictment has never been made public. The OSA had made a demand on Duncan's bonding company and there was a possibility of civil litigation. Information about the investigation had to remain undisclosed until any civil suit was settled.

On May 21, 2001, OSA Special Agent Patrick Dendy and FBI agents Brian McCarty and Mike Turner had interviewed Steve Duncan at the chancery clerk's office. Dendy's report on the interview included the following:

We began by asking Duncan about the jobs he was compensated for beginning in January 1999, referring him to the January 15, 1999, minutes of the Madison County Board of Supervisors. In those minutes the compensation for Duncan is documented as being an amount not to exceed $75,000.00 for County Administrator, an amount not to exceed $75,000.00 for Records Restoration, and an amount not to exceed $75,000.00 for Purchase Clerk. These amounts are in addition to the $75,600.00 that Duncan receives as Chancery Clerk.

Mr. Duncan said that the amount that was listed as being for Record Restoration should have been called Comptroller. . . .

When asked about the monies paid to him by the Board of Supervisors for 2000, Duncan said that the Board of Supervisors budgeted him $75,000.00 for Purchase Clerk, $75,000.00 for County Administrator, and $75,000.00 for Comptroller. These monies were in addition to the $83,160.00 Duncan received as Chancery Clerk. In addition to these duties, Duncan said that he performs the duties as Hospital Administrator for the Madison County Hospital for no money. For 2001, Mr. Duncan said that the Madison County Board of Supervisors pays him monthly $3,465.00 each for being County Administrator and Comptroller.

Mr. Duncan was asked about the method by which minutes for the Madison County Board of Supervisors were prepared. He said that notes were written on a copy of the meeting agenda by him during the meeting. If Duncan was not present for a meeting, the notes would be taken by Deputy Chancery Clerk Kathy Gregory. In all instances, Duncan would personally type the formal minutes from the notes taken at the Board of Supervisors meeting. He said that he types the Board minutes on his laptop computer. Duncan said that the Madison county Board of Supervisors meetings are not taped.

On May 21, 2001, OSA investigator Dendy, O. T. McAlpin, deputy director of the OSA's Investigations Division, and FBI Special Agent Mike Turner interviewed Madison County District Three Supervisor David Richardson at the Woolfolk state office building in Jackson. Dendy's report on the interview included the following:

The first item about which we spoke to Mr. Richardson was the compensation paid to Madison County Chancery Clerk Steve Duncan by the Madison County Board of Supervisors. We asked Mr. Richardson about an order in the January 15, 1999, Board of Supervisors' minutes allowing Mr. Duncan extra compensation for Purchase Clerk ($75,000.00) County Administrator ($75,000.00) and Restoration of Records ($75,000). Mr. Richardson said that he did not remember any extra pay being discussed in the Board meeting. He also said that he has a copy of the draft minutes of the Board of Supervisors that do not show that order, and he would make these draft minutes available for us to copy.

Mr. Richardson said that Duncan tried to explain to him that the money being paid to him (Duncan) for records restoration was a reimbursement for record restoration work that Duncan had originally paid for. Richardson said that Duncan may have told this to other members of the Board of Supervisors.

The Madison County Board of Supervisors retained certified public accountant Wallace Collins to determine how much money the Madison County Medical Center had received from Madison County. On August 2, 2001, OSA investigators Patrick Dendy and O. T. McAlpin interviewed Collins. Dendy's report on the interview noted that Collins found documentation that money had been paid by the center to Steve Duncan and his deputy, Kathy Gregory.

Mr. Collins explained to us that from August 2000 through July 2001 there has been about $2,600,000.00 transferred from Madison County's Grand Gulf Fund [taxes received from the Grand Gulf nuclear reactor in Claiborne County] to the Madison County Medical Center. Mr. Collins said that $1,055,000.00 of this money was transferred in August and September 2000. The checks transferring the money were prepared by Chancery Clerk Steve Duncan. The monthly reports given to the Madison County Board of Supervisors by Chancery Clerk Steve Duncan during this time period show no funds being expended from the Grand Gulf Fund.

While analyzing monies sent back to the County from the Madison County Medical Center, Collins noticed that sheets were missing from the Medical Center Bank Statements showing the cancelled checks paid to the County. When asked where these sheets might be, Deputy Chancery Clerk Kathy Gregory said that they were at Chancery Clerk Steve Duncan's residence, and she then went there to retrieve them. After opening the bank statement pages, Mr. Collins noticed numerous instances in which checks were issued to Duncan, Gregory, and Brad Sellers, who is a Madison County employee. On the Madison County Medical Center Records maintained by Duncan, the payments to Duncan and Gregory are posted as being paid to Madison County. Mr. Collins provided me with copies of the documents he had gathered concerning this situation.

Steve Duncan wrote the following memorandum in early August 2001:

To: Mr. David Richardson
President, Madison County Board of Supervisors
From: Steve Duncan
Date: August 6, 2001
Re: Resignation and Other Matters

It has been brought to my attention that while I have been away for medical attention that my and Mrs. Kathy Gregory's names have been removed as signatory authority for all Madison accounts and that this followed a visit to the State Auditor's Office. David, I want you to know that if Kathy and I have done anything it has working [*sic*] very hard and caring about Madison County and being loyal to you. I do not care what Wallace Collins says. Always remember that hired guns make their money be [*sic*] finding fault with those who do the job day and day out [*sic*]. . . . I am sure you will find this out when you get his bill. Kathy and I have been loyal employees day in and day out and have gone the extra mile to see that every thing runs smooth for you. It is awful hard for us to feel that we are that we are [*sic*] not being treated fairly now. As you know for my part I appreciate what you have done for me but feel that in light of all this that it is best that I move on and let you make the changes you obviously want to make, so please accept this as my resignation as Chancery Clerk and from all the all the [*sic*] other positions I hold for the county, effective immediately. I still value your friendship and will be available to help you whenever you need it and I have enjoyed working with you. Kathy has worked has worked [*sic*] here for 18 years and has 2 small children to support and I have left her decision on her continued employment here to her, but know she is also terribly hurt.

I have left all my computer equipment in my office on my desk that belongs to the county.

Kathy Gregory submitted her resignation as deputy chancery clerk and as the secretary of the Madison County supervisors on August 6, 2001.

Apparently Duncan's resignation did not actually become effective until December 2001. In a December 6, 2001, memo on Madison County Board of Supervisors letterhead, to eighteen county officials, none of whom were supervisors, Duncan resigned again. This memo stated: "As you know, my health has been failing for a number of months, and on the advice of my doctor, I am being forced to make a career change, and I resign as Madison County Chancery Clerk and all my other County Positions, effective immediately."

In his synopsis report on this case dated April 4, 2002, OSA Special Agent Patrick Dendy made the following points:

(a) Three board of supervisors orders (March, 17, 1998, January 15, 1999, and January 4, 2000) pertaining to the compensation paid to Steve Duncan for the positions of county administrator, purchase clerk, and restorations of records were not legally adopted by the board. Payments were made to Duncan for each of these jobs during 1998, 1999, and 2000. For 1998 Duncan received illegal compensation totaling $41,133.76 for these three jobs. For 1999, the amount was $179,575.53, and for 2000 it was $194,575.20.

(b) Accounting records for county check 37405 issued to Duncan on April 15, 1999, state that this check was in the amount of $10,000 and that it was for "gross wages for county administrator and records restoration compensation." The check was actually for $21,000, and the original copy of his check indicates that it was for "attending court." The $11,000 difference was removed from the county's accounting records, and it showed up on Duncan's fee journal as a payment to himself.

(c) County check number 50800 was issued to Duncan May 16, 2000, for $15,260.10, but accounting records had been modified to show this check at $10,500. According to the banner copy of the check the total $15,260.10 was made up of $3,500 each for county administrator, purchase clerk, and records restoration, and $4,790.10 was termed a "refund."

(d) As the supposedly noncompensated chief financial officer of the Madison County Medical Center, from October 2000 to May 2001, Duncan issued checks to himself totaling $60,000. He also issued checks to Deputy Chancery Court Clerk Kathy Gregory for $15,000 and to Brad Sellers, another Madison County employee, for $3,000. The board of supervisors had not approved any of these payments, which totaled $78,000. On May 22, 2001, Duncan wrote two checks totaling $62,000 from the chancery clerk's clearing account to Madison County and in newspaper interviews claimed that these payments were reimbursements of monies that had been paid by the Madison County Medical Center to himself and Kathy Gregory.

(e) Also on May 22, 2001, Duncan wrote checks of $32,000 and $30,000 from the Madison County operational fund bank account to himself and deposited them into the chancery clerk's clearing account. To conceal the fact that these monies were paid to him, Duncan recorded these checks in the county's accounting records as being paid to Merchants and Farmers Bank.

In May of 2002, State Auditor Phil Bryant sent a letter to Steve Duncan's bonding company demanding payment of $680,853.62. The amount was calculated as follows: illegal salaries paid in 1998—$41,133.76; illegal salaries in 1999—$179,575.53; illegal salaries in 2000—$194,575.20; monies illegally obtained from the Madison County Medical Center through altered checks—$78,000; monies illegally obtained from Madison County through altered checks—$15,760.10; an exception from a financial audit of Madison County—$11,144.14; interest—$135,615.77; and cost of recovery—$25,049.12. The demand was turned over to Mississippi Attorney General Mike Moore for collection. CNA Surety bonds covered Duncan on three of his county jobs. The bonding company initially balked at paying the interest demanded on two of the bonds. State Auditor Phil Bryant, Attorney General Mike Moore, and CNA Surety finally agreed that the maximum due from the insurance company under the bonds was $397,254.90.

Phil Bryant announced in late January 2003 that his office had recovered $397,254.90, which was the total amount covered by Duncan's public officials bond. Jesse Bingham, director of the OSA's Investigations Division, personally delivered the check to the board of supervisors. Bryant stated, "It is always difficult to uncover public corruption in any form. This was a particularly difficult case due to the tragic death of Mr. Duncan. However, our pursuit and recovery of the tax dollars was never compromised. We believe the facts of the case were clear and undeniable. This matter is now officially closed with the recovery of these funds."

In addition to Duncan's being charged with embezzlement, at the time of his death he was the subject of a corruption probe. He had been expected to be the star witness in a wider probe of Madison County business. The probe ground to a halt with his death. Mike Moore, whose office led the investigation that included the OSA and the FBI, said, "That's what happened."

David Richardson and Bill Banks indicated that they were glad to get the money and that this should end the matter. Banks said, "There ought to be a point at which the dead man can be at rest. It was a bad time, bad things happen, but I think this is the closure of it." Richardson said, "It certainly says everyone is exonerated and brings the matter to a close." Jesse Bingham said that no one else was being investigated. Phil Bryant said, "Barring new information, this closes the case involving Mr. Duncan." Attorney General Mike Moore had a slightly different slant on matters. He said that should new information come to light he would reopen the investigation. Moore said, "It's a mess up there. I hope one day it gets cleared up."

On March 27, 2003, OSA closed the Duncan case, noting that the insurance company that bonded Duncan had paid $397,254.90 on January 15, 2003. As noted above, the money had been returned to the taxpayers of Madison County.

On November 10, 1998, the OSA Investigations Division received a referral against Union County Chancery Clerk Larry Koon alleging embezzlement. The referral was based on the work of OSA County Auditor Beverly Thompson, who had discovered possible embezzlement in her audit of Union County records. The referral mentioned the failure to receipt and deposit all revenue from court filings, improper deposits to the clerk's court account, and improper disbursements to Koon and his family. An investigation was started on November 18, and OSA Special Agent Burt Haney was assigned to the case.

Interviews conducted by Haney revealed several practices in the chancery clerk's office that could facilitate embezzlement and cover-up by the clerk. Larry Koon controlled the incoming mail, which often contained cash and checks, made the bank deposits, and wrote checks. Receipts were not always prepared for monies coming into the clerk's office over the counter. In July or August 1998, the clerk's office began using general ledger sheets to record receipts of these monies unless written receipts were specifically requested. Koon had allegedly told at least one employee not to write receipts for certain types of payments. He also directed an employee to hold a personal check that he had written to reimburse the county for payments to him that exceeded the fee cap. Haney's interviews also revealed rumors of extramarital affairs, gambling, use of alcohol, high-priced clothes, and other expensive tastes.

In early February 1999, the *New Albany Gazette* reported that Larry Koon was at a loss to explain rumors "which have spread like the proverbial wildfire" about his tenure in office. Koon said, "I have not resigned any of my positions and I have not been asked to resign." One rumor was that while in Jackson meeting with audit officials he had been handcuffed at a restaurant and led away in an attempt to force him to resign. "How in the world could all this [have been] started and gotten out of hand?" he said. Koon noted that he had received about a hundred calls in the previous week from people asking about the rumors. Koon had reported to the board of supervisors that the auditors were checking his records, primarily to determine whether he had been overpaid. While declining to comment on the rumors, Langston Moore of the OSA confirmed that a routine annual audit of Union County was ongoing. Moore said that overpayment of fees was not unusual.

In early April 1999, the OSA issued an audit report on Union County listing thirty-five findings that needed to be addressed. The audit report noted that the chancery clerk failed to maintain a cash journal for office expenses, and that Koon had cashed a personal check from land redemption funds. Cashing the personal check appeared to be an illegal loan even though it was later repaid. Koon said, "I didn't realize that was wrong. I've done it for years and don't think it is an illegal loan." He further stated, "My conscience is clear. If I have to go home because of it, I will . . . if I can't weather this I probably don't need to be here anyway." Claiming that he had been too busy, Koon said, "I have too many jobs." (He was chancery clerk, clerk of the board of supervisors, county administrator, and purchases clerk.) "I wanted to get out of the administrator's job before all of this came up but the supervisors did not want me to." Koon's work with the county involved more than forty separate funds and more than $12 million. The investigation into the clerk's office was ongoing.

On June 28, 1999, Larry Koon resigned and withdrew from the August primary election in which he had been planning to seek a fourth term as chancery clerk. Mississippi Attorney General Mike Moore had charged him with two counts of embezzlement. In his resignation letter to the board of supervisors, Koon wrote, "I take this action reluctantly and with a heavy heart. I enjoyed serving the honorable men of the Union County Board of Supervisors and the good people of Union County. This action became necessary after a recent audit indicated shortages in monies that were under my control. I accept full responsibility and sincerely hope that my actions do not tarnish the integrity of this board or the Union County Chancery Clerk's office." Koon faced a maximum of twenty years in prison and a $5,000 fine on each charge.

On June 28, 1999, Koon waived indictment and requested that the case against him proceed in Union County Circuit Court on a bill of information charging two counts of embezzlement. Count one alleged that between March 1992 and April 1995, Koon embezzled from Union County $11,800, the proceeds of lease payments made by Stratford Company, also known as Mohasco Furniture. Count two alleged that between December 1995 and May 1998, Koon embezzled from Union County $30,600, the proceeds of lease payments made by Stratford Company and Master-Bilt Corporation.

The Union County Board of Supervisors appointed John David Pennebaker to fill Koon's unexpired term. Koon's resignation resulted from an eight-month investigation by the OSA. The three-term chancery clerk admitted embezzling $42,400 in lease payments to the county over a six-year period. He repaid the money before announcing his resignation. He now faced two felony charges.

As noted above, when he resigned from office, Koon withdrew from the upcoming primary election; even so, he received more than 7 percent of the vote in the August primary.

On October 21, 1999, Koon pled guilty to the two counts of embezzlement contained in the bill of information. Circuit Court Judge Henry Lackey sentenced him to five years in prison but suspended three years, leaving two to be served. Koon was freed on his own recognizance and awaited a January 2000 hearing, when his sentence would be reconsidered. Joey Langston, Koon's attorney, said that it would have been difficult for the state to prove criminal intent because of the way monies in the clerk's office were comingled.

State Auditor Phil Bryant issued a demand on Koon and his bonding company December 6, 1999, in the total amount of $172,873 for improper conversion of fees. The demand letter showed that this total was computed as follows: embezzlement of monies paid to the county on lease agreements for county-owned facilities (1992–1998)—$42,400; salary in excess of state-imposed fee cap (1996–1998)—$107,180; interest at 1 percent per month from the date of loss—$36,153; cost of recovery (hourly rate for staff)—$29,541; less $42,400 paid to Union County on June 28, 1999.

On January 7, 2000, Circuit Court Judge Henry Lackey refused to reduce Koon's sentence and ordered him to report to the Department of Corrections on January 10 to begin serving his sentence.

As noted above, before announcing his resignation in 1999, Koon repaid $42,400 to Union County. In August 2000, the OSA received the maximum amount payable from Koon's bonding company, $100,000. Jesse Bingham of the OSA delivered the $100,000 to the Union County Board of Supervisors on September 18, 2000. The OSA closed the case on May 5, 2003.

Lynn Presley, Jackson County Chancery Clerk

In the 1990s, Jackson County Chancery Clerk Lynn Presley played a sophisticated shell game with county money, but his ruse started to unravel in 1997. The county port authority demanded access to a fund that was supposed to contain $1 million in bond money. Presley couldn't produce it in a timely manner, and he was unable to keep the port authority from complaining about it. The shell game had worked as long as no one attempted to reconcile all of the county's accounts at the same time. In 1997, the board of supervisors engaged the CPA firm Moore and Powell to perform an independent audit of the county's records. Presley's dealings came to light early in 1998 when the CPAs were auditing the county's 1996 books and found problems with the clerk's accounts. The auditors notified the OSA, and this triggered an investigation by state and local authorities that eventually led to Presley's downfall.

Lynn Presley, who had served eighteen years as chancery clerk, was removed from office in August 1998 after he pled guilty in a state court to eight counts of embezzlement of public money. Under a plea agreement, Presley pled guilty to embezzling about $320,000; the prosecutors agreed to dismiss twenty additional charges that would have brought the total to more than $1.2 million. Presley had used county money for personal expenses and investments. He had transferred funds to a personal account from a chancery court trust fund that held litigants' money and a land redemption fund that contained money paid to the county by landowners who were delinquent in paying their taxes.

Presley came into office in the 1980s as a new face, someone who was reform minded. In fact, he helped the young Mike Moore, who was district attorney at the time, oust some corrupt county supervisors. Prior to the legislature imposing a fee cap on chancery clerks in 1996, Lynn Presley fared sumptuously. Before the fee cap, chancery clerks could legally keep all of the money that flowed into their coffers from fees after they paid the costs of running their offices. They didn't even have to pay all of those costs, because boards of supervisors paid several of their expenses, such as facilities costs. The clerks' main costs were the employees' salaries. Before the fee cap was imposed, chancery clerk positions were some of the most highly paid in the state, especially in populous areas like Jackson County. It appears that Presley had been able to support his lifestyle and many outside ventures before the advent of the fee cap. Apparently, after he became constrained by the fee cap, he started a shell game with county money.

After pleading guilty, Presley told retired Circuit Court Judge Walter "Jack" O'Barr, who had been appointed to hear the case, "Judge, I unlawfully converted public funds to my own use. After obtaining the funds, I returned them." Presley faced a minimum of three years in prison, assuming his promised cooperation measured up to expectations. Each of the eight counts actually carried a maximum sentence of twenty years. "How long he will spend in jail will depend on him," District Attorney Dale Harkey said. Judge O'Barr made it clear to Presley that he was not bound to follow the prosecutor's recommendations, and that he had some questions about the plea bargain. The judge ordered a presentence investigation report and said that he would sentence Presley within ninety days. O'Barr ordered the board of supervisors to take immediate action to appoint a new chancery clerk. The chancery clerk has check writing responsibility, and the county needed to be able to pay its employees and bills.

The board of supervisors soon discovered that Presley's shell game with county money had left the county in a precarious financial position that would necessitate a tax increase. The $1 million balance that Presley told the board the county had in its general operating fund one year earlier did not exist. During his final months in office, Presley had failed to pay a $450,000 bill for the county's sanitary operations. The county would also have to pay the $420,000 balance that remained on a $2.9 million bond issue that the board had approved in 1995 to fund Presley's efforts to computerize the county's land records. Presley had promised to pay off the bonds out of fees he collected, but the promise was nonbinding, and there would be a new chancery clerk elected in November. Presley had also illegally mixed general fund money with the proceeds of a 1994 bond issue that were to be used to renovate the chancery court side of the courthouse. This manoeuvre allowed him to use the bond money for county operating expenses instead of the renovation. The chancery clerk had put all of the county's operating funds, bond issue proceeds, and tax money collected from the county's forty-four separate tax districts into two bank accounts. He knew where the money should have gone and personally controlled the checkbooks for the accounts. Presley used the county's money to fund a growing number of personal businesses that included an eighteen-hundred-acre cattle farm, a fast-food restaurant, and a car wash. Presley also made loans of county money to personal acquaintances; some people were said to consider him a financial genius.

While indicating that the investigation was incomplete, District Attorney Dale Harkey said that so far it had shown that all the money Presley had taken had been returned. However, he noted, "This does not eliminate the possibility that some monies are outstanding." State Auditor Phil Bryant said that his investigators had at that point looked at accounts back to 1993, and he indicated that investigators would look at earlier accounts.

The plea bargain required Presley to cooperate with a broader investigation being conducted by the FBI, the U.S. Attorney's Office, the Mississippi Attorney General's Office, and the OSA. Under the plea bargain, Presley could still face federal charges, but the agreement called for any additional sentence he might receive to run concurrently with the state court sentence. Harkey would not disclose what the federal investigation was about except to say that it involved the expenditure of public money. He would not comment on who might be a target or what charges they might face.

In late August 1998, the Biloxi *Sun Herald* reported that the federal investigation was far-ranging and that the U.S. attorney had deputized District Attorney Harkey and Special Assistant Attorney General Lee Martin to assist with the federal proceedings. The federal authorities had already reviewed some of the following issues: the elaborate land map system known as GIS, which had cost taxpayers more than $3 million but was not complete; the purchase of a Heinz pet food plant in Pascagoula; the purchase of several empty buildings in Pascagoula that the county was not using; the purchase of 480 acres of pine savannah to mitigate a highway project after the state had written to say that it had already mitigated it; and an Ocean Springs land deal known as Cedar Point in which the county paid $3 million to land speculators who had doubled their money in one day.

Judge O'Barr in late August 1998 sentenced Presley to ten years in prison. At the sentencing hearing, prosecutors said that Presley had failed to cooperate with the ongoing investigation, and that he had lied to protect himself and others. Prosecutors met with the judge behind closed doors and gave specific examples of Presley's failure to cooperate. The plea bargain had called for a three-year sentence, but District Attorney Harkey said that Judge O'Barr had made it plain that he did not sanction a plea bargain. Attorneys for Presley claimed that he had lived up to his end of the deal and immediately filed a motion challenging the sentence and asking that the agreement be enforced. Because Judge O'Barr died shortly after passing sentence, the motion was to be heard by another judge. The attorneys asked that the testimony made behind closed doors be unsealed. District Attorney Harkey said, "If the testimony is unsealed it could jeopardize and compromise a joint state and federal investigation and prematurely disclose grand jury testimony."

The following memorandum was written by Gary Carson, a supervising senior with the OSA's county audit section, who was attempting to complete the audit of Jackson County accounts controlled by the former chancery clerk.

To: Leslie Ross, Audit Supervisor
From: Gary Carson
Date: August 6, 1998
Re: Interview with Lynn Presley concerning his fee accounts

Lynn Presley in his capacity as Chancery Clerk refused either to prepare a fee journal or to provide the necessary documents so that we could prepare one for him with the consequence that the amount he owes to the Jackson County General Fund could not very well be determined. For the past two months he has repeatedly rebuffed my requests for documents, bringing this part of the audit to a virtual standstill.

When he pleaded guilty to embezzlement on July 16th and was finally removed from office, I approached the investigators handling his case for assistance. They assured me that Mr. Presley would now cooperate fully as ordered by the sentencing judge. They suggested that I prepare a list of the required documents and offered to deliver the list to him. Subsequently, Mr. Presley phoned me to set up a time for our meeting, and I requested that he deliver the documents to the audit work room. He asked if I would be willing to meet at his home instead, and I agreed, as a courtesy to him and out of respect for his feelings, perceiving that he would probably prefer not to return so soon to the scene of his recent humiliation. We set the time at 9:00 A.M. on July 31st.

When I arrived at Lynn Presley's farm on that date, my expectation was to obtain certain documents substantiating his fees and expenditures and to obtain answers to some crucial questions concerning transactions in his fee accounts. What I actually got—along with some (but not all) of the documents and some answers (however evasive) to my questions—was an increasingly bitter invective indicting in his own private court of justice the various people that he perceived had ganged up and brought him down.

At first there was no hint of the hostile and bitter attitude that he would later display. Indeed, early on in the interview Mr. Presley appeared to be willing to live up to his part of the bargain in terms of cooperating with the audit. He did provide a bundle of invoices and detailed payroll records as requested, and he seemed willing enough to describe the intricacies of his accounting system.

However, when I requested his '98 bank statements (in the interest of closing out his tenure as Chancery Clerk), this was a different story and foreshadowed the trouble to come. He offered a series of reasons, sometimes contradictory ones, as to why he could not provide these records: he was working on these himself; he could not find them—maybe they were in a bag in his garage; the investigators had not returned certain records to him; the auditor did not need these records because deposits would be made into his accounts for several months. Thus, I obtained no records, but only what I considered then and now, to be doubletalk and excuses.

At this juncture the interview began to deteriorate into a long tirade by Mr. Presley, bemoaning the injustice of his situation. Into this virtual torrent of complaint, I was hardly allowed to get a word in edgeways, much less ask a detailed audit question. He angrily recalled how he would often work late into the night on county business, with no thanks from anyone, and he styled himself as the only person in county government with real "vision." Others in county government were "stupid" or misguided, and he doubted, for example, that the budget process could continue without him. As an unwilling witness to this formidable display of rationalization and self justification, I began to doubt Mr. Presley's emotional stability, indeed his fitness to be interviewed on this subject.

However, as this torrent of words began to subside, I decided to persist in my efforts to obtain answers to certain questions.

When I asked about Joy Thomas and Cheryl Jacobs [employees paid apparently illegally by both the county and Mr. Presley's office] the hostility, previously directed at all and sundry, was now focussed on his interviewer. He accused me of "joining the witch-hunt" against him. He said that I had been influenced by what I read in the newspapers and that I had been manipulated by investigators. I tried to reassure him that I was only doing my job as a financial auditor and that he would be given every opportunity to document his position on any expenditures that we questioned. I said that my purpose was to highlight certain doubtful areas so that I could take his explanations into consideration.*

I asked about a $6,000 check to E. W. Goff, Jr. (5–14–97), and he presented an invoice reflecting that Mr. Goff had performed work as a security guard for the Market Street offices. I ask him if this was not in fact a loan to Mr. Goff, and his position shifted. He admitted that this had been a loan, but that Mr. Goff had been allowed to work it off as a security guard.

I asked about the various checks written to Internal Logistical Services (beginning 7–22–97 with the amount of $15,125) for scanning court documents. He insisted these were legitimate expenditures. When pressed, he did admit that some payments, including a payment of approximately $60,000 in 1996 were made in advance. However, he angrily maintained that actual work was performed in 1997 and that tapes were available that could document the work.

I reminded Mr. Presley that we had cooperated with him and that we expected him to cooperate with us. He shot back that he was "cooperating."

I asked about a check to Cynthia Speetjens (12–14–97) for $1664. This question again provoked an angry reaction, and he declared that this was an attorney's fee for consultation on "the flyover project," a matter dating back to 1994 when monies were expended from the road bond proceeds for the purchase of certain wetlands. I asked why the Board of Supervisors did not handle this issue and why the Board Attorney was not consulted. He was openly contemptuous of the Board Attorney, and I did not pursue the subject further. (Cynthia Speetjens later served as his defense attorney for the embezzlement charges.)**

I informed Lynn that we had noted checks in excess of $200,000 from the various accounts under his control were made payable to him but were not deposited in the fee account. I told him that at a later date he would be expected to account for each of these to show why these amounts should not be classified as fees.

At this point Mr. Presley became emotionally distraught, and tears welled up in his eyes. He said that he was not "independently wealthy," and that he could not afford to repay such sums of money. He said that we could "jump on him with our cleats" if we wanted to, but that his every effort had always been to help "the little man, the mamas and babies" who depended on him as Chancery Clerk.

I concluded the interview by reminding Mr. Presley that he should provide the '98 records at the earliest possible date and promised to deliver his own list of requests to the investigators.

*Sean Thompson and I met with Joy Thomas to discuss Lynn's fees earned in the court department. Ms. Thomas said that she had no way of determining the fees earned in Lynn's court accounts and that checks were issued to him without determining whether fees were sufficient to fund his draws. In fact, she stated that she had no way of determining the various assets and liabilities that made up the court accounts, but that she was currently working on this problem. (interview on the afternoon of August 4th)

**During the '94 audit (fiscal year ending 9–30–94), I discovered that the county had expended from the proceeds of a road bond some $480,000 for 480 acres of "wetlands." Doug Armstrong, the Audit Supervisor, informed both our technical assistance division and the Deputy State Auditor, Tommy Dyson, of this purchase and sought guidance as to its legality. Subsequently, Mr. Presley met personally with Mr. Dyson to discuss this matter, but prior to this time he did meet with the field office staff—Doug Armstrong, Greg Grenn, and me—to provide an explanation. According to Mr. Presley, he personally negotiated the land deal with Mr. Whitehead, meeting with him several times, and Lynn assured us that this was a bargain purchase, even though the property was never appraised. He said that he sought the advice of bond counsel, who assured him that such an expenditure of bond proceeds was legal. As far as I know, no audit finding was ever issued. [This refers to the 480 acres of pine savannah to mitigate a highway project after the state had written to say that it had already mitigated, as mentioned above.]

OSA records contained copies of three checks Presley wrote on Lynn Presley, Chancery Clerk Land Redemption Account, during August and September 1996. Check 2145 dated 8/1/1996 in the amount of $20,000 was payable to Lynn

Presley and endorsed by him. Check 2192 for $15,000 dated 8/19/1996 was payable to and endorsed by Lynn Presley. Check 2198 for $25,000 was payable to Presley Cattle Co., and it was endorsed by Presley. The accompanying check stubs indicated that each of these checks had been voided. Presley controlled both the checkbook and the bank statements and could thus cover his extraction of cash from the land redemption account. One of the basic principles of internal control over cash in the bank is that voided checks should be mutilated and attached to the checkbook stub. As noted above, Presley did not want to turn the bank statements over to the auditor.

Lynn Presley had been a highly respected public official. After his September sentencing to ten years in prison, several prominent public officials discussed the impact of his case. Harkey said of him, "The most stunning aspect of this case was to uncover this wrongdoing on the part of somebody no one suspected. People had a perception of Mr. Presley as an upright public official, based on his intelligence, vigor, and the way he prosecuted his office. How could people not think, 'If Lynn Presley can do something like this, then who will be immune?' I think that perception is and will be the most lingering damage that public officials in Jackson County will have to deal with." State Auditor Phil Bryant said, "What it does tell you is that no one is immune from being overcome by the perceived power and influence of these [elected] offices." Bryant also said that the case would have "a sobering effect all over the state." He indicated that the case would mean that both private and public auditors would have to take extra precautions and additional time to make sure that every one of their audits is "completed as thoroughly as necessary." Lee Martin, director of the public integrity division of the attorney general's office, said, "The real significance of the Presley case is that it restored some accountability to county government." He indicated that Presley's conviction served as a reminder that the law applies to everyone, regardless of whether he or she is a private citizen or public official.

On October 19, 1998, Phil Bryant issued a demand that Presley repay $94,443 that had been embezzled from Jackson County. Bryant acted in compliance with an order issued in August by the late Judge Walter M. O'Barr, who had sentenced Presley to prison. Noting that the demand was issued in an effort to "return these embezzled dollars to the taxpayers of Jackson County," Bryant said, "We will continue to investigate allegations of wrongdoing in Jackson County and will take the proper actions when the evidence gathered proves money has been taken from the taxpayers." By the time the OSA closed this case on February 28, 2001, restitution had been paid in full. Presley's attorney made a payment of $26,664, Presley's bonding company paid $29,613, and Presley paid $38,165.

Lynn Presley's removal from office in July 1998 created a vacancy that had to be addressed by the Jackson County Board of Supervisors. In August 1998, the board appointed an employee of the chancery clerk's office, Virginia Kirk, to serve as chancery clerk until a new clerk could be elected in November. When she was appointed, Kirk promised the board that she would not be a candidate for the office. The promise was not legally binding, and Kirk picked up qualifying papers at the courthouse on September 2, two days before the last day to file for the November election. She then called all five supervisors to inform them of her decision to run. According to the *Sun Herald*, Kirk decided not to run after learning that the supervisors wanted to hold her to her promise. She changed her mind again and filed qualifying papers September 4 to become one of seventeen candidates in the November election. Before her interim appointment, the sixty-one-year-old Kirk had worked in the chancery clerk's office for eighteen years handling duties such as maintaining the county's land records and keeping minutes of the board of supervisors' meetings.

Terry Miller, a fifty-five-year-old Mississippi Power Company retiree, was elected chancery clerk in early November and took the oath of office later that month. The defeated Kirk asked for $75,600 in pay for the ninety-one business days that she had served as chancery clerk. A 1996 state law limited the amount a fee-paid clerk could make in a year to $75,600. The law did not anticipate more than one clerk serving in a year and, therefore, a loophole apparently allowed Kirk to collect the maximum amount.

When Kirk's plans became public, county residents, county supervisors, and the state auditor became irate. Several citizens stopped by Kirk's office to express their thoughts personally. Kirk said, "It's been very unreal and very hurtful what people have said to me today, and I am not very happy about it." She maintained that the interruptions from angry constituents and the news media had made it difficult for her to get her work done. However, she had not changed her mind. She said, "I'm going to abide by the law. I'm going to do whatever the law says, and that's all I can say." Bert Patterson, the district two supervisor who has also been a candidate for the chancery clerk's office, said, "People who are very angry have called me all day. The supervisors didn't intend for this to happen, but it's out of our arena now." He also said that he had advised all callers to "be as vocal about this as they can with their state legislators who put the fee-cap system in place."

The new chancery clerk, Terry Miller, fired the interim chancery clerk, Virginia Kirk, the day he took office. When he showed up for work the Tuesday after his appointment on Monday, he walked into a hornets' nest. Kirk locked herself in her office and refused to turn over the chancery court's records. OSA spokesman Langston Moore said, "There is nothing in the law that sets down a timetable for when Kirk has to turn over the records." (Lynn Presley had not surrendered his records when he left office.) Miller began making plans to run the office without Kirk's records. "I'm setting up bank accounts and carrying on business as usual," Miller said. "The State Auditor's office is sending people down here next week to help me get the office accounts going." Miller indicated that he had borrowed enough money from a local bank to run the office until he collected fees to cover expenses.

The way the law was worded made it appear that the new chancery clerk could also pay himself $75,600 for the little over a month that he would work in 1998. Miller had promised not to do so. In late November, the board of supervisors passed a resolution saying that they opposed Kirk or anyone else taking a full year's salary for working less time. Earlier, two members of Concerned Citizens of Jackson County read a letter protesting the law to the supervisors. Mason Sumrall, a member of the activist group, said, "Why not pay her [Kirk] for the time worked, and if she is not happy, let her carry it to court and face a jury of Jackson County taxpayers."

In an early December official opinion, Attorney General Mike Moore ruled that the clerk's salary should be $75,600 multiplied by the percentage of the year served as clerk. This opinion opened the possibility that the state auditor could demand that Lynn Presley return part of the $75,600 that he had paid himself for the seven months he had served as clerk before his forced resignation. State Auditor Phil Bryant indicated that his office was considering making such a demand on the imprisoned Presley.

Virginia Kirk was back in the news in late April 1999 when she repaid the county more than $70,000. Kirk's payment covered the difference between what she earned in fees and what she claimed on her fee schedule as income when she left office in November 1998.

State Representative Danny Guice, Jr., a Republican from Ocean Springs and an opponent of paying clerks from fees they collect, determined in early December to introduce a bill in the 1999 legislature to allow county supervisors to set salaries for interim chancery clerks. "Nobody ever dreamed anyone would be brazen enough to work a matter of months and try to claim a whole year's salary," Guice said. "It absolutely amazes me. It came completely out of left field." Guice, who noted little support for a salary system in the legislature, added, "I'd love to have a salary. But if you can't pass it, a half loaf is better than no loaf at all. I'll continue to try to put them on a salary. I just don't see it happening in an election year." Early in 1999, the state legislature addressed the chancery clerk salary issue, and in March Governor Kirk Fordice signed a bill designed to correct the situation. Under the new legislation, any clerk who does not work an entire year will be eligible for pay on a pro rata basis.

Phil Bryant demanded in early March 1999 that imprisoned former chancery clerk Lynn Presley repay Jackson County $458,679. This demand flowed from the OSA's examination of the county's finances for fiscal year 1996–97. Presley took money in addition to his lawful $75,600 salary for the year, according to the audit report. The demand also included part of the $75,600 salary that Presley took in 1998 despite the fact that he worked fewer than seven months. Auditors found that Presley had often overstated expenses of operating his office while at the same time understating fees collected.

In a letter dated March 13, 2000, audit department director Norman McLeod outlined to Lynn Presley how the auditors had established Presley's personal liability for monies he received in excess of the state-imposed fee cap.

Our audit of the documentation regarding revenues earned and expenses incurred during your service as Jackson County Chancery Clerk for the years 1996, 1997, and 1998, revealed that as a result of under reported income and questionable expenses, your net income exceeded the amounts allowed under Miss. Code Ann [Section] 9-1-43 (1972) by $454,486. Having obtained additional documentation and after careful review and evaluation, it has been determined that your personal liability for the aforementioned three years is $200,927.

Of that amount owed, $116,156.86 was under reported income, $63,279. was excess and extra salaries paid but not authorized, $16,310 was unallowable travel and meal expenses, and $5,181 was questionable other expenses. Documentation is not an issue in these figures.

A yearly breakdown of the amount due to be repaid for each year is attached. By March 31, 2000, this office will afford you the opportunity to provide an explanation to justify the amounts you originally reported. After that date, any amounts not justified will be subject to recovery by whatever legal action is necessary to recover the public monies with associated costs and interest.

In May 2000, OSA investigators interviewed numerous people concerning apparently unauthorized payments made to people by Presley out of county funds. Several county employees admitted that they received several year-end payments that were not a part of their normal pay. These payments were sometimes characterized as "Christmas bonuses." After Presley's troubles started, he was alleged to have instructed at least some of the recipients not to call the payments bonuses but to refer to them as payments for overtime. This series of interviews also revealed that Presley had apparently made payments to a person not employed by the county and that he had paid persons from chancery clerk funds who also received pay for full-time work in other county jobs.

On May 25, 2000, Phil Bryant issued a formal demand to Lynn Presley and his bonding company for $186,851 for the amount Presley had exceeded the statutory fee cap for the years 1996–1998 and interest. A negotiated settlement was reached in the amount of $135,623. On November 7, 2000, Presley's bonding company paid $79,081, and on November 27, 2000, Presley paid the remaining $56,542.

In May 1999, the Jackson County Board of Supervisors revealed that the county was stuck with a debt of $1.1 million that they thought Presley had paid off with state and federal grants. The debt was to Hancock Bank for the balance of line of credit that the board had directed Presley to borrow against in April 1997 to pay for construction of the Coast Guard station in Pascagoula, the fair barn, and portions of a water line project. Presley never submitted the paperwork to secure the state and federal grants to pay off the debt, and he refused to turn over the county's original records.

In early July 1999, the federal investigation mentioned above resulted in the indictment on federal charges of Lynn Presley, Don Hearn, Sr., Jackson County land appraiser and assessor, and Don Hearn, Jr. The indictment charged the three with conspiring to operate a kickback scheme that used a Florida computer company to steal more than $1 million from Jackson County. Count one of the six-count indictment charged the three with corruption and unlawful conspiracy in accepting $1,472,971 associated with a series of Jackson County transactions involving contracts and bids. Count two charged all three defendants with unlawfully affecting interstate commerce and foreign commerce in the way they handled the proceeds of the violations mentioned in count one. Counts three and four charged the Hearns with the unlawful transfers of funds to the Cayman Islands (money laundering). These transfers were alleged to have been made with the knowledge that the funds were derived from an unlawful activity and that the transfers were intended to "conceal and disguise the nature, location, source, ownership, and control of the proceeds of specified unlawful activity." Count five charged Presley and Donald Hearn, Sr., with extorting "approximately $1,472,970 from the owner of Mainline Computer Corporation, with that person's consent, under cover of official right, which money was not due to the defendants." Count six involved forfeiture by Presley and the Hearns of all real or personal property associated with the violations alleged in counts two, three, and four. Presley and the Hearns pled not guilty to all charges. Presley's trial was set for October 4, and U.S. District Court Magistrate John Roper indicated that the Hearns would likely be tried with Presley.

The seventeen-page indictment charged that the conspiracy began in 1995 when Presley rigged the Jackson County bid process to help Florida-based Mainline Computer Corporation win a $3.1 million contract to computerize the county's land records. Presley then coerced Mainline's owner into subcontracting part of the work to Associated Services, a company owned by the Hearns, for $1.5 million. It was illegal for a company partly owned by Donald Hearn, Sr., to perform services for the county because Hearn was a salaried employee of the county and his ownership was unknown to the county. The Hearns, in turn, paid Presley $665,520. Some of the money was laundered through companies owned by Presley and the Hearns, including a company with a bank account in the Cayman Islands. The conspirators wired some of the money offshore and used some to buy cattle, vehicles, and other property, and to invest in personal retirement accounts. Presley actually used some of the money to repay the county money he had been convicted of embezzling under state charges!

The money trail associated with Presley's and the Hearns' shenanigans as untangled by investigators is convoluted. Jackson County contracted with Mainline Computer Corporation for the purchase of a land records management, processing, accounting, and imaging system in December 1995. That same month the county contracted with Associated Services for scanning other land-related records for the chancery clerk's office. Investigators documented the flow of funds from Jackson County to Lynn Presley, Donald Hearn, Sr., and Donald Hearn, Jr. through Mainline Computer Corporation and Associated Services as follows: Jackson County paid Mainline Computer Corporation $3,084,321; Mainline Computer Corporation paid Associated Services $1,472,970; Associated Services paid the Hearns $739,788; Associated Services paid Lynn Presley $665,520.

The disposition of the $665,520 funnelled to Presley through Associated Services was documented as follows:

12/27/95 - Presley Polled Hereford Account $60,000.
12/29/95 - Bent Tree Farms $135,970.

02/02/96 - Yoda Construction $10,000.

02/24/96 - D. L. Whittington $46,231.

03/03/96 - Jackson County Land Redemption Account $13,005.

03/04/96 - Jackson County Clerk - Court Account $12,024.

03/06/96 - Jackson County Land Redemption Account $7,972.

03/07/96 - Jackson County Land Redemption Account $5,074.

03/07/96 - Jackson County Clerk - Court Account $60,000.

03/14/96 - Jackson County Land Redemption Account $3,994.

04/12/96 - Jackson County Land Redemption Account $50,000.

04/22/96 - D. L. Whittington $10,000.

05/27/96 - Jackson County Clerk - Court Account $25,000.

06/01/96 - Jackson County Clerk - Court Account $25,000.

06/05/96 - Jackson County Clerk - Court Account $100,000.

04/12/97 - Jackson County Clerk - Court Account $60,000.

07/29/97 - Presley Cattle Company $7,550.*

10/13/97 - Jackson County Clerk - Court Account $9,000.

12/14/97 - M/M William Lynn Presley Hancock Bk. Acct. #102735989 $24,700.*

*Funds originated from Internal Logistic Services

As noted above, at his pleading on the state charges, Presley told Judge O'Barr, "Judge, I unlawfully converted public funds to my own use. After obtaining the funds, I returned them." The payments listed above to the Jackson County accounts totalling $371,069 are the funds he "returned." Thus, Presley used some of the proceeds of his extortion from Mainline to repay the county monies that he had stolen.

The disposition of the $739,788 funnelled through Associated Services to the Hearns was as follows: Donald Hearn, Sr., $482,722; Donald Hearn, Jr., $97,000; Variety Holdings, $60,000; Vanguard Group, $100,000.

From December 1996 to December 1997 in his capacity as chancery clerk of Jackson County, Lynn Presley wrote four checks to Internal Logistic Services in the total amount of $142,455. Presley had contracted with Internal Logistic to scan documents for the chancery clerk's office. The checks were as follows: Jackson County check 1788, December 30, 1996—$60,155; Jackson County check 2275, July 22, 1997—$15,125; Jackson County check 2389, September 5, 1997—$17,875; Jackson County check 2681, December 30, 1997—$49,300.

Internal Logistic Services in turn made the following payments totalling $118,251:

- December 30, 1997—to Royal Bank of Canada, Grand Cayman, B.W.I., Account #7359029 (Lynn Presley)—$60,155.
- July 22, 1997—to Associated Services $13,125; on July 23, 1997, Associated Services transferred $7,550—to Presley Cattle Company.
- September 5, 1997—to Variety Holdings (Donald Hearn, Sr. & Jr.) $17,875.
- December 30, 1997—payment on a line of credit $27,096 and from that $25,000 was transferred to Associated Services which transferred $24,700 to Lynn Presley.

As shown above, on September 5, 1997, Associated Services transferred to Variety Holdings (owned by the Hearns) $60,000, and Internal Logistic Services transferred to Variety Holdings $17,875. On that same day, Internal Logistic Services transferred $7,000 to Variety Holdings. These transfers totalled $84,875. On September 8, 1997, Variety Holdings paid Ann White, Jackson County tax collector, $83,358 to purchase property sold at a county tax sale.

Government agents eventually seized assets valued at $2,978,000 owned by Presley and the two Hearns. Included in this total were monies in Hancock Bank, Compass Bank, Regions Bank, and the Royal Bank of Canada, Grand Cayman, B.W.I. Also included were assets held in the Vanguard Group, stock in the Southern Company, two vehicles, a condo in Florida, a house in Ocean Springs, a car wash in Moss Point, a farm in Alabama, and a restaurant in Pascagoula. The total value of assets actually forfeited by Presley and the Hearns was $192,882, of which $71,175 was recovered from the Grand Cayman bank. Half the amount recovered from the Grand Cayman bank had to be paid to the Grand Cayman Island Government, leaving the grand total of assets recovered in forfeiture at $157,294. Presley also agreed to a forfeiture judgment of $655,520, which has not been collected.

About $83,000 of the kickback money was funnelled to Variety Holdings, which was owned by the Hearns, and then used to buy Jackson County property at delinquent tax sales. Thus, county money fraudulently paid to a vendor and extorted from that company was used to buy real property from the county at tax sales. Property bought at tax sales eventually becomes the property of the purchaser or is redeemed by the original owner, who must pay the tax sale purchaser 14 percent interest on his investment. Variety Holdings made the purchases because direct purchases by Presley or Don Hearn, Sr., would have involved conflicts of interest. Presley supervised portions of the tax sales, and Hearn, Sr., was responsible for setting the land value.

The indictment also charged that in 1996 Presley gave a second bid for scanning chancery court records to Internal Logistic Services. The Hearns had set up the company during trips to the Cayman Islands. Jackson County paid Internal Logistic Services $142,455, without knowing that it was owned by the senior Hearn.

Because of all the publicity on the Gulf Coast, Presley and the Hearns were scheduled to be tried in Natchez in October 1999. As the trial began, Presley made a last-minute bargain with the prosecutors in which he agreed to plead guilty to counts one and two of the indictment, conspiracy to commit theft of bribery and conspiracy to launder money. He also agreed to forfeit property that he had acquired with the fraudulently obtained money, and to testify against the Hearns. The charges to which Presley agreed to plead guilty carried maximum penalties of twenty-five years in prison and $750,000 in fines. Presley's plea bargain and guilty plea chagrined his codefendants and their lawyers. Calvin Taylor, the attorney for Don Hearn, Jr., asked for a delay to prepare for Presley's expected testimony. When U.S. District Judge David Bramlette denied the request, the Hearns decided to plea-bargain. The senior Hearn agreed to plead guilty to count one of the indictment and to forfeit his ill-gotten gains, and the prosecutors agreed to recommend a one-year prison sentence. Prosecutors also agreed to clear Don Hearn, Jr., of the criminal charges against him if he successfully completed a one-year probation period.

On January 10, 2000, Judge Bramlette sentenced Lynn Presley to forty-six months in prison but allowed him to serve thirty-four months concurrently with the ten-year state sentence he was serving and twelve months to run consecutively. Judge Bramlett also imposed a $10,000 fine. Even though the automated land record system would not work, no restitution was ordered according to the judge because Mainline Computer Corporation's president had promised to get the system working. The judge said that "the biggest judgment he will receive will not be from the criminal justice system, but from his conscience for having crossed the line." While noting that the federal crimes were similar to the state crimes for which he had already received a "serious" sentence, Bramlette said that "he tried to run Jackson County pretty much as his own business."

On March 20, 2000, Judge Bramlette sentenced fifty-three-year-old Don Hearn, Sr., to thirty-five months in prison and ordered him to pay restitution of $665,520 (the amount of the kickback he had paid Presley) to Jackson County. The restitution was to be $100,000 within a month and then $100,000 every three months until it was paid. As noted above, Hearn's plea agreement called for prosecutors to recommend a one-year prison sentence. Judge Bramlette refused Hearn's request for a reduced sentence, noting that Hearn still had not accepted responsibility for his crime. Hearn still maintained that the kickback to Presley was actually a loan. Twenty-seven-year-old Don Hearn, Jr., was assigned to a twelve-month program that would result in his criminal record being expunged if he followed the law.

At sentencing, Hearn's attorney, Earl Denham, maintained that the $665,520 that Hearn, Sr., had paid to Presley was really a loan and that there were no victims in the case. Judge Bramlette disagreed. "That money was not a loan, but rather a payoff, and the victims were Jackson County and the citizens of Jackson County," said the judge. Bramlett called the money "a payment by Mr. Hearn to Mr. Presley, who used his influence to see that Hearn got a contract." Bramlette went on to say, "To say this was a loan was not true. This was not a loan, it was a kickback, and the people of Jackson County are entitled to get their money back from Mr. Hearn." Denham also took issue with the presentence report recommendation, which exceeded the thirteen-month maximum sentence Hearn expected to receive. The attorney accused the prosecutors of going back on their word and acting dishonorably. He said, "The government made a deal, and now they're not going to agree to it."

Denham asked the judge to allow Hearn to change his plea from guilty to not guilty. Judge Bramlette denied the request and reminded Denham that he was not bound by the plea agreement and did not have to follow it. He indicated that he would follow federal sentencing guidelines enacted by Congress. He also reminded the attorney that his client knew that by pleading guilty he gave up his right to withdraw his plea. Finally, Judge Bramlette indicated that a motion to withdraw had not been filed in a timely fashion and that had Hearn filed such a motion shortly after entering it, he might have considered it.

On March 10, 2000, Jackson County Chancery Clerk Terry Miller wrote an interesting letter concerning the sentencing of the Hearns to Becky Luke, United States Probation Office, Biloxi. Maybe the judge took his comments into consideration, at least in sentencing the senior Hearn.

Dear Becky:

I have been asked by George Blue, Investigator for the State Audit Department, and other federal agents, to make a statement in connection [with] the upcoming sentencing of Don Hearn, Sr. and Don Hearn, Jr. scheduled for March 20, 2000.

I have been involved in the investigation of Lynn Presley, Don Hearn, Sr. and Don Hearn, Jr. as a private citizen, Commissioner of the Port Authority, and as the duly elected Chancery Clerk of Jackson County. My concern throughout this investigation has been *the need for justice* and, more importantly, what certainty we are providing to the citizens of Jackson County that *elected and public officials who participate in criminal activity will be held accountable for their actions.*

I was subpoenaed to testify in the hearing held in Natchez, Mississippi when Lynn Presley, Don Hearn, Sr. and Don Hearn, Jr. pled guilty to a money laundering scheme that defrauded $1,250,000 from the taxpayers of Jackson County. I was also subpoenaed and present at the sentencing of Lynn Presley on January 10, 2000.

Both Presley and Hearn [Sr.] were public officials at the time of their criminal activity and *each* benefited financially from this planned and fraudulent scheme. These same individuals profited considerably from business given to Associated Services, Internal Logistical Services and Variety Holdings.

My position is simple: Justice should prevail. Don Hearn, Sr. and Don Hearn, Jr. should be sentenced to a lengthy prison term with a substantial monetary fine for their planned fraudulent scheme against the citizens of Jackson County.

I am attaching an additional copy for you to forward to Honourable David Bramlett, United States District Court Judge. Please let me know if I can be of further assistance to you.

In March 2001, Presley's lawyers asked the Mississippi Supreme Court to enforce the terms of Presley's plea bargain and reduce his ten-year sentence to three years. Presley claimed that he had cooperated in the ongoing investigation of his conduct as chancery clerk as required by the agreement. Prosecutors had told the sentencing judge that Presley had not cooperated, and Judge Walter O'Barr had imposed a twenty-year prison sentence with ten years suspended. On June 14, 2001, in a 7–0 decision, the Mississippi Supreme Court ruled that Presley's ten-year sentence should stand. Writing for the court, Justice William Waller, Jr., noted that key portions of the plea agreement said that the prosecutors would determine if Presley had cooperated and that they would recommend no more than twelve years in prison on each count. Waller said that the trial judge was in a better position to determine whether Presley cooperated with the authorities as described in the plea agreement.

Lisa Jenkins, Tallahatchie County Deputy Circuit Court Clerk

Tallahatchie County is one of eight Mississippi counties that have two county seats. This is an anachronism caused by the poor roads of the nineteenth century that politics has prevented from being remedied. Charleston and Sumner are the county seats, and the Tallahatchie County Circuit Court clerk maintains offices in both places. The two county seats are located in different judicial districts, and the circuit court clerk's offices maintain separate and unconnected financial, judicial, and other records. In the late 1990s, Paul O. Eastridge was circuit court clerk of Tallahatchie County. He lived in the eastern part of the county and spent most of his time in Charleston.

On December 16, 1997, Eastridge registered a complaint with the OSA alleging embezzlement. The complaint named former deputy circuit court clerk Lisa Jenkins, a Webb resident and a six-year employee of the clerk's Sumner office, who had been terminated on December 12, 1997. There was a question about a $900 restitution payment made to the clerk's office that had not been reported properly. OSA investigator Walt Drane was assigned to the case on the day of the complaint. Drane advised Eastridge to contact District Attorney Robert Williams about the missing funds. The district attorney requested the assistance of the Mississippi Department of Public Safety Criminal Investigation Division.

Drane reviewed the circuit clerk's 1997 bond and fees account and found that Jenkins had transferred approximately $18,000 from that account to Circuit Clerk Eastridge's personal account. He also found that Jenkins wrote checks to Eastridge from the personal account, signed Eastridge's name, and cashed the checks at the Union Planters Bank in Sumner. The district attorney's office was notified, and a decision was made to review the accounts for the years 1992 through 1997.

Drane's extended review revealed that on several occasions during the period 1992 through 1997, Lisa Jenkins transferred funds from the bond and fees account to Eastridge's personal account, wrote checks on the personal account to Eastridge, forged Eastridge's name on the checks, and cashed them at the Union Planters Bank in Sumner. Bank statements had not been reconciled to accounting records. The total amount embezzled in this way over the entire period was $29,110.00. Drane also found that over the same time period $7,591 had been collected in fees but not deposited.

Lisa Jenkins made a voluntary statement to the Mississippi Department of Public Safety on December 18, 1997. Jenkins claimed that she "wasn't getting enough money so Paul [Eastridge] paid me an extra $350 a month out of his personal account, which I was supposed to write the checks to Paul and endorse his name to the checks. Sometimes I paid myself more than I was supposed to." Jenkins went on to state, "I would take the monies out of the bond and fees account and put it into Paul's personal account and write the checks from that. I was also using the bond money to cover the overdraft accounts.

I've used some of the funds for my personal use other than what I was supposed to. I can't tell how much money I've taken out of the public funds. I've
also taken money away from the criminal receipt docket, but, I can't remember how much or which ones."

In an eleven-page handwritten document dated December 19, 1997, Eastridge outlined developments that caused him to report the suspected embezzlement to the OSA. He had received several complaints over about a year
concerning things going wrong in his Sumner office. His trusted deputy,
who had proved to be very competent, was always able to provide "a ready
and prompt answer *anytime* I asked her about *anything.*" He also wrote, "I
had absolutely no idea she was 'dipping in the till.'" According to Eastridge,
the first indication of the embezzlement came to light when a man was arrested on a bench warrant for nonpayment of court-ordered restitution. In
fact the defendant had made the required payment to the circuit clerk's office in Sumner but had not been given credit for the payment. Eastridge wrote
that when he checked the fines registry to see how much the man was in ar-
rears, he found that the balance was more than the original amount owed.
Lisa Jenkins was said to have explained the situation by saying that she had
added $900 back rather than deducting it as she should have. When asked to
get the book in which the receipt should have been recorded, Jenkins couldn't
produce it. Eastridge's statement indicated that the receipt book was eventually found under circumstances that showed Jenkins had lied and attempted
to deceive him.

Further review of conditions in the circuit clerk's Sumner office revealed
several problems. Lisa Walker, another employee of the circuit clerk, told Eastridge that Jenkins had carried "a big box of papers and things to the third
floor on December 12." Eastridge wrote that he retrieved the box from the
third floor and "There were checks for garnishments that had not been processed and a whole bunch of mail, some dating as far back as August that had
not even been opened. A stack of judgements that had not been recorded. Cash
in the amount of ten one dollar bills paper clipped together. The cash journal
was in this box loose leaf. Some bank statements unopened and an old check
book was found. . . ." Subsequently, Eastridge phoned the OSA and requested
its assistance in clearing things up in his Sumner office.

Investigators interviewed four employees of the Sumner branch of Union
Planters Bank about the circuit court clerk checks made out to Paul Eastridge
and cashed by Lisa Jenkins. Such checks were cashed at the bank about twice
a month. The checks, which were usually for about $400, were cashed by the
bank employees because they knew that Jenkins was a long-time deputy cir-

cuit clerk. The bank employees indicated that sometimes Jenkins would deposit approximately $200 to her personal account and take the remaining $200 in cash. On other occasions, Jenkins would take the whole amount in cash. Jenkins explained to bank employees that the money deposited to her personal account was money owed to her by Eastridge for extra work she did during elections and for travel and court work.

When investigators interviewed Lisa Walker, she said she had cashed at the bank a circuit court check made out to Eastridge for Jenkins. Walker said Jenkins told her and another employee of the clerk's office that "Paul paid her some and the county paid her some." Walker said Jenkins repeated to her several times that both the county and the circuit court clerk paid her.

Faced with facts documented by the OSA and the Criminal Investigation Division of the Mississippi Department of Public Safety, thirty-six-year-old Lisa Jenkins worked out a plea agreement with District Attorney Robert Williams. Jenkins waived indictment and pled guilty May 22, 1998, to a bill of information that charged her with embezzling $36,701 from Tallahatchie County. Jenkins entered her plea before Circuit Court Judge George C. Carlson, Jr., at the Panola County Courthouse in Batesville. Based on the plea agreement, the judge signed a Plea of Guilty and Order of Non-Adjudication. Jenkins was required to immediately pay $37,701 in restitution and investigative costs to the state auditor, and to pay court costs of $1,500 in equal annual payments of $500 beginning one year from the day of the plea. Jenkins was also placed on three years' probation. Upon satisfactory completion of the probation, the judge was to issue an order dismissing the case. Under Mississippi law, Jenkins could have been sentenced to ten years in prison and fined up to $5,000 on the one count of embezzlement.

Jenkins made the court-ordered $37,701 payment as required, and the OSA closed the case May 28, 1998.

Linda Kay Olsen, Pontotoc County Deputy Circuit Court Clerk

In early March 1998, an employee at Crawson's Used Cars in Pontotoc complained to Pontotoc County Circuit Court Clerk Tracy Robinson about not getting money from garnishments paid to the circuit clerk's office. Robinson met with Hodge on March 9 and reviewed a partial list of monies due Crawson that Crawson claimed had been paid to the circuit clerk's office. Robinson attempted to verify these amounts and found that receipts had not been prepared for some of the payments. Deputy Circuit Court Clerk Linda Kay Olsen admitted to Robinson on March 10 that she had been stealing money. Olsen wrote a check for $1,186 to cover the amount she thought she had taken over the past couple of weeks. Olsen claimed that she had been taking money since about 1996. Robinson immediately terminated Olsen's employment and told her to take her things and leave. The next day Olsen called to tell Robinson that the thefts probably actually started in late 1995. Olsen agreed to help determine the actual amount missing.

Robinson notified Sean Thompson of the county audit section of the OSA, and Thompson referred the alleged embezzlement to the Investigations Division March 11, 1998. Special Agent Johnny Shannon was assigned to the investigation. Shannon met with Kay Olsen, her father, James E. Stegall, Pontotoc County Chancery Court Clerk Reggie Collums, Phil Tutor, attorney for the Pontotoc County Board of Supervisors, and Tracy Robinson at Tutor's office. At this meeting, Olsen voluntarily explained how she stole the money. A memorandum written by Shannon on March 12 outlined what he learned at this March 11 meeting.

> She was asked to explain what exactly she did to acquire money from the office. She stated that she would take checks that came to the office on garnishments and deposit them to the criminal account instead of the civil account and not write up a receipt. She took the equivalent amount in cash from the criminal funds. This according to her would keep the accounts balanced on the books. She acknowledged that she had taken several thousand dollars but did not know how much. I asked if she had ever cashed any of the garnishment checks, she stated she had not. She said that she had meant to pay the money back but it got so out of hand that the only amount she ever repaid before yesterday ($1,086.00) was a couple of weeks ago she wrote a check for around $500.00 and had it deposited. She stated that this was the only type of money that she had taken. She said she would pay the money back as soon as the amount was determined. I explained to her that there would be investigative costs and interest in addition to the principal amount to be paid. She also wanted it to be known that Tracy had nothing to do with it and had no knowledge of any of this prior to yesterday [March 10]. She said she was sorry and again said she wanted to pay the money back as soon as a figure could be determined. I also informed her the State Auditor's Office was required to notify the Governor and District Attorney regarding this matter.

The investigative auditors were able to tie down what had actually happened. Olsen's stealing had started long before 1995, and it involved monies other than garnishment payments. Special Agent Shannon's synopsis report dated April 16, 1999, contained the following paragraphs:

> After reviewing the deposit information on the criminal account, I determined that $126,315.76 in various civil funds (marriage license fees, civil court costs, garnishments, etc.) were deposited to the criminal account to replace cash taken. Included in this amount were some instances of criminal money deposited but not receipted. A comparison was made of each deposit with the corresponding receipts for that deposit. Deposits were not made in a timely manner. Olsen not only receipted funds, but also posted the journals and made the deposits.
>
> In addition, it was determined that a deposit slip was prepared by Olsen on March 9, 1998, in the amount of $1,486.00. This money was not deposited on this date though the deposit slip prepared by Olsen indicated that it was.
>
> I also determined that $2,632.00 in criminal funds were taken by evidence of altered receipts. There were 16 instances whereby receipts were changed though the accounts receivable ledger maintained by Olsen indicated a larger amount being paid.

The March 18, 1998, edition of the *Pontotoc Progress* ran a story about the investigation in which Circuit Clerk Robinson is quoted as saying: "At this time any alleged wrongdoing is simply that, alleged. Any person or persons suspected or accused remain innocent until proven guilty. But I will assure all Pontotoc County citizens that I will continue to ensure the complete integrity of my office."

During the course of this investigation, the circuit clerk's office received numerous calls from individuals who claimed they had not received their money on garnishments which they said were paid into the circuit clerk's office. Some of these amounts had been paid and actually deposited into the civil account as required. But those funds possibly could have been used to settle existing obligations for which the funds received were deposited to the criminal account to cover cash shortages in that account. This appeared to be a simple lapping scheme.

A Pontotoc County grand jury indicted Linda Kay Olsen on sixteen counts of embezzlement and twenty-two counts of embezzlement by false entry in early December 1998. She was arrested and released on a $15,000 bond. Phil Bryant said, "Ms. Olsen was arrested on an indictment for allegedly embezzling approximately $129,000. The investigation of Ms. Olsen regarding additional instances of embezzlement is continuing."

Circuit Clerk Tracy Robinson said the indictments covered a period of time that started prior to her election in 1991 and continued until she fired Olsen in March of 1998. Robinson commented, "I have worked closely with the Mississippi Department of Audit since discovering these discrepancies and reporting it to the audit department. The alleged wrongdoing by Ms. Olsen extends back beyond my initial term of office, while she served as either deputy clerk or as acting circuit clerk. I intend to vigorously urge the prosecution to compel total repayment by Ms. Olsen of any missing public funds. While I feel badly for her and her family, she must take personal responsibility for any wrongdoing in this matter."

In the spring of 1999, under a plea agreement, Olsen pled guilty to six counts of embezzlement and four counts of embezzlement by forgery. These charges involved the embezzlement of more that $148,000. The other thirty counts were retired to the file. On August 4, 2000, Circuit Court Judge Tommy Gardner sentenced Kay Olsen to twenty years in prison with fifteen years suspended. Olsen was also ordered to pay restitution of $203,930.76 and fined $942.

Under the headline "Sadness grips courtroom as clerk sentenced," the *Pontotoc Progress* reported on the sentencing hearing as follows:

> Before final sentencing Friday morning testimony from family and friends was heard before Judge Gardner. Dennis Stegall, Greg Herndon, Larry Olsen, and finally Kay herself spoke to the judge.
>
> Stegall, her brother who lives in Troy, said he had seen Kay suffer for two years through this ordeal. "Her family needs her," he said. "I'm worried about how it will affect my mother if she goes to prison."
>
> Herndon is Olsen's pastor. "I've known she and her family since they moved into our county from Arkansas about 15 years ago," he said. "I called her the day we heard of the crime. She has never made light of it. She is placing herself at the mercy of the court. I'm convinced she will follow the court's rules."
>
> Olsen's husband, Larry, testified about what they have done to pay back the money that was taken. He also asked the judge to allow her to remain free so she could help her family.
>
> Olsen herself apologized. "First I want to apologize to Tracy, you (she looked at Judge Gardner), and this county for what I did. If you could see fit not to take me away from my family. Some people think I've gotten away with it, but they don't know what I've put my family through." She cried. "I just have to have my boy. What I've done is wrong and the consequences don't come easy. There are no words that will make it right with people. We've lost everything, we are starting over."

Assistant District Attorney Clay Joiner outlined the restitution owed by Olsen. "There are $148,217 taken from the office," he said. "She has paid back $44,202 since then." Joiner said there is an interest charge of more than $52,000 and more than $47,500 for cost of recovery in this matter. "That leaves a total of $203,930 to pay. It pains me to be here as well. She (Kay) showed me a great deal of kindness when I started out. But the very nature of this crime is the betrayal of public trust. Tracy is still feeling the effect of this crime."

Joiner reminded the court of recent court sentencing in other cases of this nature in the state. "The purpose is to maintain trust of the people who are in government working in those institutions," he said. "She says she is sorry and will replace the money and I believe her. We retired 30 counts, but she could have been charged with thousands of counts." Joiner said the state recommended some sort of term in prison and proper time to be suspended pending repayment.

"This is a painful experience to me," said Judge Gardner. "I like everyone else have known you. I'm saddened by the fact that I'm here and you are here. I've thought about this sentence for a long time. I'm charged with protecting the integrity of our government and on some occasions, it is painful. We are called upon to do our duty." With that, the judge handed out concurrent sentences of 20 years with 15 suspended.

District Attorney John Young said the sentence was a just one. "Considering the large sum of money she admitted to taking, the sentence was fair," he said. "She was in a position of trust to properly take care of the court's money. Hopefully a sentence such as this will discourage people who are in a position of trust from violating that trust."

The person who is most relieved to see the ordeal get over is Circuit Court Clerk Tracy Robinson. "I'm grateful it's over for Pontotoc County," she said. "This will help my perspective get back to everyday business. It has been a heart wrenching situation for me and my entire staff. This is the hardest thing I have ever lived through in my public office. It has been a personal challenge to me to make sure that everything was finalized."

Robinson explained that the county was only bonded for $5,000 each term so the bonding company would only cover $10,000 of the theft. She also said that the money taken by Olsen was garnishment money that comes into the office, and not money for fines and other fees.

Robinson was the person who caught Olsen stealing. "I worked diligently for eight months trying to catch her. The state auditor told me that if I hadn't done it they would never have caught her." She said an audit is done every year in her office.

ry and Circuit Clerks

"I do appreciate the people of Pontotoc County supporting me through all of this. I intend to continue to make this a place of integrity so that they can know that their business is taken care of in a professional way."

Judge Gardner signed an order January 14, 2002, authorizing Olsen to pay off the entire amount she had been assessed at the rate of $150 per month. The order noted that Olsen was indigent. The OSA normally holds each case open until the entire amount owed by the defendant is paid. The Olsen file contains a report written by Agent Shannon dated August 30, 2002, that includes the following paragraph:

On Friday August 30 2002, I went to the Pontotoc County Circuit Clerk's Office at the Pontotoc County Courthouse in Pontotoc, Mississippi, and obtained a copy of the accounts receivable ledger sheet for former Pontotoc County Deputy Circuit Court Clerk Linda Kay Olsen. Since my last report on July 3, 2002, Ms. Olsen has made two (2) additional payments in the amount of One Hundred Fifty ($150.00) each. These payments as per receipt numbers 7167 and 7276 were paid on July 30, 2002, and August 28, 2002, respectively. This leaves a balance as of the date of this report, of Two Hundred Three Thousand Five Hundred Eighty-Two Dollars and Seventy-Six Cents ($203,582.76).

Another report dated July 19, 2004, written by O. T. McAlpin, deputy director of the OSA's Investigations Division, noted that it was not cost effective to continue to monitor this case and recommended to the division's director, Jesse Bingham, that the case be closed, which it was.

At $150 per month it would take more than 113 years to pay the restitution assessed by the court.

Gregory Jones, Supervisor of Finance, Harrison County Circuit Court Clerk's Office

On September 19, 2001, the Harrison County Circuit Court Clerk's Office received a telephone call from Diana Williams at Peoples Bank about a $78,000 check drawn on the Harrison County Registry of the Court Account. Williams asked to speak to Gregory Jones, the supervisor of finance. Because Jones had taken the day off, the call was referred to Harrison County Circuit Clerk Gayle Parker. Williams told Parker that a man was at her bank wanting to obtain a cashier's check to replace the $78,000 check drawn on the court account, but that the account lacked sufficient funds to cover that amount. Parker asked for the cause number on the check, investigated the matter, and found that there was no order signed by a judge authorizing the funds. Parker learned that Gregory Jones had delivered the check to the man. Parker then asked Williams to tell the man to bring the check to her office. (He never did.) The circuit clerk checked the Registry of the Court Account and found other checks that had been issued to Legacy Sound and Lighting, a company owned by Jones. Parker's signature stamp had been used on each of these checks without her authority. Parker notified the OSA and the Harrison County Sheriff's Department, and an investigation was started immediately. Gregory Jones was arrested on September 20.

Gayle Parker told OSA investigators that Gregory Jones served as her bookkeeper and that he had authority to prepare checks but not to use her signature stamp. She indicated that only Deputy Clerk Connie Ladner had authority to use her signature stamp in her absence and that the deputy made copies of checks she stamped for Parker's review. Parker said that before signing checks from the Registry of the Court Account she always compared cause numbers on the checks with court orders. She stated that the signature stamp was kept in her desk, which was locked when she was absent. Connie Ladner was said to be the only other person who had a key to the clerk's office. Parker also said that Jones reconciled the bank statements.

On September 20, OSA Special Agent George Blue interviewed Rick Hamm, owner of PA Systems and Lightings; he was the one who had attempted to obtain the cashier's check for the $78,000 check. Blue's September 21 report on the interview included the following:

Mr. Hamm said he had known Mr. Jones for about one year. He said Gregory Jones would come into his business a couple of times a week. Mr. Hamm said Gregory Jones told him that Jones was coming into a large sum of money because of the settlement of a court suit. He said that Jones wanted to order some expensive sound equipment, and Mr. Hamm told Jones that he would have to receive a cashiers check for the equipment purchase. Mr. Hamm said about two weeks ago Gregory came into his business and told Hamm to order the equipment.

Mr. Hamm said Gregory Jones brought him a check drawn on an account of the Harrison County Circuit Clerk. When Mr. Hamm was asked if he thought anything was strange about the check being drawn on an account of the Circuit Court Clerk, he said he did not think anything about it because Gregory Jones had previously told him Jones was going to come into some money through a court suit, and this check was a draw on the money Jones was to receive.

Mr. Hamm was asked why he went to the Peoples Bank to obtain a cashiers [check] and he said his bank, Hancock Bank, would not let him deposit a check as large as this one and then write a check for a large amount. Mr. Hamm also said the factory he was ordering the speakers from required a cashiers check because he was a new customer and this was a large order. Mr. Hamm then exhibited a bill for speakers and other equipment in the amount of $78,190.00. Mr. Hamm said he only charged Gregory Jones 5% over his cost for the speakers and other sound equipment.

Mr. Hamm said when the Peoples Bank would not give him a cashiers check he called Gregory Jones. Gregory Jones came to the business location of P A Systems and Lighting and picked up the check. Mr. Hamm said Gregory Jones said he would take care of the check. When Mr. Hamm was asked if he received a replacement check he said he has not seen or heard from Gregory Jones since Jones picked up the check.

On September 29, 2001, Harrison County Circuit Clerk Gayle Parker was quoted as saying "upward of $200,000" appeared to be missing from her office after the arrest of Gregory Jones, a trusted employee who had been in charge of finance and accounting in the clerk's office. When he was arrested on September 20, Jones was charged with six counts of embezzlement and one count of uttering forgery based on an investigation conducted by the OSA, the Harrison County Sheriff's Department, and the district attorney. Jones had worked in the circuit clerk's office as chief financial officer since August 1997.

Jones, a former senior accountant and field auditor for the OSA whose duties included auditing Harrison County's financial records, had helped Parker set up a new accounting system for the clerk's office. Parker, who had been in office since 1992, hired Jones for about $50,000 a year based on his audit work. Parker said, "That's one of the main reasons I hired him, because he had been with the auditor's office . . . I've been in shock . . . That's what we are checking on now, all the investigators, to see when this started. It looks like it really started hitting in May and June of this year." Parker also said she believed that Jones had been writing checks to a business he ran on the side. Parker and others involved in the investigation said they didn't believe any other employees of the circuit clerk were involved.

In a September 20, 2001, interview with the investigators, Troy Carpenter and Kevin Jackson of the Harrison County Sheriff's Department, Jones admitted using Circuit Clerk Gayle Parker's signature stamp to write himself several checks without authorization. Jones claimed to have written, over about a two-year period, five checks totaling about $91,000 and depositing them to the bank account of his business, Legacy Sound and Lighting. He indicated that the proceeds from these deposits were used to cover normal business expenses. He also admitted depositing a check that he had forged for $16,000 in his personal bank account. Finally, Jones admitted forging the $78,000 check to PA Systems and Lighting that the bank refused to honor for lack of funds.

The investigation revealed twenty-two checks totaling $204,698.32 that were fraudulently disbursed by Jones during his tenure in the circuit clerk's office. Using the stamp of Gayle Parker, Jones had issued checks to himself, to his wife, and to his sound and lighting business. Jones later admitted that he embezzled all of the money associated with these checks. Jones had also charged numerous personal purchases on an American Express credit card issued to the circuit clerk's office and paid the credit card bills out of various accounts controlled by the circuit clerk. Jones also claimed that he had practiced Gayle Parker's signature but never attempted it on a check.

On December 9, 2002, Gregory Jones was indicted on two counts alleging forgery and embezzlement. He was charged with forging a check on a court account for $78,190 to PA Systems and Lighting in September 2001 and with embezzling more than $250 from five court accounts. The embezzlements were accomplished by charging personal expenses to the clerk office's credit card. The former chief financial officer for the circuit clerk faced up to fifteen years in prison for forgery and up to ten years in prison for embezzlement.

Jones and his attorney, Dean Holleman, entered into a plea bargain with prosecutors on May 5, 2003. The plea agreement called for Jones to plead guilty to the embezzlement charge in count two of the indictment. The district attorney agreed to recommend a sentence of ten years with nine years suspended, leaving one year to serve, and a $1,000 fine. Jones acknowledged that he had embezzled $204,698.32 from the Harrison County Circuit Clerk's Office between October 23, 1998, and August 27, 2001, and that he could be sentenced to a maximum of twenty years in prison and fined a maximum of $5,000 based on his guilty plea. Jones also agreed to pay restitution totaling $246,105.40 including interest and investigative costs. The agreement outlined how the restitution was to be paid—$100,000 by certified check, waiver of any claim to $28,000 seized from a bank account, $24,676.54 from Jones's state retirement account, estimated proceeds from the sale of seized equipment $5,000, with the balance of $88,428.86 plus the $1,000 fine to be paid in monthly installments. Any monies received from Jones's bonding company would reduce the balance to be paid by Jones.

In May 2003, Senior Special Agent Ben Norris of the OSA delivered a $246,105 demand letter to Gregory Jones. The demand included $204,698.32 in principal, $33,545 in interest, and $7,861 in investigative cost.

Gregory Jones pled guilty on May 5, 2003, to embezzlement of public funds before Circuit Court Judge Stephen Simpson. The judge delayed sentencing and ordered a presentence hearing. The state did not prosecute the uttering forgery charge, count one of the indictment, and passed it to the file, i.e., not prosecuted. After the plea hearing, State Auditor Phil Bryant recovered $100,000 from Jones in partial restitution. Bryant said, "Mr. Jones violated the public's trust, and this office will not tolerate embezzlement. We appreciate the work of the district attorney and his staff for prosecuting this case, and the Harrison County Sheriff's Department and the circuit clerk's office for their full cooperation. By recovering $100,000 today, this will begin the efforts to make the circuit clerk's office and Harrison County whole." Circuit Clerk Gayle Parker said, "I will not tolerate anything less than full accountability, absolute honesty and fair dealing with the public. This has been a tragedy for everyone involved. In the end it's proven not to be a burden for the taxpayers of Harrison County."

On May 13, 2003, the *Sun Herald* published the following letter to the editor:

Former County employee Gregory E. Jones pleaded guilty of embezzling more than $204,000 from the Harrison County Circuit Clerk's Office.

He could receive a 10-year sentence with nine years suspended, and the judge might agree to allow the remaining year to be served under house arrest.

The Sun Herald reported that he will pay $100,000 immediately and the rest at $500 per month until the other $104,000 plus interest is paid back to the county.

It must be nice to steal over $200,000 and pay it back at a monthly rate less than some car notes. That will go on for 292 months or 24 years. Maybe the few current taxpayers who are alive in 2027 can send him a big "thank you" note for his repayment . . . if he lives to be 70 years old. He's 46 now.

What happened to selling everything a thief owns and sending him to jail for 20 years? It makes one wonder.

Tommy Rand
Long Beach

On July 28, 2003, Circuit Court Judge Stephen Simpson sentenced Gregory Eddie Jones to ten years' imprisonment with nine years suspended, leaving one year to serve in the Mississippi Department of Corrections. The year was to be served in an intensive supervision program—house arrest. Upon completion of the intensive supervision program, Jones was to serve five years of probation. Jones was to pay court costs and restitution of $246,105.46. The judge noted that Jones had already paid approximately $155,000 in restitution and ordered that he begin paying $500 every month on the balance.

The Gregory Jones case presents a classic example of how embezzlements are often discovered. He was not at work the day the fraudulent check payable to PA Systems and Lighting was presented to the bank for payment. Because there were insufficient funds in the account on which the check was written, a bank employee called the circuit clerk's office and asked to speak to Jones, who was the supervisor of finance. Had Jones been at work that day, it is quite possible that he could have covered his tracks. Since he wasn't there, the circuit clerk addressed the matter and Jones's fraudulent schemes soon came to light. A basic principle of internal control over financial matters is that everyone who deals with cash and accounting records should be required to take a vacation and someone else should do their work while they are gone.

The Jones case is especially tragic because he was a former employee of the Office of the State Auditor who had gone bad.

2. Tax Assessors/Collectors

Each of Mississippi's eighty-two counties elects a tax assessor/collector every four years. A brief review of the duties of this politically charged office will set the stage for the six cases briefed in this section.

The tax assessor/collector submits a proposed budget for the upcoming fiscal year to the county board of supervisors (BOS) at its July meeting. The board, which must adopt a budget by September 15, may accept or modify the proposed amounts. Subsequently, the board appropriates a lump sum for the tax assessor/collector's budget on a quarterly basis at the first meeting of each quarter beginning on October 1, January 1, April 1, and July 1. The quarterly appropriation must be equal to one-fourth of the annual budget unless the assessor/collector requests a different amount. The budget includes amounts to cover necessary expenses of providing equipment, supplies, and personnel to properly operate the tax assessor/collector's office. No deputy tax collector can be paid a salary that is greater than the tax assessor/collector. According to Mississippi Code Sections 25-15-101 and 25-15-103, the budget should include amounts for theft insurance and for bonds for the tax assessor/collector and his deputies as the BOS deems necessary. The board may revise the tax assessor/collector's budget at any of its regular meetings.

The tax assessor/collector files a report of all his office's expenses during the previous month with the BOS. This report, which must be in a form prescribed by the OSA, is considered at each regular (first Monday) board meeting. After board approval, disbursements are made by check by the chancery clerk. Any appropriated funds not expended by the end of a fiscal year are settled to the county's general fund.

The tax assessor/collector is required to maintain a system of internal controls to safeguard assets and to strengthen accounting and recording functions. One of the basic features of an internal control system is a requirement that all deputies who make collections must operate separate cash drawers. Other control features include requirements to record all transactions on a daily activity listing sheet; prepare a daily check-up sheet that summarizes all of the daily activity listing sheets and reconciles to cash on hand; maintain a tax collector's journal that tracks all cash receipts and disbursements; prepare a monthly bank reconciliation; and maintain an investment journal.

The tax collector's journal, which includes more than forty columns, is the most important record maintained by the tax assessor/collector's office. Collections and receivables reported on the daily check-up sheets are recorded daily in the journal. Payments from the State Tax Commission for the legislative tag credit are recorded in the journal when received, and disbursements are recorded when made. The journal gives the tax collector current information and provides the basis for making monthly and annual settlements (transfers of collected funds to appropriate parties).

The tax assessor/collector prepares a report as of September 30, the end of the fiscal year, which identifies the distribution of all funds held by or due to the tax collector. This is necessary to ensure that these assets are included in the county's financial statements. The report specifies the revenues due to the general fund, other funds, state government, local government, and others. It also identifies amounts owed to or by the tax collector. The report must be filed with the chancery clerk by October 31 of each year.

Evan Doss, Jr., Claiborne County Tax Assessor/Collector

The story of the embezzlements perpetrated by former Claiborne County Tax Assessor/Collector Evan Doss, Jr., would be far from complete without a review of his convoluted political career. Doss was a member, deacon, and trustee of Mercy Seat Baptist Church when he first took office in 1972. In a biography published in *Mississippi Black History Makers*, Evan Doss, Jr., is reported to be the first black county tax assessor/collector in Mississippi history. The embezzlement conviction that eventually landed Doss in federal prison was simply the culmination of a series of events that in retrospect seem almost unbelievable. Doss served as Claiborne County Tax Assessor/Collector from 1972 through the end of 1995. During his time in office numerous events pointed to his instability and incompetence.

In 1983, Doss protested the decision of the Claiborne County Board of Supervisors to hire Mason Shelby as county administrator. Enmity between the two men came to a head in June 1986 in the form of a fistfight during a meeting of the board of supervisors. Doss and Shelby sued each other over the incident, but in the end no one was held responsible.

In 1986 Doss failed to prepare the county's tax rolls on time. This delayed tax collections and caused the county to have to borrow $1.9 million to pay its bills and employees.

In 1988, Doss physically attacked S. J. "Skippy" Tuminello at a BOS meeting. Tuminello was the architect for a courthouse renovation project, and his firm had previously sued Doss over another project. For this incident, Doss was convicted of misdemeanor assault and battery charges in municipal court, fined $300 and given a sixty-day suspended jail sentence. The verdict was appealed to the circuit court, where an all-black jury took twenty minutes to acquit Doss.

Late in 1988, Doss feuded with the BOS over whether he had to post a $50,000 bond for each of his positions, tax assessor and tax collector. He had acquired a bond for the assessor position and claimed that was sufficient. The BOS disagreed, and after it threatened to declare the tax collector position vacant, Doss posted the other required bond.

In December 1989, Doss threatened to close his office if the BOS did not restore $46,000 to his budget. The county's revenues had dropped significantly because of a Mississippi Supreme Court decision regarding taxes collected from the Grand Gulf nuclear power plant. The court ruled that the revenue was to be divided among all forty-five counties served by Mississippi Power and Light Company, whereas previously Claiborne County had received most of the tax payments. Deputy Attorney General Robert Gibbs said a shutdown of the tax collector's office would be in violation of state law. Gibbs said the BOS could sue Doss for revenue lost to the county because of any shutdown, and they should be able to collect from the companies providing Doss's two $50,000 bonds.

The pugnacious Evan Doss took on district one supervisor Albert Butler in 1991. After a May BOS meeting, one of the men slammed a door in the other's face, and Doss struck Butler in the face. In an affidavit, Butler claimed Doss pushed a door into him as he was leaving the BOS meeting and struck him in the face with a fist. Charges were filed against Doss, and he subsequently filed an affidavit claiming Butler pushed the door in his face and accused Butler of harassment and of provoking the incident. A hearing was held on the charges filed by Doss and Butler on June 14 in city court. This marked the fourth time that Doss had been taken to court on assault and battery charges following incidents in or around the BOS meeting room. Doss ended up dropping his charges and pleading no contest to the charges against him. He was fined $100 and ordered to pay $19 in court costs.

An early September 1991 altercation between Doss and Claiborne County Administrator James Miller had to be broken up by sheriff's deputies. Miller claimed Doss attacked him in the courthouse after Miller had impounded political campaign materials for which Doss had illegally used county supplies. The men filed assault charges against each other and were released on $200 bonds. Doss eventually pleaded no contest, was fined $100, and assessed court costs.

In the August 1995 Democratic primary, Doss was declared the winner over incumbent Albert Butler in the district one supervisor's race. Butler challenged the defeat in circuit court. Butler's lawyer, Cynthia Stewart, pointed out in court that 127 of 142 people who received federal homeless shelter assistance voted in district one. The Mississippi Supreme Court appointed Circuit Court Judge Keith Starrett to hear Butler's challenge. In November, the judge ruled that Butler's allegations were substantiated by the evidence and voided Doss's nomination. Soon afterwards, Judge Starrett ordered a new election, ruling that there had been election fraud and that Doss was ineligible to run in district one because he lived in district three. Doss was excluded from the new election, which was to be between the Democrat Butler and an independent candidate. In December, Attorney General Mike Moore issued an opinion that allowed Butler to stay in office until a successor was elected. Doss appealed Judge Starrett's ruling to the Mississippi Supreme Court. The court dismissed his appeal in April of 1996. A new election was set by Governor Kirk Fordice for July 1996. Albert Butler won the election.

It was after Doss stepped down as tax assessor/collector on December 31, 1995, that his legal troubles really began. On January 23, 1996, the OSA accused Doss of misappropriating $260,660 of public funds and issued a demand for repayment. In a February 20 one-sentence reply to the OSA's demand, Doss claimed that he didn't owe anything. The following May, Attorney General Mike Moore filed charges against Doss accusing him of embezzling $652,368 of Claiborne County tax collections from October 1, 1993, through January 12, 1996. Doss was arrested and released on $10,000 bond. Doss said, "This is a slap in my face, on my integrity, considering all the years of service I have rendered to the people . . . Certainly I'm going to deny the allegations brought forth."

Referring to the OSA's demand, Steve Patterson, then the state auditor, said, "He didn't take me too seriously. Obviously he does now." Mike Moore said that his office had been investigating Doss for about five months, and the head of the attorney general's public integrity division, John Emfinger, said the office had received numerous complaints about Doss in recent years.

Attorney General Moore said employees of the tax collector took in money and prepared deposit tickets and then gave the money to Doss. Moore said,

"The money did not wind up in the bank." Patterson indicated that the tax collector's books were in order, but comparisons with bank deposit records showed that money was unaccounted for. According to Patterson, "He was robbing Peter to pay Paul from one year to the other in order to make the settlements, to reconcile the books. What actually caught him was when he went out of office." Patterson also said that, while no earlier demands had been made, OSA reports for the past four years had notified the BOS of irregularities and called for corrections. Patterson added, "I am probably the third state auditor who has tried to bring a case against Mr. Doss. I think that we have probably gotten further than anybody else."

Doss immediately claimed the arrest and charges were politically motivated. Referring to the upcoming special election for district one supervisor and the local "power structure," he said, "They are applying the pressure to the attorney general and the state auditor to do something to character assassinate Evan Doss because if they don't, there is a good chance Evan Doss will win." He suggested that the investigators should instead be looking at Claiborne County Administrator James Miller and a former employee of the tax assessor/collector's office.

Miller said, "I have no earthly idea why he said that, and I can only speculate that when the ship is sinking he had to do something. The only one who handled finances was Doss." Special Assistant Attorney General John Emfinger said, "He hasn't provided any information . . . If he has got any information, we would gratefully receive it." Steve Patterson said, "The buck stops with the tax collector. It's odd to me in a very desperate situation like this Mr. Doss would try to bring somebody else into the picture." Patterson also said that he did not even know Doss was seeking the position of supervisor.

Doss had filed for corporate bankruptcy (Evan Doss Corporation) in October 1994 and for personal bankruptcy in October 1995. He was scheduled to face a bankruptcy hearing in Jackson in May 1996. In late March 1996, U.S. Bankruptcy Judge Ed Ellington approved a motion by Mike Moore for time to file a request for an adjourned "341 meeting of creditors" of Doss. The judge granted Moore's request and allowed the attorney general until April 15 to add the state of Mississippi to the list of creditors in the personal bankruptcy case. In a related action, he gave Steve Patterson until July 15, 1996, to object to the dischargeability of debt and/or to object to the debtor's discharge as well, to protect and preserve the rights of the taxpayers of the county and state and the state auditor. The judge had originally ordered the debts discharged until the attorney general and auditor objected. The discharge was rescinded and the order granting more time was issued on March 26.

May 1996 also found Evan Doss in trouble with the federal government. He was arrested May 13 and charged with embezzling $652,358.78 of county funds. The U.S. District Court in Jackson issued a subpoena for him to testify before a federal grand jury. He was also ordered to produce daily journals, deposit slips, checkbooks, bank statements, and other records from October 1994 through December 1995. Doss commented to the media, "I think it is another attempt to destroy me politically because I am running for supervisor. This is still another attempt to destroy my name, my honesty, my integrity, my reputation, and my political career."

In mid-January 1997, Phil Bryant, the new state auditor, presented the Claiborne County Board of Supervisors a check for $100,000 that had been received from Evan Doss's bonding company. This represented payment in the full amount of the former tax collector's surety bond, and it came just ten days short of a year after former State Auditor Steve Patterson had issued the demand for repayment of $260,660. Bryant said in a news release, "The citizens of Claiborne County were not well served by Evan Doss. His violation of the trust placed in him is legendary in Mississippi. Today's recovery of funds is the result of allegations and investigations that go back for years. I intend to continue working to recover more money for the taxpayers of Claiborne County."

Three days after the $100,000 was presented to Claiborne County, Doss was indicted in the U.S. District Court of the Southern District of Mississippi on nineteen criminal counts. Counts one through twelve charged that Doss embezzled $5,000 or more from the Claiborne County Tax Assessor/Collector's Office twelve times between June 29 and September 26, 1994. Counts thirteen through eighteen charged that Doss embezzled $5,000 or more from the Claiborne County Tax Assessor/Collector's Office six times between October 6, 1994, and August 21, 1995. Count nineteen accused Doss of embezzling more than $5,000 from the Claiborne County Tax Assessor/Collector's Office during November 1995. The indictment noted that Claiborne County received federal assistance in excess of $10,000 during each of the federal fiscal years in which the embezzlements took place, thus making the thefts violations of Section 666 (a) (1) (A) of Title 18 of the United States Code. Possible maximum penalties on each count were ten years' imprisonment and a $250,000 fine.

Doss said, "All along I've maintained my innocence. I look forward to having my day in court." But Doss was livid about the proximity of the indictment and the $100,000 payment by the bonding company. He questioned this, saying, "That's the most outrageous act that the bonding company could do.

That was without my approval and that was without my consent. You have to question the timing of this. It further shows a conspiracy."

Attorney General Mike Moore had turned his office's findings, which had put the loss at $652,368 from October 1, 1983, to January 12, 1996, over to the U.S. attorney. But U.S. Attorney Brad Pigott pointed out that only individual transactions of $5,000 or more could be prosecuted under federal law. Moore said that he had asked the U.S. attorney to handle the case because "[w]e felt that we could get a fair and expeditious trial in federal court."

Chokwe Lumumba, a Jackson lawyer and friend of Doss but not his attorney in this case, indicated that the move to federal court was intended to avoid a predominately black jury pool from Claiborne County. In federal court, jurors would be drawn from the Western Division of the U.S. District Court of the Southern District of Mississippi, an area that included Claiborne and seven other counties, Adams, Issaquena, Jefferson, Sharkey, Warren, Wilkerson, and Yazoo. Lumumba said, "The federal courts are famous for taking cases away from black folks so that they can create a jury pool which dilutes the black population, and putting black officials before a jury that is not of their peers. If Claiborne County is the place where these ills are alleged to have taken place, then Claiborne County is where it should be tried."

Relating the charges against Doss to the distribution of taxes from the Grand Gulf nuclear power plant, Lumumba said, "We feel all the charges are false and the only embezzlement or larceny that is going on has been the state itself stealing large portions of the income from Claiborne County. The state ought to be embarrassed to be bringing these charges against Mr. Doss, given the contributions he has made to Claiborne County."

Evan Doss was in serious legal trouble, but he was not without friends willing to put him on a county payroll. The day after his indictment on the federal embezzlement charges, his name appeared on a routine list of school district requests for teaching certificates that was presented to the Mississippi State Board of Education. Frank Melton, a board member from Jackson, noticed his name on the list and asked state Superintendent of Education Tom Burnham if this was the same Evan Doss who was on the front page of the January 17 State/Metro section of the *Clarion-Ledger*. Burnham withdrew Doss's name until his staff could answer some questions. Melton (who became Jackson's mayor in 2005) asked sarcastically, "What's he teaching, business management?" The Jefferson County school district had requested that Doss be given an emergency certificate to teach social studies. Jefferson County borders Claiborne County on the south. Doss had held a teaching certificate in

social studies, but it had expired in 1975. The Jefferson County schools superintendent would not comment on the Doss application.

Doss went to trial on the federal charges in May 1997 before U.S. District Judge David C. Bramlette. The prosecutors had consolidated the original
nineteen charges into nine counts, three of embezzlement and six of money
laundering. Doss's attorney, Mark Pearson, admitted that bank deposits were
not made in a timely manner, "but it is not a federal crime." He claimed that
there had been a robbery at the former tax collector's office, which probably
explained some of the missing funds, and he noted some former employees
had been fired for stealing. U.S. Attorney Robert Anderson told jurors that
the tax collector waited weeks and even months to make bank deposits of tax
payments made by checks and cash.

During the four-day trial, Claiborne County Chancery Clerk Frank Wilson
said that reports of a safe burglary and accusations of thefts by employees
occurred before October 1, 1993, which was the beginning of the time period
during which Doss was accused of taking county funds. Wilson described the
burglary as "rumored" and noted that someone tried unsuccessfully to burn
the hinges off a safe. When pressed by defense attorney Mark Pearson about
whether the safe was actually opened, Wilson admitted that he did not know.
Wilson indicated that, although Doss did not report a safe theft to the board
of supervisors, he requested and received money to buy a new safe. Wilson
also testified that Doss was sometimes as much as three months late in paying
money to the county treasury. State law requires that money collected in one
month be turned over to the county by the twentieth day of the next month.
Wilson testified that Doss did not turn over money for the three months before he left office, October through December 1995. Bank records introduced
as evidence showed deposits made as much as three months later than the
handwritten dates indicating when the deposits were prepared. Carol Burk,
a clerk who worked in the tax collector's office, testified that Doss made the
deposits. The prosecutor showed sixty bank deposit records that had been altered with correction fluid.

Bill Jones, former director of audit for the OSA, testified that he found cash
shortage of $285,886.84, and that Doss had operated a "lapping scheme." Jones
had examined sixty deposit tickets on which multiple days of collections had
been combined. The pattern reflected several days' worth of checks deposited but only one day's worth of cash being deposited. The other days' cash
collections that had been recorded on the books of the tax collector's office
did not show up in the bank deposits, according to the auditor. Jones testi-

fied that money collected over a five-day period in March 1994 and shown on a deposit ticket dated March 1994 was not deposited in a bank until June 30, 1994. In describing the lapping scheme, Jones testified, "As monies were collected, they were used in some part to cover monies that were already short. It can continue indefinitely until the source of that income is cut off. In this case, Mr. Doss left office."

FBI financial analyst Kimberly Abby supported the auditor's testimony. She testified that on some of the dates when the tax deposits did not include cash collections Doss deposited cash into his personal bank accounts at Mississippi Southern Bank and Port Gibson Bank. These deposits totaled $68,780 between December 1993 and December 1995. Abby also testified that sometimes Doss withdrew money immediately after a deposit by writing a check to the Evan Doss, Jr., Corporation. However, neither the auditor nor the FBI analyst could directly link the missing cash tax collections to Doss's personal accounts.

On May 22, after nearly four hours of deliberation, the jury rendered guilty verdicts on all nine counts. Prosecuting attorney Robert Anderson said, "I think Claiborne County has been waiting for this day for a long time." Anderson noted that while documents and testimony in the trial accounted for about $70,000 of the $285,886 embezzled between October 1, 1993, and January 22, 1996, as having been deposited in Doss's personal accounts, "We have never been able to find the rest of it." Defense attorney Mark Pearson immediately announced that the verdicts would be appealed. Doss faced maximum penalties of 120 years in prison and $3.75 million in fines. Sentencing, originally scheduled for June 21, was later changed to July 28.

During the trial, Judge Bramlette cut off Doss's main defense argument and refused to let him fire his attorney. Defense attorney Pearson argued that the missing cash might be explained by the rumored burglary and employee thefts. Judge Bramlette did not allow witnesses to these incidents to testify before the jury because the burglary was supposed to have taken place in 1988, before the period covered by the indictment. When Judge Bramlette refused to allow testimony about these incidents, Doss asked for a mistrial, a new lawyer, and a new judge. The judge rejected all three motions.

Doss called the judge unfair, saying, "This is the heart of our defense here, and this jury has got to understand why this shortage occurred and why we were taking money to cover a shortage." Doss further stated, "You have taken away all the evidence I would ever have, and that at this point in time, I see no reason we would even continue with this trial." Saying that he did not quibble with his attorney's performance, Doss maintained that "[t]he court is making this job impossible for him to do. I am not getting justice here, and if this trial is to go on, it's under protest." The judge replied, "You certainly have a right to do that. This trial will go on under protest."

The judge's ruling left Doss with character witnesses and friends who testified that the cash deposited in his personal accounts could have come from fund-raising efforts on his behalf. Eight witnesses claimed that they had raised money for Doss's political campaigns, to help him in his financial troubles, to assist his struggling radio station, and to help him pay his legal bills. The radio station had been listed as an asset in his bankruptcy proceedings. Delores Polk-Mack of Port Gibson testified that she was chair of the Evan Doss Legal Defense Fund, and that some of the money had recently been paid to help Doss with his defense. Doss had declared that he was indigent and had a court-appointed lawyer paid for by the taxpayers. Noting that "[t]he government doesn't like paying for lawyers when people have legal defense funds and other assets," prosecuting attorney Robert Anderson indicated that the U.S. Attorney's Office would consider what, if any, action to take.

Doss filed motions in U.S. District Court to have his convictions thrown out and to be granted a new trial. He challenged the makeup of the jury and the federal laws under which he was convicted. Prosecuting attorney Robert Anderson characterized the latest legal maneuver as a "kitchen sink motion" that is fairly routine after convictions.

On July 28, 1997, Judge Bramlette sentenced Evan Doss to a maximum of four years and three months in prison and three years' probation. He also imposed a fine of $186,000. Doss said, "The money was deposited. But they are saying, 'Here we got a nigger, here we can show others we can convict. I even have witnesses that were out in the hallway that overheard conversations of some of the things they were saying." Prosecuting attorney Anderson countered, "I've heard that several times . . . This case had nothing to do with race." Judge Bramlette agreed, saying, "I saw nothing to indicate that it is true." Citing Martin Luther King, Jr., the judge indicated that Doss had been judged by the content of his character, not the color of his skin. He added that Doss was sworn to serve the public, but "this defendant served himself. Anything that is done illegally must be brought from the dark corners to the sunshine. There will be no tolerance from the government for corruption in this county or state."

Judge Bramlette had federal marshals take Doss into custody immediately after sentencing, and he was escorted to a waiting car in handcuffs. The judge explained that Doss might be a threat to prosecution witnesses. "The risk of flight does not concern me . . . but he's been involved in altercations over the years in Claiborne County."

Delores Polk-Mack chose to continue the race theme in Doss's defense. "He's been railroaded from Day 1 . . . from the all-white racist jury to the white racist attorney and the white racist judge. Contrary to what they are telling the court, Claiborne County supports Doss 100 percent. Once we get out of the state of Mississippi, we are confident we will win on appeal."

Doss appealed his embezzlement and money laundering convictions to the United States Court of Appeals for the Fifth Circuit. The appeal alleged that the district court erred in denying Doss's motion to dismiss the indictment for lack of subject jurisdiction (he claimed no federal funds were involved). Doss also claimed the court abused its discretion in failing to grant his motion for continuance and by excluding two defense witnesses. Finally, Doss claimed the district court erred in changing venue from the Western Division to the Jackson Division of the Southern District of Mississippi. The appeals court affirmed the district court verdict in all respects in August 1997.

In January 1998, Doss, the Evan Doss, Jr., Corporation, and Leola Dickey, Doss's sister, were indicted for conspiracy to conceal assets from the trustee in the bankruptcy in the cases of Doss and his corporation. Doss and his corporation were alleged to have transferred assets belonging to their bankrupt estates to an account opened by Leola Dickey. In June of 1998, while he was in prison for embezzlement and money laundering, Doss was sentenced to an additional thirty months for the bankruptcy offense. U.S. District Judge Tom S. Lee dismissed the charges against Dickey without prejudice at the request of Assistant U.S. Attorney Robert Anderson in August 1998. Doss appealed his conviction on the bankruptcy charge, but the U.S. Court of Appeals for the Fifth Circuit upheld the verdict in March of 2003.

In his appeal of the embezzlement conviction, Doss maintained that "I did not steal or embezzle any taxpayer money." In May 2002, the court of appeals upheld the embezzlement and money-laundering convictions. In December 2002, when he was in a halfway house in Jackson completing his sentence that had only six months to run, Doss appealed his embezzlement and money-laundering convictions to the U.S. Supreme Court. In this appeal, Doss claimed that prosecutors failed to show that the charges against him violated any federal law. According to Doss's petition, "This case raises the question of how far Congress has gone, and under the constitution may go, to federalize crime—here the alleged crime of theft of local county funds." Doss asserted, "The alleged crimes they convicted me of were all state offenses." The Supreme Court refused to hear the case.

Claiborne County's pursuit of funds under the control of Evan Doss, Jr., continued through April 2004. When he was tax assessor/collector, Doss had an account with Mississippi Southern Bank in his name as tax assessor. When Doss left office, the bank interpleaded the funds. That is, the bank sued Claiborne County, Evan Doss, Jr., and Doss's bankruptcy trustee, Derek A. Henderson, in Claiborne County Chancery Court, asking the court to decide the rightful owner. By January 31, 2004, the balance in the account had grown to $29,326.05. Doss, his attorney, Johnnie McDaniels, and Claiborne County's attorney, Allen L. Burrell, reached an agreement in April 2004 that the money, now totaling $29,345.34, belonged to Claiborne County. Doss, his attorney, and the county's attorney appeared in chancery court on April 13, 2004, to finalize the agreement. Bankruptcy trustee Derek A. Henderson refused to participate because he did not consider the funds in question the personal funds of Evan Doss. Chancellor Kennie Middleton issued a judgment April 13, 2004, ruling that the funds belonged to Claiborne County and calling for the bank (now State Bank and Trust Company) to remit the funds to the county. On April 14, 2004, the bank paid the money to Claiborne County by check.

In August 2004, Judge Lee sent Doss back to prison for failure to gain employment or make any payment during his period of supervised release. Doss had been ordered to pay $192,549.92 to Derek A. Henderson. Doss's corporation and Doss himself had been ordered to pay restitution of $81,832.11. Doss was to report to prison by October 4, 2004.

Mary Jones, Claiborne County Tax Assessor/Collector

On July 17, 2002, the OSA's Investigations Division received a referral from the county audit section concerning delayed bank deposits of Claiborne County tax receipts. The director of the county audit section, Ed Yarborough, indicated that the audit work which generated the referral was accomplished by the CPA firm of Lyles and Sinclair and that Tracey Sinclair had performed the field work. Special Agent Patrick Dendy was assigned to the case.

On September 16, 2002, Dendy contacted the attorney general's public integrity division, which had already done some work in the Claiborne County tax assessor/collector's office. Roger Cribbs and Kyle Wilson of the AG's office met with Dendy, Special Agent Bubba Gabbert, and Jesse Bingham to discuss the case. The AG representatives reported that a deputy tax collector, Doretha Rankin, had been cashing personal checks which were included in daily deposits. The checks were returned for not sufficient funds (NSF). When the checks were returned by the bank, the deputy would intercept them in the mail and destroy them. Cribbs indicated that the deputy used this method on three occasions in August of 2002 to embezzle about $7,000. The OSA and AG personnel proceeded with a joint investigation of the apparent embezzlement by the deputy and the apparent failure of Mary Jones, Claiborne County tax assessor/collector, to deposit tax receipts in a timely manner.

During a cash count conducted at the Claiborne County tax assessor/collector's office on October 10, 2002, investigators discovered Tax Collector's check 1773 dated September 30, 2002, payable to the Claiborne County Board of Supervisors. The check had been returned by the bank because there were not sufficient funds in the account to cover the amount of the check. Tax collector Mary Jones was interviewed, and she admitted that she had taken envelopes containing deposits to her home and used the currency they contained.

Patrick Dendy's report of October 10, relates what happened next:

Ms. Jones was asked if she would go to her residence, which is located at 308 Cedar Street, Port Gibson, Mississippi, and retrieve the envelopes with an agent accompanying her. Ms. Jones said she did not want anyone going into her house with her. Because of this a search warrant was obtained by [AG investigator] Mr. Wilson for Jones' residence.

Claiborne County Sheriff Frank Davis, Mr. Wilson and [OSA investigator] Mr. Gabbert went to Ms. Jones' residence. They found bags containing numerous deposit envelopes. Mr. Gabbert returned to the Claiborne County Courthouse and informed [OSA performance audit division director] Mr. Goodwin and I about the large number of items at the residence. We all returned there to examine the envelopes at Ms. Jones' residence. Since there was not a good place at the residence to allow for the examination of the contents of each envelope, Sheriff Davis suggested that we take them to the conference room in his office to inventory the contents of each envelope. Ms. Jones agreed to this and personally carried the envelopes to the sheriff's office, riding with the sheriff in his vehicle.

At the sheriff's office, an inventory was prepared listing the contents of each envelope. A copy of the inventory was provided to Ms. Jones, and Mr. Wilson took possession of all the original items.

While conducting this inventory, we learned that Ms. Jones had voluntarily resigned as tax collector. This resignation was submitted to the Claiborne County Board of Supervisors, and I was provided a copy. [Jones had been elected tax collector in January of 1996, and she had worked in the tax collector's office for twenty-seven years. She had worked for and followed Evan Doss as tax collector.]

OSA investigator Patrick Dendy documented the amount of an exception the agency was to take against Mary Jones in a February 14, 2003, report:

Based upon my analysis of the collections and deposits for the Claiborne County Tax Collector's Office, there appears to have been currency in the amount of One Hundred Ten Thousand Five Hundred One Dollars and Fifty-Three Cents ($110,501.53) embezzled from that office from money collected from June 19, 2001 through June 25, 2002. In addition to this, checks collected by that office totaling Seven Thousand Five Hundred Ninety-Nine Dollars and Sixty-Six Cents ($7,599.66) could not be accounted for.

The deposit slips for the collections of June 19, 2001, June 25, 2001, and August 27, 2001, appear to have been altered by former Claiborne County Tax Collector Mary Jones. For these three (3) deposits, the currency amounts on the original deposit slips have been covered with white out, and lower currency amounts listed in their place. . . .

Deposit slips for several days' collections, dating from December 10, 2001, through April 4, 2002, appear to have been altered as well. On twenty-seven (27) occasions during this time, additional checks were substituted in deposits for cash that had been collected. I have prepared a schedule documenting these collections and deposits, many of which were deposited into the bank weeks later than [when] they were collected. This delay allowed Ms. Jones to receive the checks sufficient to cover the currency she was removing from the collections.

Analysis of the deposit slips related to these deposits revealed that, in many instances, the additional checks were simply added to the bottom of the list. On some occasions an entirely new deposit slip was prepared. We have obtained the original correctly prepared deposit slips for several of these days, which, when compared to the new deposit slips, reveal the extra checks added to the deposit.

On October 10, 2002, we obtained numerous deposit envelopes from Ms. Jones' personal residence, most of which contained deposit items that she had taken to her house rather than deposited in the bank. Twenty-four (24) of these deposit envelopes contained some of the checks collected on the dates listed on the envelope. Also contained in these envelopes were deposit slips filled out in the office as the checks were collected. The checks not in the envelopes had been used to substitute for cash in other days' deposits. Some of these envelopes also contained change that had been left in them, but none of the currency was left.

The same day we obtained thirty-seven (37) envelopes from Ms. Jones' residence containing checks from those days' collections. In the case of these envelopes, all of the checks collected were still inside. Other than some change in a few of the envelopes, only the currency appeared to be missing. These envelopes also contained deposit slips that were prepared in the office as the checks were collected.

Each of the days' collections and deposits was analyzed on a schedule prepared by me. This schedule shows the currency and check overages and shortages for each day. When interviewed, Ms. Jones admitted swapping checks for cash to enable her to pull cash from the daily collections and still remain in balance for the day. After a while, she simply took the deposit envelopes home, and ultimately stopped making deposits.

In December 2003, fifty-year-old Mary Levon Jones was indicted by a Claiborne County grand jury on three counts of embezzlement. Count one charged her with embezzling $1,600 during the period June 19 through August 30, 2001. Count two charged that she embezzled $9,692 in December of 2001. Count three charged her with embezzling $99,209 during the period January 1, 2002, through June 28, 2002. Jones was arrested on December 9, 2003. She pled not guilty and was immediately released on a $15,000 bond.

Former Claiborne County Tax Assessor/Collector Mary Levon Jones pled guilty to all three counts of the indictment on May 25, 2004. Circuit Court Judge Lamar Pickard sentenced her to serve a term of ten years on each count with the sentences to run concurrently. She was ordered incarcerated for the first five years of the sentence, and the last five years were suspended. She was to be placed on three years of postrelease supervision after she got out of prison. Jones was also ordered to pay court costs of $248, a $300 bond fee, a $2,000 fine, and $110,502 in restitution. If she has not paid the restitution, fees, and fines before she is released from incarceration, Jones is to be placed in a state restitution center and is to remain there until all are paid.

On July 6, 2004, Phil Bryant sent a demand letter to Mary Jones and her bonding company, Zurich North America, for $160, 377. This amount was computed by adding the amount embezzled ($110,502), checks not deposited ($7,264), interest calculated at 1 percent per month from the date of loss ($30,719), and cost of recovery ($11,820). The insurance company paid the

$100,000 maximum on the claim, and Jesse Bingham presented a check to the Claiborne County Board of Supervisors for that amount on October 5, 2004.

As noted above, a deputy in the tax collector's office, Doretha Rankin, also embezzled money. In January of 2004, Rankin pled guilty to embezzling $20,898 and was sentenced to six months in prison. Phil Bryant issued Rankin a demand letter on January 12, 2004, for $25,099, which included interest and costs of the investigation. The demand was paid in full on January 13, 2004. The OSA returned $24,500, principal and interest, to Claiborne County on February 24, 2004.

Carla Chris Haley, Lincoln County Deputy Tax Collector

Lincoln County Tax Assessor/Collector Jerry E. Bailey filed a complaint with the OSA in early October 1997 alleging that one of his deputies, Carla C. Haley, had embezzled money from the tax collector's office. Bailey reported that Haley failed to properly record approximately $3,000 in real property receipts collected in December 1996. The receipts were actually reported in August 1997, signaling some type of lapping scheme. The OSA assigned investigator Charles Robinette to the case on October 10, 1997.

The problem with real property receipts was discovered when the bookkeeper in the tax collector's office, Mary Wallace, detected an entry called "Various Land Receipts—$2,376.00—all in cash" in an August 1997 daily settlement. The taxpayers had been issued receipts in December 1996, but the receipts were not included in Haley's daily settlement with the bookkeeper at that time. Without the August entry to clear the taxes due, the properties would have been sold at public auction for non-payment of taxes. Haley, who had worked as a deputy tax collector since September 11, 1995, was fired by Bailey on September 30, 1997. She was bonded for $25,000.

An August 16, 1999, report by OSA investigator Charles Robinette documented how Haley was able to extract cash from auto tag receipts and still have her daily paperwork balance. A cash receipt dated June 4, 1997, retained in the tax collector's office for tag MK3 323, showed collection of $79.31 in cash, a credit for a prior tag of $200.77, and a legislative tax credit of $479.34. The auditor's work revealed that the credit for the prior tag actually due was only $2.71. The taxpayer was asked to bring her copy of the receipt to the tax collector's office. The taxpayer's copy, which properly reflected the legislative tax credit, showed that she had paid $279.17 in cash. The auditor determined that Haley stole the difference between what the taxpayer paid in cash ($279.17) and what was reflected on the tax collector's copy of the receipt ($79.31), or $199.86.

The OSA worked with Wade Motes of Delta Computer Systems, Inc., of Gulfport to extract needed information from records on the state network maintained by the State Tax Commission. A computer program was developed and used to identify car tag transactions originating from Chris Haley's drawer in Lincoln County that had been changed or deleted. The program identified twenty-eight such items during the period October 23, 1996, through September 19, 1997. The OSA audited each of these items to help tie down monies missing from car tag transactions.

As the OSA's investigation continued into early December 1999, Haley failed to show up for several scheduled meetings with the auditors. In a December 14, 1999, interview with OSA Special Agents Robinette and Patrick Dendy that was audiotaped, Haley gave a rambling story of how money came up missing from her drawer and how she covered up the problem. The former deputy tax collector claimed that in December 1996 her cash drawer began to check up hundreds of dollars short and that, instead of telling her supervisor, Mary Wallace, or tax collector Jerry Bailey, she began placing her own money in an envelope to repay the missing money. Haley also claimed that she did not have the ability to reprint receipts for car tags for lesser amounts than actually received from taxpayers and to use the smaller amounts to make deposits and settlements. However, she admitted her initials were on several receipts that had been altered, including two that had been changed to show exactly $100 less than actually collected. Although she initially denied taking any money for personal use, she later admitted taking this $200 to pay for groceries. She initially claimed not to know who could have been going into her cash drawer and taking money but later said it could have been a former deputy clerk. Haley gave several explanations of how she had replaced money missing from her drawer and covered it up by altering documents. She finally admitted taking about $100 from the cash drawer for herself every other week and estimated the total amounted to approximately $1,500. She claimed to have done this because she had personally repaid so much money to cover the money that had been taken from her drawer. Haley said she would repay any monies found to be missing.

The former deputy tax collector wrote and signed a document witnessed by three people and dated 12/14/99 that reads as follows:

Between Dec. 96 – March or April 97 my money draw[er] would come up short 150.00 to 600.00, not on any given day, once or twice a week. In order to repay or to cover the money missing, I would hold land tax receipts in my money bag. I also altered other documents to cover this amount. (heavy truck, car tags p/p)

The money started missing when I came upon information about M/H [mobile home] taxes that were not being paid by employees. Nancy Jordan confronted my [me] about this and she told me to "leave her children's business alone." It was common knowledge that other employees M/H taxes were not paid.

Chris Haley
I am giving this Statement voluntarily and of my own free will. ch

On December 15, Haley again contacted OSA Special Agent Patrick Dendy and denied any involvement with embezzlement of approximately $8,000 from land taxes in 1996. She claimed that another person had taken the money out of her cash drawer. Haley also claimed to have repaid $1,500 in March 1997 that she admitted taking. The auditors could find no evidence of this repayment.

Carla Chris Haley was indicted by the grand jury of the Fourteenth Judicial District of Mississippi during its January 2000 term on two counts of making false entries and for one count of embezzlement. The offences were alleged to have occurred while Haley served as Lincoln County Deputy Tax Collector from December 1996 through September 1997. She was charged with failing to deposit the proceeds of taxes collected and on two separate occasions making false entries in official records to cover up the thefts.

On February 23, 2000, OSA investigators Robinette and Dendy met with Haley, District Attorney Jerry Rushing, and Haley's attorney, Joe Fernald, at the Lincoln County courthouse. The purpose of the meeting was for the OSA and district attorney to provide discovery information. The investigators showed Fernald the results of their work to date, which had been assembled in an incomplete file for discovery purposes only. The investigators also explained the process they had gone through to document missing monies handled by Haley. Fernald asked for copies of documents included in the file, and the documents were delivered to him on February 25, 2000. At Fernald's request, Haley's December 14, 1999, written statement was also faxed to him on the twenty-fifth.

At the request of Lincoln County District Attorney Jerry Rushing, the OSA produced a summary of exceptions for the Lincoln County tax collector. This summary, dated March 15, 2000, was used in negotiating a plea bargain.

Principal Items

Realty Receipts included in the indictment	$2,739.00
Automobile Receipts included in the indictment	8,461.03
Other Receipts not properly settled	6,434.61
Total Principal Items	$17,814.64

Interest

Associated with Realty	$1,082.09
Associated with Automobiles	2,741.06
Associated with Other Receipts	2,434.01
Total Interest	$6,257.16

Cost of Investigation	$12,000.00
Total Exception	$36,071.80

A subsequent review reduced the total exception to $35,395.

In early May of 2000, thirty-five-year-old Carla Chris Haley pleaded guilty to one count of embezzlement and two counts of making false entries. On May 5, 2000, she was sentenced by Circuit Court Judge Keith Starrett to a suspended eight-year prison term and placed on probation for five years. On the embezzlement count, she was also ordered to pay $17,815 in restitution, $6,257 in interest, $12,000 for the cost of the investigation, and $246 in court costs. On the two false entries counts, Haley was also given an eight-year suspended prison term and placed on probation for five years. The two sentences were to run concurrently.

On May 12, 2000, former Lincoln County Deputy Tax Collector Carla Chris Haley made a partial payment of $18,312. During fiscal year 2000, she also repaid $400 directly to Lincoln County. State Auditor Phil Bryant issued Haley a formal written demand in the amount of $16,784 on August 10, 2000. A month later, the demand having not been paid, Bryant transferred it to the office of the attorney general for collection. In May 2003, CNA Security paid the demand, and the OSA closed the case June 23, 2003.

Anna Addison Langston, Sunflower County Tax Assessor/Collector

In July 2002, Sunflower County Chancery Clerk Paula Sykes requested that the Performance Audit Division of the OSA help ascertain why actual tax settlements were less than budgeted amounts. Jeff Goodwin, director of the Performance Audit Division, wrote to Clanton Beamon, president of the Sunflower County Board of Supervisors (BOS), on August 28, 2002, and summarized the auditors' findings. The five-page single-spaced letter noted numerous problems in the tax assessor/collector's office, including the following:

(a) Erroneous assessed values were used for budgeting purposes.

(b) There were unexplained differences between projected tax collections based on assessed values and actual collections.

(c) There were unexplained decreases in the assessed values of automobiles and ad valorem taxes collected on automobiles.

(d) There were significant disparities in the amounts settled among funds when compared to assessed values and millage rates, indicating settlement and perhaps collection problems.

(e) Monthly reconciliations were not made between computer-generated settlement sheets and handwritten spreadsheets actually used to make the settlements.

(f) Some parcels of land on which year 2000 property taxes had not been paid had been held out of 2001 tax sales. In 2002, the tax collector was still accepting payments on these proprieties. If proper procedures had been followed, the chancery clerk would have been accepting land redemption payments. The taxes due on these properties totaled $32,657, of which some had been received but not properly accounted for.

(g) The tax collector was improperly accepting partial tax payments.

(h) The tax collector was selling automobile licenses and improperly holding checks after individuals had received license plates.

(i) Bad checks received as tax payments were not being followed up on properly.

(j) The tax collector had not sold sixteenth section leasehold interests at tax sales when the lessees had not paid their taxes.

(k) The tax collector had not properly notified the board attorney of bankruptcies to facilitate collection efforts against bankrupt delinquent taxpayers.

(l) The tax collector claimed to be unaware of remedies provided by state law for collection of unpaid personal property taxes.

(m) People who paid personal property taxes were not always provided receipts.

(n) Nonprofit and ecclesiastical bodies had been improperly granted exemptions to ad valorem taxes on vehicles.

(o) In excess of $200,000 was outstanding in uncollected solid waste fees.

Because of its limited resources, the OSA recommended that the BOS contract with a private firm to perform a more in-depth review of the tax assessor/collector's operations.

The board of supervisors subsequently engaged the CPA firm Moss and Killibrew to perform an evaluation of the tax collector's office and to assist Langston with her monthly settlements to the county and other entities.

It could be surmised from the OSA's findings that first-term Sunflower County Tax Assessor/Collector Anna Addison Langston was either grossly negligent in carrying out her duties, incompetent, or engaged in criminal activities. It could also be predicted that, absent immediate effective actions, Sunflower County would soon experience major financial problems. The OSA's Performance Audit Division recommended that the Investigations Division open an investigation into possible embezzlement. The OSA opened such an investigation August 27, 2002, and assigned Special Agent Rick Moody to the case.

In September 2003, the Sunflower County Board of Supervisors asked all county agencies to cut back 10 percent from their budget for the upcoming fiscal year, which was to begin October 1. The new county budget totaled about $14 million. The board indicated that lower property assessment, embezzlement of county funds, and a desire not to raise taxes caused the across-the-board reductions. County Attorney Johnny McWilliams said, "It was a true slashing. We cut as much as we could. There will be no employee raises." During the prior year, supervisors noted financial difficulties and raised taxes about 6 percent. The board also asked State Auditor Phil Bryant to analyze tax collection procedures.

The OSA found many financial discrepancies and contacted District Attorney Frank Carlton. The OSA's work led to the September 4, 2003, indictments of Sunflower County Tax Assessor/Collector Anna Addison Langston, Deputy Tax Assessor/Collector Dandreier Bush, and county purchases clerk Gwen Ailes. Langston was indicted on one count of embezzling more than $10,000 and one count of changing vehicle tag receipts and underreporting monies collected by her office. All three of the women had worked for Sunflower County for more than twenty years. Langston and Bush were accused of taking county money between December 1, 2000, and August 29, 2003. Langston was also alleged to have loaned Ailes at least $500 of county money. The BOS immediately suspended Bush and Ailes with pay and shortly thereafter fired both of them.

Langston won the Democratic primary for a second term in August 2003, and she faced no opposition in the general election scheduled for November.

Arrested on September 5, 2003, she remained in office, although the BOS asked her to take paid leave.

A citizen petitioned the BOS September 5, 2003, asking for a refund of the money he had paid to redeem his land that had been sold for delinquent taxes. The petition shed light on one of the ways tax payments were being embezzled and how such chicanery adversely affected individual taxpayers.

To: The Board of Supervisors
Sunflower County Mississippi
Sunflower County Courthouse
Indianola, MS 38751

Re: Parcel no. 1133 0500000 0000200
Legal Description: 1.9 ac pt lot 8 N of Bayou

On December 13, 2002, I, Edwin Searcy, paid $544.62 into the Sunflower County Tax Assessor/Collector's Office as payment for my 2002 county property taxes. I attach hereto a copy of the tax receipt where I paid these taxes.

I have since learned that my property was sold on the April 7, 2003, tax sale for delinquent taxes. I have attempted on several occasions to talk to the Sunflower County Tax Assessor/Collector's Office to get this matter resolved, without any success. Because my mortgage company had received an incorrect report on these taxes being delinquent, I redeemed this property from the sale paying $641.38 into the Sunflower County Chancery Clerk's Office on release number 20,792.

This petition is to request that the Board authorize the Chancery Clerk to refund the redemption and release from the Tax Sale and refund the $641.38 to me. Thank you for your consideration and approval of this request.

Edwin Searcy

On October 14, 2003, by way of Executive Order 890, Governor Ronnie Musgrove suspended Anna Langston from her position of tax assessor/collector. Under state law, the governor has the power to suspend "alleged defaulting tax collectors pending the investigation of their respective accounts." It had been more than twenty years since a governor had taken such action. When sheriff's deputies and an officer from the OSA delivered the governor's executive order, Langston vacated her office immediately. Langston, who earned $51,516 annually, was to receive her salary until the matter was resolved.

In October 2003, Dandreier Bush pled guilty to embezzling less than $500, and Gwen Ailes pled guilty to conspiracy to embezzle. Both agreed to testify against Langston, whose trial was set for November 14, 2003. Both women were ordered to make restitution, and each received pretrial intervention because they agreed to testify against their former boss.

OSA Special Agent Ricky Moody's synopsis report, dated August 17, 2004, explained clearly what the investigators found. It includes the following paragraphs:

> The field work in this investigation began on November 21, 2002. Special Agent Ricky Moody, along with Special Agents Bubba Gabbert and Pat Dendy, Senior Special Agents Ben Norris and Denver Smith conducted an unannounced cash count of the office and conducted interviews with the deputy tax collectors. We also met with Gay Moss [of the CPA firm], who advised that there appeared to be a serious problem with timely deposits of daily cash collections, and possibly that all collections made were not being receipted. Moss also advised that internal controls were not in place and that Addison knew all the deputies' passwords to enter their computer terminals. At this time Senior Special Agent Denver Smith met with Paula Sykes, Chancery Clerk, and all passwords were changed.
>
> The first step in the investigation required a subpoena of all deposit items for the Tax Collector's Office for the calendar years 2001–2002. The county depository was Planters Bank & Trust of Indianola, Mississippi. After a preliminary matching of a sample of daily collection data with the corresponding deposits, it became apparent that timely deposits were not being made and checks were being substituted for cash. At this point, a detailed analysis of each day's collections matched with the corresponding deposits was compiled. This analysis indicated that, for daily collections and corresponding deposits ranging from July 1, 2001, through December 31, 2002, a total of Forty-Seven Thousand Six Hundred Fifty-Five Dollars and Seventy-Three Cents ($47,655.73), in cash, had been collected, but not deposited. Included in this analysis were four (4) days' collections that were never deposited. These collections are as follows:

Date	Cash Collected	Checks Collected	Total
March 21, 2002	$4,718.75	$17,375.70	$22,094.45
March 22, 2002	$8,208.38	$10,087.62	$18,296.00
August 1, 2002	$4,636.30	$11,175.11	$15,811.50
September 3, 2002	$7,076.42	$13,046.51	$20,122.93

> The checks collected for these four days were ultimately deposited in other days' collections, allowing the cash in those days' collections to be removed.

Also, a deposit of Forty Thousand Three Hundred Ninety Dollars and Forty-Five Cents ($40,390.45), made on April 25, 2002, contained a check from Tarrant Apparel totaling Thirty Nine Thousand Ninety-Nine Dollars ($39,099). This check was for personal property and realty taxes for Rocky Apparel in Ruleville, Mississippi. This check was deposited, but the personal property taxes were never posted into the computer system, nor settled to the county. It should be noted that the collections of March 21 and 22, 2002, which were never posted, totaled Forty Thousand Three Hundred Ninety Dollars and Forty-Five Cents ($40,390.45).

On January 29, 2003, Anna Addison [Langston] was interviewed by Special Agents Ricky Moody and Pat Dendy. The purpose of this interview was to question Addison about cash shortages on certain deposits. When questioned about these deposits and comparing them with corresponding collection sheets, Addison could give no explanation. After several attempts to gain information, Addison stated that she wanted to contact her attorney. At this point, Addison refused to cooperate any further with the investigation.

On October 7, 2002, the day Gay Moss was to begin work at the Tax Collector's Office, Addison made two (2) cash deposits, one for Eight Thousand Three Hundred Eighty Dollars ($8,380.00) and another for Nine Thousand Nine Hundred Five ($9,905.00). The following day, October 8, 2002, Addison made a cash deposit of Seven Thousand Dollars ($7,000.00). There were no collection sheets to substantiate these deposits. According to Moss, when questioned about the large cash deposits, Addison stated that the cash had been in the vault, and she (Addison) had not had time to make a deposit.

Through the investigation it was determined that Gwendolyn Ailes, Purchasing Clerk for Sunflower County, had been receiving loans from Addison. Ailes stated that Addison would hold checks for her (Ailes) and give her cash in return. According to Ailes, the cash that she received was from receipts collected through the Tax Collector's Office. Ailes stated that she would make the checks payable to the Sunflower County Tax Collector, but Addison would hold the checks and not send them to the bank. Ailes states that, in late September or early October 2002, Addison called her (Ailes) and stated that she (Addison) needed Ailes to repay the cash as soon as possible. Ailes stated that she and Addison agreed that she (Ailes) owed approximately Ten Thousand Dollars ($10,000.00). Ailes stated that she went to her brother, Henry Palmer, and borrowed Five Thousand Dollars ($5,000.00), and to a friend, Annette Turner, and borrowed Three Thousand Dollars ($3,000.00). The rest of the money, Ailes stated, came from personal funds. Ailes stated that, when she secured the funds, she contacted Addison. Ailes stated that, the next day when she went home for lunch, Addison was at her house waiting to pick up the money. Ailes stated that as soon as she gave Addison the money, Addison called the Tax Collector's Office and requested Dandrier Bush, Deputy Tax Collector, to come to Ailes house. Ailes stated that when Bush arrived, Addison gave her (Bush) the money and instructed her to make a deposit. The facts of this statement were later confirmed through an interview with Bush. Ailes stated that, at a later date, Addison provided her (Ailes) with the checks that she (Addison) had been holding. Ailes stated that she (Ailes) destroyed the checks.

Through a subpoena of Addison's personal bank records, it was determined that on October 7, 2002, Addison secured a personal loan from Community Bank of Indianola, Mississippi. The loan was for Seven Thousand Dollars ($7,000.00). It was determined that, upon securing the loan, Addison cashed the loan check at Community Bank on October 7, 2002, and received Seven Thousand Dollars ($7,000.00) in cash.

On July 25, 2003, Gay Moss made an unexpected appearance at the Tax Collector's Office. Addison was not at work that day. Upon arrival, Moss noticed that several days' collections were in the vault and had not been deposited. Moss instructed Deputy Dandrier Bush to get all the collection receipts together and make out deposits to take to the bank. According to Moss, Bush came to her (Moss) and stated that there was not enough cash on hand to cover the deposits. Moss then contacted the Office of the State Auditor and Senior Special Agent Denver Smith met with Special Agents Ricky Moody and Bob Woods at the Sunflower County Courthouse. Upon arrival, it was determined that the cash shortage for collections of July 21, 2003, was Four Thousand Three Hundred Seventy-Nine Dollars and Twenty-Nine Cents ($4,379.29), and the cash shortage for collections of July 24, 2003, was Three Thousand Thirty-One Dollars and Forty-Four Cents ($3,031.44), for a total cash shortage of Seven Thousand Four Hundred Ten Dollars and Seventy-Three Cents ($7,410.73). Through subsequent interviews with deputies, it was determined that Addison had taken this cash and had told them that she would repay the cash before Moss arrived. The deputies also stated that Addison would order them (deputies) to delete the dates from the car tag receipts and hold the cash for her (Addison). The deputies stated that Addison had threatened them with termination if they did not comply with her requests. Each deputy interviewed stated that Addison always told them that she was only borrowing the cash and was repaying it later. The deputies also stated that some realty and personal property taxes had been received but were never receipted into the computer system. This became evident when the April Tax Sale was published in the local newspaper, and several citizens were complaining about their property being sold for delinquent taxes when the taxes had already been paid.

In a sworn statement given to the OSA, Juliana Bell, deputy tax collector, identified what might have been the major cause of Langston's chicanery. She wrote that Langston had her write personal checks to about five different pay-day loan companies. According to Bell, Langston said she was going to use the checks to get money to gamble at the casinos. Bell also indicated that Langston would take cash in amounts of $300 to $500 out of Bell's drawer and tell her she was going to the casinos.

The trial scheduled for November 14, 2003, never took place. Langston was indicted again on December 16, 2004, on six counts of embezzlement totaling $13,720 and two counts of making false entries. Based on a February 11, 2005, plea agreement with the district attorney's office, Langston pled guilty in Sunflower County Circuit Court on February 25, 2005, to two counts of embezzlement. The two counts on which Langston pled guilty were count one of the first indictment, which charged embezzlement of more than $10,000 during the period July 1, 2001, through August 29, 2003, and count five of the second indictment, which charged embezzlement of $9,372 on or before November 20, 2001. The 2002 sentencing law requiring at least one year prison time for anyone convicted of embezzling $10,000 or more of public monies was not in effect because the charges covered time periods before July 1, 2002. Circuit Court Judge Margaret Carey-McCray sentenced the former elected public official to five years in an intensive supervision program (house arrest). Judge Carey-McCray also ordered Langston to make restitution of $97,767 to Sunflower County and $13,720 to the state tax commission. She was also fined $250 and ordered to pay $5,000 in court costs and another $5,000 to the crime victims' compensation fund. In addition, Langston was to serve five years' probation after release from the intensive supervision program.

After imposing sentence, Judge Margaret Carey-McCray ordered Langston's immediate removal from the office of Sunflower County tax assessor/collector. The board of supervisors removed Anna Addison Langston from office on March 1, 2005. The board immediately appointed Carolyn Ray to the position of tax assessor/collector until a special election could be held in November 2005. As noted above, Ray was already serving in that capacity, having been appointed by former Governor Ronnie Musgrove when he suspended Langston.

On March 10, 2005, Phil Bryant issued a letter to Anna Addison Langston and Saint Paul Fire and Marine insurance company demanding payment of $164,178. The total comprised the amount Langston embezzled, interest at 1 percent per month from the date of loss, cost of bank records, and cost of OSA staff time. The OSA recovered money from both Langston and the bonding company. Phil Bryant presented two checks totaling $164,178 to the Sun-flower County Board of Supervisors on June 6, 2005.

Stacy Montgomery, Lincoln County Deputy Tax Collector

While working on the investigation of Lincoln County Deputy Tax Collector Chris Haley, OSA Special Agent Charles Robinette found a problem regarding the work of Stacy Montgomery, another Lincoln County deputy tax collector. On August 27, 1999, he filed a complaint with the Investigations Division of the OSA alleging that tax collections were not being properly reported. The OSA opened an investigation August 30, 1999, and assigned Robinette and Special Agent Pat Dendy to the case.

Stacy Montgomery began work in the tax office in July 1993. She took ma-ternity leave for three months in both 1995 and 1999, and she was off from work for a short time in 1997 after undergoing surgery.

Special Agent Robinette's January 13, 2000, report summarizes important events in this case. The report was prepared as a synopsis of significant dates and the sequence of events that led to the exceptions which had been pre-pared as a result of an investigation into the work of former Deputy Tax Col-lector Stacy Montgomery:

1. Stacy D. Montgomery becomes an employee of the Lincoln County Tax Collector's Office, July 19, 1993.

2. October 6, 1997 – State Auditor's Office opens original investigation with Chris Haley as the subject.

3. Month of September 1999 – While auditors are present working at the Lincoln County Tax Collector's Office, customers come to the various col-lection windows to purchase renewals for car tags for which there is no rec-ord of their prior year's purchase. Auditors copy their expiring car tags on the copy machine and in [some] cases, obtain [a] copy of the tag receipt for which there is no record at the office. These no-record items are from a year gone by, i.e., 1998.

4. August 19, 1999 – Additional research work that had been performed by Delta Computer Company from the back-up material supplied by Lincoln County leads to a listing of car tag receipts that have been deleted off the Lincoln County computer system by using "TNRMD" commands, i.e., de-letions. Names from individuals listed in 3 begin to show up on her [Mont-gomery's] work. The listing shows an unusual source of user identity to

access the system—drawer "oo" for which there has never been such a designation used.

5. September 23, 1999 – The State Auditor's Office opens a separate case, #2307, against Stacy D. Montgomery.

6. October 19, 1999 – Bob Woods (certified polygraph operator) of the OSA polygraphs Deputy Tax Collectors Tammy Foster and Renae Sharon Lofton.

7. On October 20, 1999 – Bob Woods polygraphs Deputy Tax Collector Mavis Stewart and office bookkeeper Mary Wallace. Each of the four employees pass all questions that center on land tax monies that are missing and automobile tag monies. They are also asked whether they have ever manipulated any other deputy's records.

8. October 22, 1999 – Stacy D. Montgomery confesses to Bob Woods, Patrick Dendy, and Charles Robinette that she had embezzled funds out of the Lincoln County Tax Collector's Office in the Judge's Chambers located on the second floor of the courthouse. She leaves and brings back the receipts which do not appear in her work. On her own volition, she fills out a resignation letter and leaves the building.

OSA investigators conducted interviews with deputy tax collectors Mavis Stewart, Tammy Foster, and Renae Lofton during the fall of 1999. They all denied taking any money from the tax collector's office, and each reported suspicions about Stacy Montgomery. Montgomery was said to have reconciled the monthly car tag decal report to one issued by the State Tax Commission and that she didn't want anyone else doing this work. It was reported that Montgomery came in on weekends when she was on maternity leave to perform the reconciliations. According to the interviewees, Montgomery had suspicious amounts of folded money in her cash drawer on several occasions. On at least three occasions, other deputies had checked up exactly $100 short at the end of a day, and on each occasion, Montgomery had gone into the other deputy's drawer to make change during the day. Montgomery was alleged to have gotten several phone calls at work each day from bill collectors.

In its January 2000 term, the grand jury of the Fourteenth Judicial District of Mississippi indicted Stacy Montgomery for embezzlement. She was accused of unlawfully taking $9,563.92 of public funds while she was an employee of Jerry Bailey, tax assessor/collector of Lincoln County. The thefts were said to have taken place between May 1998 and March 1999. According to the indictment, Montgomery "willfully, unlawfully, feloniously, and fraudulently failed to deposit taxes collected, from which she received the proceeds to which she was not entitled . . ." At the time of the indictment, the Bogue

Chitto resident was an unemployed twenty-eight-year-old married mother of two. On February 3, 2000, Montgomery waived formal arraignment and pled not guilty in Lincoln County Circuit Court. The same day, in an application for appointment of counsel, Montgomery claimed to be unable to afford counsel and asked the court to appoint an attorney to represent her. Circuit Court Judge Keith Starrett appointed Lesa Harrison Baker.

Stacy Montgomery pled guilty to the charges against her in Lincoln County Circuit Court on March 10, 2000. Sentencing was set for March 20, and she was given until sentencing to pay $10,014 in restitution, $1,817 interest, and $5,791 in investigation costs. District Attorney Jerry Rushing recommended a seven-year prison sentence with all seven years suspended and five years of probation. The DA also recommended that Montgomery be sent to a restitution center if the restitution was not paid at sentencing. Montgomery was unable to pay the required restitution on time, and she was given a ten-day extension.

Montgomery soon came up with the money. Jesse M. Bingham, director of the OSA's investigations division, in a letter to the Lincoln County clerk dated April 26, 2000, reported that Montgomery had paid $17,623.84. State Auditor Phil Bryant returned this money to Lincoln County on April 1, 2000. The OSA closed the case May 30, 2000.

An order dated April 26, 2000, noted that the sentencing order dated March 20, 2000, was not worded properly and set it aside. The intent of the parties had been that, if restitution was made, at the end of one year the court would retain jurisdiction, and that Montgomery would receive a nonadjudication. A new sentencing order was entered reflecting the intent of the parties. This corrected order placed Montgomery on nonadjudicated probation for eighteen months. Circuit Court Judge Keith Starrett issued the revised order, which was agreed to by District Attorney Jerry Rushing and the attorney now representing Montgomery, Ronald Whittington. An order signed by Judge Starrett dated September 20, 2001, dismissed with prejudice the charges against Stacy Montgomery.

Stephanie Taylor-Beam, Itawamba County Deputy Tax Collector

In late September 1996, a taxpayer contacted Itawamba County Tax Assessor/ Collector Johnny Riley and complained that his company had purchased tag decals for two trucks but had not received the decals. The taxpayer had cancelled checks and receipts to prove the payments had been made. On September 29, 1996, Tommy Gann, an employee of the tax assessor's office, brought Itawamba County Deputy Tax Collector Stephanie Taylor to Riley's home to discuss the situation. According to Riley, Taylor confessed that she took the money but insisted that she planned to replace it. Riley told Taylor that he would have to consult with an attorney.

According to Riley, when he contacted attorney Stacy Russell on September 30, he was advised that Taylor should make restitution and resign. Riley contacted Taylor on October 4, and she came to his office October 7 where it was explained to her that she should resign and make restitution. When asked if there were any other instances of embezzlement, Taylor claimed that there were not and said she had intended to pay the money back. She claimed to have been busy with her new baby since she had taken maternity leave in August. Taylor said she had confessed to the Lord and felt good about this. She also apologized to each employee of the tax assessor/collector's office. Taylor, who made no restitution at that time, resigned October 16, 1996. During October, Riley received two additional complaints from taxpayers who had paid for decals for tags but had not received them. On October 21, 1996, Riley talked to Russell again and was advised to notify County Attorney Billy Funderburk.

Taylor's father, Eddie Hood, Funderburk, and Riley talked on October 25. Funderburk telephoned Assistant District Attorney Sam Reedy, who talked to Hood and told him that he could repay the amount the investigators knew his daughter had embezzled. By this time it was evident that Taylor had stolen at least $4,700. Riley told Hood he would accept a check, but it would not be deposited until the amount of embezzlement was firmly established. Hood apparently did not make any payment. Riley contacted the OSA, and investigator Johnny Shannon was assigned to the case on October 28, 1996.

Shannon interviewed Riley and three of his deputies. These interviews revealed that Stephanie Taylor often made entries into the computer system "correcting" tax receipts when the taxpayer was no longer in the office. Such "corrections" were improper and without legal basis. In fact, Taylor had allegedly given one of the deputies an unauthorized credit on a tag she bought in January 1996 before she was employed by the tax collector. When another deputy confronted Taylor about tag receipts hidden behind boxes, she maintained the receipts had errors on them and were not any good. At Shannon's request, Riley contacted a taxpayer, Cecil Johnson, Jr., and they helped the investigator document three apparently unauthorized credits totaling about $423 that Taylor entered in the system on February 1, 1996. Johnson said that Taylor had helped him because of some problems he had with heavy truck tags. The problems he referred to were actually caused by Taylor's handling of the transactions. In this particular case, it appears that Taylor did not actually take the $423, but she had no authority to reduce the amount Johnson owed.

The OSA's work on this case involved contacting approximately fifteen hundred Itawamba County residents by letter or phone and requesting copies of tag receipts. The copies received were matched with the amounts settled per the tax collector's tag report. Discrepancies were documented with the aid of records maintained by the tax collector and copies of checks obtained from the depository bank. The auditor's work covered the time period October 1994 through August 1996. Schedules were prepared documenting the total amount of missing funds. Unaccounted-for funds were as follows: heavy truck tags, $35,620; auto tags, $97,450; tags for F. L. Crane & Sons, Inc., $11,808; tags for Cecil Johnson, Jr., $450. The total was $145,328.

In a report dated June 10, 1998, Shannon noted that Taylor had been responsible for handling heavy truck tags. His report gave a detailed explanation of all fifty-nine instances that were included in the $35,620 missing funds associated with heavy truck tags. Instance number forty-four serves to illustrate what happened.

On October 19, 1995, Nolan Bennett Trucking Company wrote a check to the Tax Collector's Office in the amount of $5,575.25. This check (number 0910) was for tags for the following trucks: 1990 International $1,349.75, 1990 International $1,351.00, 1988 International $999.75, and 1996 International $1,874.75. None of these amounts were posted to the Daily Cash Count Sheet. According to officials at the Bank of Mississippi in Fulton, the check was cashed though the endorsement on the back of the check stated, "Pay to the Order of the Bank of Mississippi For Deposit Only Johnny E. Riley, Tax Collector 932-02253712." No one at the bank could explain why the check was cashed with that endorsement. On October 25, 1995, Ms. Taylor's Daily Cash Count Sheet reflected an amount for Heavy Trucks that included the amount of $1,001.00. A remittance advice on October 27, 1995, to the State Tax Commission for this amount was for a tag for Nolan Bennett Trucking. A review of the deposit itself did not reflect this amount being paid. It appears that a check from F. L. Crane and Sons, Inc. in the amount of $4,056.07 was used to cover this amount. Two other Daily Cash Count Sheets dated April 30, 1996, and May 7, 1996, respectively, indicated amounts of $13.00 on each from Nolan Bennett Trucking Company for replacement tags on one of the 1990 International trucks and the 1996 International truck. There is no indication that these amounts were paid by the taxpayer. Both of the receipts for $13.00 were prepared by Ms. Taylor. As a result of these transactions, there is at least $5,575.25 unaccounted for.

Shannon explained the $97,450 associated with auto tags as follows:

This Investigator also reviewed the checks which made up each deposit to ascertain if any Auto Tag money was unaccounted for. Each check was compared to the Daily Cash Count Sheets (if available) and the monthly tag report as generated by the State Tax Commission. The tag report is based on information supplied by the Tax Collector's Office each day. As a tag is entered into the system at the local level, the information is downloaded to the State system each day, subsequently at the end of a month this tag report is compiled and sent to the Tax Collector's Office. In addition, this Investigator acquired through the District Attorney's Office a printout titled "Mississippi State Tax Commission Motor Vehicle Title/Registration System Audit Registration Records for a Particular County, County Seat Fulton, Ms." This document indicates those decals which are entered in the system more than once. There were also 1500 letters sent requesting copies of tag receipts since based on interviews with employees of the Tax Collector's Office, Ms. Taylor discarded many receipts. After the review of these records, it was determined that there is $97,450 of Auto Tags unaccounted for. Due to the large number of receipts in question, this Investigator will not attempt to discuss in detail each transaction. However, this investigation has determined that receipts were issued for the correct amounts, but later another receipt was prepared for a lesser amount and entered in the system. On those instances whereby checks were written by the taxpayer for the receipt, the checks were deposited and the amount of cash was taken to reflect the difference between the original and fraudulent receipt. All of these fraudulent receipts showed additional amounts for credits (privilege and/or ad valorem) which were in excess of the original receipts. There were numerous instances whereby the original receipt was issued by one deputy and the fraudulent receipt reflected a different deputy. Some of these instances were brought to the attention of two of the current deputies in the Tax Collector's Office who were also employed at the time Ms. Taylor was there. There were other instances whereby an attempt was made to implicate one of these deputies by falsifying the initials on the fraudulent receipts. It appears Ms. Taylor was responsible for initialing these receipts.

Shannon documented the problems associated with the $11,808 tags for F. L. Crane & Sons and the $450 tags for Cecil Johnson, Jr., in similar fashion.

In a memorandum to the file dated June 11, 1998, OSA investigator Johnny Shannon noted a complete lack of internal controls in the Itawamba tax collector's office during the period covered by the investigation, October 1994 through August 1996. Deputies operated out of one cash drawer until about April 1996, when Tax Collector Johnny Riley changed the system to require separate cash drawers for each deputy. The office failed to maintain the "Daily Activity Listing Sheet" for each cash drawer required by the Mississippi County Financial Accounting Manual. The activity sheet should document detailed information about each transaction and facilitate the checkup process at the end of the day. Shannon also noted that, although Riley was bonded, the deputies were not. According to Riley, OSA county auditors had failed to call attention to the internal control weakness during their annual audits. Riley also maintained that someone at the OSA told him that his bond was the only one he could have for his office. The control deficiencies were not mentioned in the Itawamba County audit reports issued by the OSA during the time covered by the investigation.

Stephanie Taylor failed to show up at the office of her attorney, Roy Farrell, for a scheduled July 21, 1998, meeting with investigative auditors Johnny Shannon and Burt Haney. Farrell, who had not heard from Taylor in more than a week, acknowledged that Taylor was to be in his office at 9:00 A.M. The attorney attempted to contact Taylor by phone but was unable to do so. Taylor did not cooperate further with the investigation.

In October 1998, Stephanie Taylor was indicted on five counts of embezzlement (count one—$400, count two—$400, count three—$300, count four—$400, count five—$143,828). On January 21, 2000, Taylor pled guilty to all five counts before Circuit Court Judge Frank Russell. No plea bargain was struck in this case.

At the request of Tax Collector Johnny Riley and the Itawamba County Board of Supervisors, Assistant District Attorney Dennis H. Farris recommended a prison sentence of fifty years with thirty-five years suspended, leaving fifteen years to be served. Farris also recommended that Taylor be given five years' probation, that she be required to pay restitution totaling $315,096 (including interest and investigative costs), and that the statutory minimum fine be imposed.

The following, which is taken from the transcript of the defendant's January 21, 2000, sentencing hearing, is especially relevant in light of the district attorney's recommendation and subsequent developments.

THE COURT: Let's take up State of Mississippi versus Stephanie Taylor Beam, B-E-A-M. This is Cause Number CR98-123 in the Circuit Court of

Itawamba County, Mississippi. Ms. Beam earlier entered a plea of guilty to five counts of embezzlement as charged pursuant to Mississippi Code Section 97-11-29. That plea was entered on the first day, or those pleas, were entered on the first day of October 1999 at the Chancery Building—at the Justice Complex in Lee County, Mississippi. I'm prepared for sentencing at this time.

Before I impose sentence would you, Mr. Farrell, or your client, Ms. Beam, desire to state anything to the court?

MR. FARRELL: Yes, Your Honor.

THE DEFENDANT: Your Honor, I know I was wrong for what I done. I'm at the mercies of the Court, and I want to do better. I've learned a lot. I made a lot of mistakes but I want to do better.

THE COURT: Anything else that you want to tell me, feel free to tell me.

THE DEFENDANT: I'm sorry for all that I hurt, and I want the forgiveness of the people.

THE COURT: Is that all?

THE DEFENDANT: Yes, Sir.

THE COURT: Very well. Mr. Farrell, anything that you desire to state to the Court?

MR. FARRELL: Your Honor, briefly, Stephanie has come before this Court previously and pled guilty to these crimes. She is now here before the Court for sentencing. Your Honor, there is, as filed by the District Attorney's Office, recommendations that are what we would consider extreme, Your Honor. We recognize that as an agent, as a fiduciary or a public official, that Stephanie really had duties and obligations to the public and that a breach of—of those duties is a very serious offense. But at the same time, Your Honor, we'd ask the court to balance that with the fact that she is a first offender with a very serious case, that she is human, subject to the same frailties as any other person with the same propensities, Your Honor. In her family there is a problem with a bipolar disorder. Your Honor, there are some suggestions by individuals who have talked with her that she may suffer from this bipolar disorder and OCD, Your Honor. She has not been treated for that at this point. Unfortunately this case has certainly got to a critical point and—and she should have had some treatment prior to this. I bring that to the Court's attention because I clearly want to convey to the Court that—that this young lady is—is a fine young lady. She has a tremendous heart. She is—she is a fine person and—and she is clearly capable of rehabilitation with some help, some professional help. Now, Your Honor, she understands, and the family understands, that because of the crime, you know, she is going to have to serve some time for this. That this is just too serious not to. But we ask the Court, Your Honor, to—to balance those and to consider this case in the context of the constitutional proportionality of sentencing. What the State has suggested in the filing is—is, we would suggest to the Court, clearly contrary to the principal of constitutionality of sentencing. In fact, I would submit to the Court that if you view the sentences that have been given to public officials throughout the State of Mississippi for the same or similar type crimes, you would find that the sentences have not exceeded five years. Your Honor, we certainly would ask the Court to be on—on the low end of that. Respectfully, Your Honor, we'd ask the Court to be as lenient as possible under the circumstances of this case, recognizing that this—this young lady is clearly capable of rehabilitation. She's capable of earning a living and paying restitution to this county, making Itawamba County whole in that respect, Your Honor. And we would ask the Court to be as lenient as is judicially possible under these circumstances, Your Honor. Thank you.

THE COURT: Very well. Does the State desire to make any statement?

MR. FARRIS: Your Honor, the sentencing recommendation has been filed, and the statement is in that.

THE COURT: Very well. It is always sad when a public official or a public employee or a deputy public official is before the Court having pled guilty or been convicted of breaching the public trust. And today the same is true. Ms. Beam, you pled guilty to five counts of embezzlement, each count carries a possible ten-year sentence and/or a fine in the amount of twice the amount taken. The Court strives to impose a sentence that is just, and fit, and proper in view of all the premises, in view of all the circumstances that exist. You are a first offender, first time you've been convicted of a felony. I take that into account. You were born, raised in this county. The Court is aware of your family background. To my knowledge, none of them have ever been in trouble with the law, serious trouble with the law, and it is indeed, I'm sure, embarrassing and disgraceful for you to stand here before the Court. However, the Court, on the other hand, has to take proper steps to punish you, hopefully rehabilitate you, hopefully deter others from acting as you have done, taking funds which belong to the people of Itawamba County and converting them to your own use. I am aware of sentences that have been meted in this District and in this State. Just recently we had a Circuit Clerk in—I mean a Chancery Clerk in Union County [Larry Koon—see chapter one] that was sentenced to five years, with three suspended, two to serve for embezzlement. That amount, I understand was probably half of what you have pled guilty to, half the amount. And he had made restitution in full prior to being sentenced. Now I realize he was an elected public official, and you were a non-elected deputy to an elected official. Also we have other cases where we have City Clerks and Deputy City Clerks to embezzle in this District and the sentences they received. And I'm aware of the Presley [Lynn

Presley—see chapter one] case down on the coast, where the Chancery Clerk has been sentenced in state and federal court for wrong doings dealing with public funds. I'm not going to sentence you to 15 years to serve as has been recommended. That's too much in the Court's opinion. I think the proper sentence in your particular case will be some time in the penitentiary and then an extended period of time under supervised probation or post-release supervision, mainly to give you ample time to repay the county. Because that's one of the goals, I hope to achieve by imposing the sentence I'm about to impose. I'm somewhat disappointed that you have not made any effort to repay any of it since you were charged and since you pled guilty. That disappoints me. If it had been just whatever you could pay, I would feel better about it. But not a penny has been paid by you directly since this occurred and I would—I would have taken that into consideration had an effort been made to this particular point to repay the County of Itawamba for the monies that were taken. However, I do fully intend to see that you do repay it.

As to Count I, you've got a five-count indictment. As to each count, I'm going to do it this way. As to all five counts, you're sentenced to serve ten years in the custody of the Mississippi Department of Corrections at the facility to be designated by that department. In Count I, I'm going to suspend seven of those years, leaving you three to serve, followed by five years post-release supervision under the provision of Section 47-7-34 of the Mississippi Code. On the other four counts I'm going to suspend the imposition of the ten-year sentence pending you violate no law of any city, county, state or of the United States and pending also that you make full restitution. On each count, it will be ordered that you make full restitution to the County of Itawamba and that restitution in the Court's opinion, the reasonable restitution is $145,328. That is the principal that I understand you have taken. This Court has never before in this District ordered interest on any restitution in criminal cases. I want you to make that restitution in that amount, and in order to see that this gets done on Counts II, III and IV, I'm going to place you on five years post-release supervision after you have served your incarcerated time and your post-release supervision on Count I. In other words, I've got you for 20 years to get this money repaid. Hopefully, it won't take that long. Counts II, III and IV, the post-release supervision in those counts will run consecutively to each other and to Count I. In essence, what you're looking at, if you don't mess up is three years to serve, followed by 20 years post-release supervision in order that hopefully we can get this 145,000 some odd dollars paid back to this county.

In Count V, you'll be sentenced to 10 years. As I indicated earlier, it'll be suspended pending you violate no law of any city, county, state or of the United

States. Now, Ms. Beam, if you don't get a job and don't start paying on a regular basis once you're released from your incarceration, the Court is going to send you to the restitution center and you're going to flip burgers at McDonald's or you're going to work in a catfish skinning plant, possibly waste management, or some other public job that probably pays minimum wage. And I'm going to keep sending you there, keep sending you there on each of these post-release supervisions until this county gets repaid $145,000. So you need to start making plans to pay it back. I realize it's like pay for a house, but you took it and you've got to pay it. And this county is entitled to get the money back. You're getting a break by not paying interest. You're getting a break by not paying the investigative cost of the Audit Department. But that's what they are there for to make these investigations. It would be really totally unrealistic for me to order you to pay $135,000 plus interest accruing at the rate of one percent per month, hereafter. You would never be able to pay the interest, much less pay the principal, one percent a month is $315 a month. So, I think that's the reasonable restitution that needs to be paid in your particular case.

After you serve your three years and are released, you'll be on supervised probation for a total of 20—possibly 20 years and we're going to set you up a payment plan. If you make it, working out here in the—in the general public, I'll allow you to do it. If you don't, you'll be sent to a restitution center and be in essence incarcerated at night and work during the day. You're also assessed court costs. Do you have any questions?

THE DEFENDANT: No, sir.

THE COURT: Mr. Farrell?

MR. FARRELL: No, Your Honor.

THE COURT: All right. You'll be in the custody of the Itawamba County Sheriff to await transportation to a facility to be designated by the Mississippi Department of Corrections. Good luck to you.

After her release from incarceration, collecting the ordered restitution proved to be difficult. In April 2003, she was required to come before the circuit court again for failure to make restitution payments. Taylor-Beam (she was now married) was arrested in August 2004 for failure to make restitution payments. After a formal hearing, Circuit Court Judge Paul Funderburk issued the following Order.

THIS CAUSE having come to be heard this day on the State's Petition for Revocation of Probation the Court finds as follows:

This cause was set for hearing because of non-payment by Defendant on her account.

The Defendant showed proof that her account balance was brought current as of twenty-four (24) hours before the hearing and she currently had a six hundred dollar ($600) credit on her account.

The Court stated that the Defendant had been brought before the Court on two (2) separate occasions for non-payment and that it would not tolerate any further non-payment or any other violation of probation.

Upon the Defendant's showing that her account was current, the State moved an ore tenus motion to dismiss the petition for revocation.

The Defendant asks the Court to issue a Writ of Garnishment so that her account would stay current. The Court hereby authorizes her attorney, Lori Nail Basham, to provide a Writ of Garnishment to the Court.

IT IS THEREFORE ORDERED, ADJUDGED, AND DECREED that the State's Petition for Revocation is hereby dismissed.

SO ORDERED, this the 20th day of August 2004.

An Order for Garnishment was issued by Judge Funderburk the same day. The Order noted that Taylor-Beam still owed Itawamba Circuit Court $136,151, and that she had been ordered to make monthly payments of $600. Belden Foam and Fiber, Inc., Taylor-Beam's employer, was ordered to garnish $600 a month from her paycheck and pay that amount to the Itawamba County Circuit Court. On August 31, 2004, Circuit Court Clerk Carol Gates sent the Itawamba County treasurer, Chancery Clerk Jim Witt, a check for $6,428, which was the amount of restitution recently received from Taylor-Beam.

On April 18, 2000, the OSA issued a demand letter to Stephanie Taylor-Beam demanding payment of $326,376. This amount was computed as the amount embezzled, interest, cost of the bank copying records, and the OSA's cost. In July 2004, the OSA closed the case, leaving the circuit court with the sole responsibility for monitoring restitution. The failure of Itawamba Tax Assessor/Collector Johnny Riley to bond his deputies had come back to haunt Mississippi taxpayers.

3. Justice Court Clerks and Sheriffs' Employees

Mississippi counties elect sheriffs every four years. Boards of supervisors fund the operation of sheriffs' departments through county budgets. Money is collected by sheriffs in the form of fines, bonds, and payments from other government entities. Monies are "settled" by sheriffs to the county, other government units, and to individuals, e.g., return of bond money. Sheriffs are charged with properly establishing accountability for monies received and with depositing receipts in a bank. Sheriffs are also required to properly document and account for all disbursements. The first case briefed in this section involves a sheriff's clerk who embezzled more than $150,000.

A basic appreciation of the way justice court clerk offices operate is necessary to understand how the four embezzlements from such offices that are outlined in this section were possible. A brief summary of how money flows through these offices will suffice to set the stage.

The justice court is a highly visible part of county government, and a lot of money goes through the office of the justice court clerk. The justice court interacts with individuals, state and local law enforcement agencies, businesses, and the county board of supervisors. A justice court clerk is appointed by, and reports to, the board of supervisors in each county. Although the clerk collects various fees, the clerk is not paid under the fee system, as are chancery and circuit clerks. The justice court clerk is paid a salary, and the board budgets for the operation of the clerk's office. Under Mississippi law, justice court clerks and each of their deputies must be bonded in the amount of $50,000.

Mississippi law requires justice court clerks to give any person paying the court money a uniform receipt designed by the attorney general. The purpose of the payment and the form of payment (cash, check, or money order) should be indicated on the receipt. All receipts should be posted to the appropriate accounting journal. The OSA requires separate cash drawers for each person who collects money, and the OSA has prescribed journals to assist in

Justice court clerks are encouraged to install a system of internal controls that includes proper segregation of duties to safeguard assets and strengthen the accounting function.

Justice court clerks are required to maintain three journals—civil, criminal, and clearing. Receipts of monies result in debits to cash in the appropriate journal, and checks written by justice court clerks result in credits to cash in the appropriate journals. The journals carry a running cash balance, which is supposed to be reconciled to the bank statement monthly. Mississippi law requires a clearing bank account, and separate civil and criminal bank accounts may be used.

Monies the justice court clerk receives from the following sources are normally deposited into the civil account: court fees, constable fees, sheriff fees, bank interest, state court education fund fees (law library), and court constituents funds.

Monies the justice court clerk collects for the following sources are usually deposited into the criminal account: clerk fees, general fines, litter fines, traffic violation fines, implied consent law violation fines, game and fish law violation fines, other misdemeanor fines, court constituents funds, criminal justice funds, state court education fund fees (law library), bank interest, constable fees, county attorney fees, Crime Stoppers fees, highway patrol citation fees, adult drivers training fees, hunting violation fines, and compulsory motor vehicle liability insurance fines.

Monies the justice court clerk collects from the following sources are deposited in the clearing account: judgements, restitution, bail bonds, appearance bond fees, and bank interest.

The state has a uniform set of fines for criminal violations, e.g., $31 for traffic violations and $44 for game and fish violations. Various types of assessments, e.g., bond appearance fee assessment and state criminal justice fund assessment, are added to these fines. The state also has a uniform set of assessments in civil cases, e.g., state court education assessment and local citation assessment. Justice courts have no authority to suspend assessments. Fines and assessments may be paid to the justice court clerk by cash, check (Mississippi residents only), or money order. The court may also authorize assessments being worked off.

All collections must be deposited daily to the county treasury, which is administered by the chancery clerk. This process is called a "settlement," and it requires a daily report that shows the total amount of receipts by category. The OSA has prescribed a daily check-up sheet that must be prepared for each cash drawer at the end of each business day. This sheet reflects receipts by type, a cash count, and to which accounts the receipts should be deposited. A recap daily check-up sheet is used to summarize information on all the daily cash check-up sheets and to support the required daily bank deposit. Fees, costs, fines, penalties, and bond forfeitures must be reported to the board of supervisors monthly, and the chancery clerk must settle the assessments monthly to the state and others as required by law. The OSA has designed a court assessment/fine settlement form that must be used in the report to the supervisors and as an aid in the chancery clerk's settlement with the state.

Fines and assessments may be refunded under any one of the following conditions: overpayment has been made due to a collection error; a court directs a refund; or a conviction has been overturned on appeal. There are strict rules for documenting and accounting for refunds.

Cora Lou Thrash Carnley, Jackson County Sheriff's Department Bookkeeper

When he succeeded Jackson County Sheriff D. B. "Pete" Pope in December 1999, the new sheriff, Mike Byrd, wanted to make a clean start. Byrd asked the OSA to conduct an audit of the sheriff's department because of "irregularities in prior audit reports." The CPA firm Moore and Powell performed the 1996 county audit, which included the sheriff's department. The CPAs were unable to perform many regular audit procedures because some of the sheriff's records were not available. Sheriff Pope and Lou Thrash Carnley, bookkeeper for the sheriff's office, maintained that the records had been discarded by accident.

The OSA performed the county audits for 1997 through 1999 and reported the following problems in the sheriff's office:

- Month-end balances were not carried forward properly in the cash journal.
- Bank accounts were not reconciled properly to the cash journal.
- A running balance was not shown in the checkbook.
- Settlements or payments to other depositories were not made promptly.
- Internal control was lacking because the bookkeeper performed incompatible functions. The bookkeeper deposited cash, made disbursements, and maintained the accounting records. These activities should be segregated for good internal control.
- Sheriff Pope did little to address these problems.

In early 2000, while performing an audit of the 1999 records of Jackson County, the county audit section of the OSA discovered what appeared to be embezzlements in the sheriff's department. The problem was referred to the Investigations Division, and Special Agent Darrell Chance was assigned to the case on April 17, 2000.

Eddie Scarbrough was convicted of a minor offense in Jackson County Justice Court in July 1999. When he was trying to set up a payment plan, Justice Court Deputy Clerk Lisa Fairley reminded Scarbrough of a 1996 fine that was still shown on justice court records as unpaid. Scarbrough contended that he had paid the fine when he forfeited a cash bond that he had made for the offence. La'Shea Lowe, bookkeeper for the justice court, located the case file and found a July 1, 1996, receipt for the $109 bond and a $25 sheriff's processing fee. Lowe contacted Marie Long, a new bookkeeper in the Jackson County Sheriff's Office, because the justice court had no record of having received the money from the sheriff. Lowe's review of settlement reports from the sheriff's office to the justice court revealed that the $109 was never paid to the justice court.

When a person did not show up for court, or otherwise pay a fine, e.g., by forfeiting a bond, the justice court clerk sent a letter asking him or her to come in and pay the fine. According to Fairley, there had been several instances of people contacting the justice clerk's office after receiving such letters, claiming that they had posted and forfeited a bond for the offense. Fairley thought those instances had occurred because the sheriff's former bookkeeper, Lou Carnley, would not remit cash bonds to the justice court for up to three months after collection.

Kim C. Tran was found not guilty of a charged offense in Jackson County Circuit Court, and Tran requested a refund of the bond he had posted with the sheriff's office in July 1998. Tran presented receipt 0374 for the $3,075, but circuit court personnel told the sheriff's bookkeeper, Marie Long, that the circuit court had never received the money from the sheriff's office. Long was able to find a copy of the undated and unsigned receipt in the sheriff's bound receipt book, but she could not find it posted to the sheriff's cash journal. The cash journal did not reflect the receipt or settlement of the money to the circuit court.

Lou Carnley served as Sheriff Pete Pope's bookkeeper during his entire term of office, January 1988 through December 1999. Work performed by OSA investigators revealed the following conditions that allowed Carnley to embezzle in excess of $100,000 from the sheriff's office during her employment.

Most of the time that she served as bookkeeper, Carnley received cash and checks, made bank deposits, wrote checks, kept the cash journal, and reconciled bank statements. Pope was "hands off" when it came to bookkeeping. Sometimes, Carnley took accounting records to her home to catch up.

As noted above, auditors had reported a lack of segregation of duties in the sheriff's office and recommended that Carnley not write checks and reconcile bank statements. During most of the last two years of her employment, other employees signed checks (after Carnley determined the payee and the amount) and reconciled bank statements.

Bank deposits were not made on a daily basis. Sometimes, months went by between the actual receipts in the sheriff's office and related bank deposits. Carnley made nearly all of the bank deposits.

Also as noted above, some records (bank records, copies of receipts, and a cash journal) had turned up missing during the time Carnley served as bookkeeper. Carnley claimed that a prisoner who was serving as a trustee and working in the sheriff's office had thrown them away by mistake.

OSA investigators determined that Carnley extracted cash receipts and covered up her thefts by not recording transactions properly and by substituting checks for cash when making bank deposits. Four examples illustrate how this was done.

Check number 8371 from Circuit Clerk Joe Martin in the amount of $1,390.51 was properly recorded on the sheriff's office receipt 4021 dated July 8, 1999. This check was deposited to the sheriff's bank account July 13, 1999. But the supporting cash journal page for July 13, 1999, listed a series of twenty-three receipts totaling $1,019.00 and another series of receipts totaling $371.51, which, combined, equaled the deposit of $1,390.51. Receipt 4021 was recorded in the cash journal as only $47.38. Carnley could not explain the difference of $1,343.13, which had obviously been extracted in cash.

Special Agent Darrell Chance noted that Carnley paid back some of the money she had stolen by depositing checks drawn on her personal account to the sheriff's account. In a report dated September 7, 2000, which recorded the results of an August 24, 2000, interview, Chance wrote:Special Agent Darrell Chance noted that Carnley paid back some of the money she had stolen by depositing checks drawn on her personal account to the sheriff's account. In a report dated September 7, 2000, that recorded the results of an August 24, 2000, interview, Chance wrote:

[OSA Special Agent George] Blue showed Carnley a copy of check number 1199, dated October 1, 1999, in the amount of $918.00 drawn on Carnley's checking account, number 31-004-23 at the Merchants and Marine Bank. Carnley confirmed she had deposited this check in the Sheriff's bank account. Carnley explained that she had cashed the check because she needed the cash. Carnley commented that she knew that was not proper.

Blue showed Carnley a copy of check 1319, dated January 4, 2000, in the amount of $5,472.00 also drawn on Carnley's checking account. Carnley explained that when she was closing out Pope's bank account, she was short and needed that much money to close out the cash journal. Carnley said she had that much money from her husband's insurance. [Her husband had died of cancer.] Carnley explained that she had made mistakes in the cash journal. Carnley commented that she did not believe anyone had taken the money but she honestly did not know what had happened. Carnley did not tell Pope about having to make the deposit. Carnley confirmed that if there were other shortages, they were less than $50.00. Carnley thought she remembered being about $20.00 short one time, perhaps from a 2% bond fee collection.

Receipt DR2407, dated July 24, 1999, showed a $425 cash payment made to the sheriff's office. Carnley admitted recording this transaction in the cash receipts journal on September 20, 1999, at $25 to cover up her theft of $400.

Four checks from the Mississippi Department of Finance that were receipted properly were not recorded properly on the cash receipts journal. Receipt 3942 was for $225, receipt 3943 was for $750, receipt 3944 was for $225, and receipt 3945 was for $2,382.25. Carnley posted the first three checks to the cash receipts journal at $25 each, and the last one at $155. Carnley admitted to OSA investigators that she used this method to make up for cash she had stolen from other payments received by the sheriff's office.

On August 24, 2000, Lou Carnley gave OSA investigators the following written statement:

> I, Lou T. Carnley, furnish this statement to Darrell Chance and George Blue, who have identified themselves as investigators of the State Auditor's Office. This statement is furnished free and voluntarily. No threats or promise's [sic] have been made to have me make this statement. I took cash money from the Sheriff's Dept. and covered it by using check's [sic] to make the deposits to the bank come out even with the cash journal. I regret the path I took to pay off debts for my son who was addicted to crack.
>
> Lou T. Carnley

Chance's September 7, 2000, report also contained the following:

When asked how far back did she begin taking money, Carnley estimated that she began taking money in 1995, perhaps fiscal year 1995–1996. Carnley said that she often times gave the money to her son so he could pay the drug dealer. Carnley was afraid that the dealers would kill her son if he did not pay them.

OSA investigator Darrell Chance observed, "To me it is sad that Lou did not have enough confidence in her department to arrest her son's drug dealer so she just kept on paying him with [stolen] money."

Carnley said that neither Sheriff Pope nor Chief Deputy Ferron Jeanne knew or had any idea that she was taking the money. Carnley commented that they trusted her completely. Carnley said that she had never given any of the money to Pope for his campaign for sheriff. Carnley said that she had never given any of her own money to Pope either.

On March 8, 2001, Carnley took a polygraph test administered by OSA Special Agent Bob Woods. During the test, Carnley said she began taking money about 1991 and that she had taken money because of her son's drug problem and to pay her son's child support, trailer note, and medical bills. She added that some of the money had been used to make her own house payment and to buy groceries. Carnley again stated that Sheriff Pope had received none of the money. Woods found no reactions that indicated deception.

While Lou Carnley obviously had family problems that caused financial pressures, she and her family also spent money on luxury items. An interview conducted by OSA investigators with a fellow sheriff's office employee revealed that Carnley had purchased gifts for certain sheriff's department employees and their families. Among the gifts was at least one set of diamond earrings. Shortly before his death, Carnley's husband, a county road employee, had purchased a Cadillac.

Special agents from the OSA and sheriff's deputies arrested former Jackson County Sheriff's Department bookkeeper Cora Lou Thrash Carnley October 17, 2001, and charged her with embezzlement. The sixty-seven-year-old Vancleave resident had been indicted September 28 on one count of embezzling more than $100,000 between October 1996 and December 1999. The longtime trusted bookkeeper for Sheriff Pete Pope was released on a $10,000 bond. The OSA investigators' work revealed that Carnley embezzled $170,890 from cash bonds, process fees, and bond fees between 1996 through 2000. OSA investigator Chance said, "I believe the amount would have been much greater if all the records would have been available for my review."

Former Sheriff Pete Pope issued a statement saying, "As sheriff and employer, I placed great trust in my employees believing they would perform

their sworn duties as assigned in a professional manner. To my surprise and
sorrow, things were going on that I had no knowledge of. In the future, as I
have in the past, I will place my confidence in the judicial system."

Sheriff Byrd issued a written statement saying that Carnley admitted guilt
and that she had assisted in the investigation by answering investigators' questions. Byrd went on to say that he had added extra checks and balances by
having his bookkeeper's work checked by both the chancery clerk and the
county financial officer.

In December 2001, the OSA issued a formal demand to Carnley for $235,577,
which included principal, interest, investigative costs, and copying costs.

On May 15, 2002, Mississippi Supreme Court Justice C. R. McRae issued
an order appointing William F. Coleman as a special judge in the Carnley
case. Judges Kathy King Jackson, James W. Backstrom, and Dale Harkey of
the Nineteenth Circuit Court District had all requested recusal from the case.
No doubt the recusals were the result of the judges' dealings with the sheriff's
office during Carnley's tenure as bookkeeper.

On January 21, 2003, Cora Lou Thrash Carnley pled guilty to one count
of embezzlement before Circuit Court Judge William Coleman. She faced up
to ten years in prison and a $5,000 fine. Assistant District Attorney Wendy
Martin recommended a five-year prison sentence. Phil Bryant said, "In this
instance we support the recommendation of the district attorney for sentencing. Ms. Carnley violated the public's trust and this type of behavior will not
be tolerated." Judge Coleman ordered a presentence investigation and allowed
Carnley to remain free on bond. When she pled guilty, Carnley had not paid
any of the money previously demanded by the OSA.

Former Sheriff Pope said he was "sorry and saddened that the crime occurred on my watch as sheriff of Jackson County. Those who have known
me, as a professional law enforcement officer and administrator, know that
in no way can I condone this crime or burden placed on the taxpayers of
Jackson County. I place great confidence in our judicial system. Contrary to
what some have said, I was aware of this investigation several months before
I left the office of sheriff, and I assured the representatives from the State Auditor's Office that I would cooperate to the fullest extent of the law in reference to this matter."

On March 14, 2003, Judge Coleman sentenced Carnley to five years in
prison with four years suspended. She was to serve the remaining four years
of her sentence on nonsupervised probation. She was ordered to pay restitution of $178,192. Carnley was to start making monthly restitution payments
within sixty days after release from confinement. Because of the large amount

of restitution agreed to in the plea agreement, the district attorney recommended that no fine be imposed, and none was. The four years of nonsupervised probation provision reflects Carnley's sixty-eight years and the fact that she was not considered a threat to society.

The Lou Thrash Carnley case is very sad. By the time of her sentencing, she had lost two husbands and a son who had a drug problem. Her second husband died of cancer, and her son was killed in an automobile accident. Numerous letters to Judge Coleman touted her many virtues and pointed out her desperate condition as she tried to provide for her extended dysfunctional family. At sentencing, friends and family described her as a mother and wife who was desperate to support her family. When she entered her plea before Judge Coleman, she cited her situation and admitted guilt. The court records contain a handwritten letter by an obviously young grandson.

Dear Judge Coleman,

Please don't send my grandma to jail. I love her too much. She is the nicest person in the whole world. I would die to be away from her. Please, please, don't send her to jail. She is too nice and loving. I would give everything I have for her.

Sincerely,
Curtis Thrash

Lou Thrash Carnley actually served only three months in prison. She was released and placed on house arrest in July 2003. While on house arrest, Carnley was allowed to work at a job, but she had to be home by 6 P.M. each day. A representative of the Mississippi Department of Corrections, Susan Singletary, said that Carnley went before the department's joint placement committee and asked for release from prison. According to Singletary, who would not elaborate further, "She met the criteria set by the committee and was allowed for release." Assistant District Attorney Wendy Martin, who had prosecuted the case, was not happy with the release. She said, "I feel like white collar crimes are not being taken seriously and something needs to be put in place to deter people from committing the crime."

As of May 2005, only $2,300 of the required restitution had been repaid.

This case vividly illustrates all three components of the fraud triangle—pressure, opportunity, and rationalization. Carnley was under tremendous pressure because of family problems. The accounting system in the sheriff's office was such that she could receive cash and not record the receipt in a way that would establish accountability. Finally, she was able to rationalize her actions probably because of her felt need. When the embezzlement started, she might have even planned to pay the money back.

Jennifer Green, Jasper County Deputy Justice Court Clerk

The Investigations Division of the OSA received a complaint from a Jasper County official on January 12, 1998, alleging that not all collections for overdue fines and court costs (mittimus payments) were reported by the justice court clerk. Apparently citizens who had not been given credit for such payments had complained to county officials. An investigation was immediately opened and investigators Patrick Dendy and Bob Woods were assigned to the case.

The following portions of a January 16, 1998, report prepared by Patrick Dendy explain how the investigators identified the culprit.

The purpose of this report is to document the events of this investigation to date. On January 15, 1998, Investigator Bob Woods and I arrived at the Jasper County Court House in Bay Springs, Mississippi. The purpose of our being there was to investigate problems that had been brought to our attention concerning the operations of the Jasper County Justice Court Clerk's Office. We had received information that there had been some problems with the handling of monies collected at the Jasper County Sheriff's Office from overdue fines and court costs in the Jasper County Justice Court Clerk's Office. These are referred to in that office as Mittimus payments.

We interviewed the three employees of the Justice Court Clerk's Office: Justice Court Clerk Jolene Page, Deputy Justice Court Clerk Linda Pittman, and part-time Deputy Justice Court Clerk Jennifer Green, who is the wife of Supervising Senior Accountant Tony Green of the County Audit Section of the State Auditor's Office. From these interviews, each of which have separate reports, we were told the process for handling the Mittimus payments made from the Sheriff's Office to the Justice Court Clerk's Office.

Based on information given to us in these interviews, we asked Deputy Justice Court Clerk Jennifer Green to show us where envelopes containing Mittimus payments were kept in the Justice Court Clerk's Office. She took us to a locking filing cabinet that the Mittimus envelopes were placed in when received from the Sheriff's Office. Ms. Green pulled out a bank bag from the cabinet and opened it to see if there were any of the envelopes in the bag. She pulled out one envelope for a Mittimus payment and placed the bag back in the drawer. Bob

Woods got the bag back out and looked in it, and there were four other envelopes for Mittimus payments in the bag, all of which we seized.

We went back across the hall with Ms. Green to ask her if she knew of any other Mittimus envelopes that may be located in the Justice Clerk's Office. She told us that the ones we had from the filing cabinet were the only ones in the office. She left and went back to her office. A moment later, Mr. Woods and I went to Ms. Green's office to see if there were any other Mittimus envelopes located in her desk. With Ms. Green standing there, we looked in her desk and found several of these envelopes, though she had told us there were no other ones in the office. When asked by Mr. Woods if we could look at the contents of her purse, Ms. Green took out a bundle of Mittimus envelopes that she had just placed in there. These envelopes were all seized by us at that time. At this time, she asked us to close the door and said that she had been taking money from the office.

Ms. Green told us that she wanted to call her husband, Tony Green, to be there with her. We told her that we had no objections to her making that call. She told Tony that she had been taking some Mittimus money and that we were there with her. I spoke to Tony on the phone for a minute, and he seemed to be completely surprised that this had happened. Tony came to the Courthouse about one hour after receiving this call.

At this time I contacted Managing Accountant Ben Norris [senior special agent who was Dendy's supervisor] concerning the developments that had taken place in this case, and to see if there were any instructions concerning what should be done at this time. I notified Mr. Norris that Ms. Green had indicated a willingness to us to give a statement concerning the money she had taken from the Justice Court Clerk's Office. I was told not to interview Ms. Green unless a representative of the Jasper County Sheriff's Office was present at the interview. I was also told that we could not tell Ms. Green to resign her job at the Justice Court Clerk's Office or to inform the Jasper County Board of Supervisors or the Justice Court Clerk that we knew of any problem that would merit placing Ms. Green on administrative leave.

At 1:15 p.m., after Mr. Tony Green had arrived at the Jasper County Courthouse, Ms. Green voluntarily wrote out a letter of resignation for her job as Deputy Justice Court Clerk. This letter was delivered by her to Jasper County Justice Court Clerk Jolene Page.

At 1:20 p.m., Jasper County Sheriff Kenneth Cross arrived, and Ms. Green was notified of her rights by Investigator Woods. After notification, Ms. Green gave us a statement admitting taking money from the Mittimus payments made to the Jasper County Justice Court Clerk's Office. She did not remember when she began taking these monies, and had no idea of how much she had taken. She said that she had never taken any other types of money from the Justice Court Clerk's Office, and did not know of any other employees in that office taking any monies. She further stated that no other employees of the office or her husband had any idea that she was taking these monies. A tape recording was made during this interview, and Ms. Green also provided us with a short written statement concerning this problem. After asking our permission, Mr. Green sat in the room while this interview took place but did not say anything.

An inventory was made of all the items that had been seized in the Jasper County Justice Court Clerk's Office. A copy of this inventory, along with all checks and money orders and twenty dollars cash contained in the records we seized was provided to Jasper County Justice Court Clerk Jolene Page for safekeeping.

In the recorded interview Green explained that she had worked in the clerk's office for about eight years. She was originally hired as deputy court clerk, became court clerk when the justice court clerk left, and then became part-time deputy court clerk. She admitted stealing mittimus payments for several years including during the time she served as clerk. Green said that sometimes she would just take the money and not prepare receipts. On occasions she said she would just delete people out of the computer so that it wouldn't show that they had been there. She also admitted "lapping" mittimus payments by applying later receipts to cover up what she had previously stolen. When asked if there was any specific reason for needing the money she was taking, Green said there was not. But when asked what she did with the money, she said, "Just different stuff. I had charged a bunch of stuff on the credit card that Tony didn't know about, and I didn't want to tell him."

On January 15, 1998, Jennifer Green gave the following sworn statement to the Office of the State Auditor:

I began taking money from the mittimus money that was received in our office. This was being done without the knowledge of my husband Tony Green nor to the knowledge of my co-workers. I do not know at this time the exact amount that was taken. As of this date I resign my position as Deputy Justice Court Clerk.

Jennifer Green

Phil Bryant issued a demand letter to Jennifer Green in the amount of $58,983 by certified mail on March 31, 1988. The total amount was determined as follows:

- Embezzlement (Green failed to deposit fines and court costs collected in the Jasper County Justice Court office from 1993 to 1997), $39,249.
- Interest (1 percent per month from the date of the loss), $11,509.
- Cost of recovery (hourly rate for staff members), $8,225.

On April 20, 1998, OSA investigators Patrick Dendy and O. David Hollingsworth met with Jennifer Green and her attorney, Bobby Shoemaker, to explain the demand and give Green an opportunity to challenge anything in the demand. Green and her attorney did not challenge the computations but asked if the investigative cost was a firm amount or if it could be negotiated. The investigators told them to discuss the possibility of a reduction with the director of investigations, Al Waits. Attorney Shoemaker requested a reduction in the investigative cost included in the demand. In a meeting on April 21, 1998, attended by Dendy, Waits, staff attorney Lynn Murray, and Assistant Attorney General Loni McMillin, a decision was made to reduce the demand for investigative cost by $2,000 because of unusual circumstances that had arisen during the case.

The unusual circumstances involved the abnormal amount of time needed to complete the investigation and process the demand. The investigation was undertaken in part to assist District Attorney Rusty Fortenberry, who was also working on the case. The district attorney requested that Green not be interviewed until the auditors determined the amount missing and that a formal demand for return of the money be made at the end of the investigation rather than pursuing recovery through an informal process. Working under these parameters increased the time OSA needed to complete the investigation, and it was determined that it would be fair not to charge the culprit for the additional time. On April 28, 1998, State Auditor Phil Bryant issued a media release stating that his office had received repayment of $56,983 from Green and noting that she was accused of embezzlement. The release stated that the results of the investigation had been turned over to District Attorney Rusty Fortenberry for his review and consideration. Bryant was quoted as saying, "When the taking or misappropriating of taxpayers' money is uncovered, it must and will be dealt with firmly by the State Auditor's Office. In this case, as in all our cases, we seek repayment of these funds in order to keep accountability measures in local and state government. Mrs. Green cooperated with our investigation and has repaid our demand in full. I expect the funds to be returned back to Jasper County the week of May 4th."

Jennifer Green waived indictment on May 22, 1998, and consented to and requested that the case against her proceed on a bill of information by the district attorney. Circuit Court Judge Robert G. Evans issued an order allowing the state to proceed by bill of information the same day. The bill of information dated May 22, 1998, states that between May 1993 and November 1997, Jennifer Green did willfully, unlawfully, and feloniously violate Mississippi law by embezzling $39,249 while employed in the Justice Court Office of Jasper County, Mississippi. Green faced up to ten years in prison and a fine of up to $1,000.

Although Jennifer Green claimed that she only took mittimus payments, the $39,249 listed in the demand that Phil Bryant had issued included only $18,938 stolen from mittimus payments. The rest of the funds came from six other sources (twice-issued receipts, suspension-clearing receipts, other suspensions cleared, criminal account shortage, civil account shortage, and subsequent items) according to OSA records. Tony Green submitted to a lie detector test, which indicated that he, in fact, did not know that his wife was stealing from Jasper County. The OSA closed this case on July 10, 1998.

On July 24, 1998, Circuit Court Judge Robert G. Evans sentenced Jennifer Green to five years in prison with the first year to be served on house arrest. If the one year of house arrest were completed successfully, the remaining four years of the sentence were to be suspended and she was to be placed on four years' reporting probation. Green was also ordered to pay court costs within thirty days and to pay all costs associated with her house arrest.

Jennifer Green's court file contained some interesting letters to Judge Evans asking lenience in sentencing Green. Two letters from Tony Green's colleagues and one from the Greens' pastor were included. The following are excerpts from these letters.

One of Tony's colleagues wrote:

I have known Tony since we were in Elementary School together, and Jennifer since they were dating. I never thought something like this would have happened to my friends. I can only wonder what was going through her mind when this was happening. I have seen people caught up in the "keep-up-with-the-Jones" problem before, and I guess this was Jennifer's motive . . . I have witnessed the pain and problem this has caused Tony and Jennifer. I hope that you can see how much they and their families have suffered due to her mistakes. They have tried to handle this mistake with as much repentance and class as they could. The day Tony found out, he called me and other people to explain what had happened and lay everything out in the open. This is the type of person he is. I know Tony and Jennifer have made every effort to amend what has happened. They have not tried to hide anything, but rather admit her mistake and make the proper restitution.

Another colleague wrote:

I have had the opportunity to talk with Jennifer concerning the theft in her former capacity as Justice Court Clerk. I firmly believe she has shown true repentance both before God and man concerning her theft. She has expressed to me very deeply her sin against God for breaking the eighth commandment, "Thou shall not steal" and her sorrow and disappointment with herself for having done what she did. It is also my understanding that Jennifer has agreed to and is submitting to counseling from her pastor concerning her sin . . . Judge Evans, obviously there is no excuse for what Jennifer has done. Yet if given the right circumstances in which the opportunity to steal without impunity exists, I believe all of us would be more susceptible and vulnerable to yield to such great temptation. It is my understanding that this was the very situation in which Jennifer served as Justice Court Clerk. In other words, speaking as an auditor, there were little if any controls to prohibit or prevent possible theft from taking place.

The Greens' pastor wrote:

I was shocked when they called for a special appointment during which Jennifer and Tony revealed the events of the previous day. Jennifer shared that she was confronted with and admitted to being involved in taking funds over a fairly lengthy period of time. Tony was not aware of what had been going on and was devastated but because of his love for Jennifer resolved to stand by her and do all that was necessary to make things right. This session was fraught with guilt, confession, forgiveness and a resolve to not let this experience destroy their lives. Since the beginning of this experience I have watched this couple, individually and together, face and deal with family, friends and others in a noble fashion. They practiced the Christian virtue of confession and openness, not skirting around personal responsibility. While this has been painful for them, they are both to be commended. Jennifer has gone out of her way to admit her wrongdoing with the hope that in some small way that she will be given the opportunity to present her side. My personal heartfelt belief is that Jennifer has come to grips with the moral fracture in her life that has led to this experience and is committed to do all that is needed to rebuild a life of integrity.

At sentencing, Green herself gave a moving and tearful statement. "I want to apologize for what I've done. I know it was wrong. I hurt more than myself; I hurt family, friends and co-workers. For that, I'm truly sorry. I'll have to live with it for the rest of my life." The judge himself called Green's cooperation with the investigation and her repayment "admirable."

Alberta Baker Longstreet, Leflore County Justice Court Clerk

State Auditor Phil Bryant issued a demand against former Leflore County Justice Court Clerk Alberta Baker Longstreet for $400,782 on October 22, 2003. Longstreet became deputy justice court clerk in 1984 and was promoted to justice court clerk in 1988. In June 2000, Ruth N. Wylie, CPA, found a $14,000 discrepancy when auditing records of the Leflore County Justice Court's Office. That finding was the impetus for an investigation that eventually resulted in this huge demand.

Wylie wrote the following letter dated June 29, 2000, to Ed Yarborough, director of the OSA's county audit division:

Dear Mr. Yarborough:

During the performance audit of Leflore County, which I performed for Gary & Dribben, I reviewed the records of the Justice Court Clerk. In reconciling the records for the Clearing Account, which handles garnishments, I could not account for a shortage of funds in the approximate amount of $14,000. It appeared that the only way the Justice Court Clerk had been able to keep a positive cash balance in the bank was by waiting two months to settle the money to the appropriate parties. Of the shortage of $14,000, approximately $8,000 represented outstanding checks from prior months. I did not attempt to determine the validity of these outstanding checks. Some of these could be for checks that had been rewritten. I am also concerned that the checks shown as outstanding and due to others were never written or mailed.

I am concerned that garnishments may have been remitted to the Justice Court Clerk, but not settled to the appropriate parties for periods other than the current months.

I have included a recommendation in the Leflore County Audit Report that the shortage in the Justice Court Clearing Account be investigated, and that the accounts be reviewed to determine if monies held in trust were settled to the appropriate organizations. I am very concerned that some of the checks shown as outstanding were never remitted.

I am enclosing a copy of the audit finding and recommendation for the Leflore County Justice Court Clerk's Clearing Account and my workpaper on the Justice Court Clearing Account, which should be self-explanatory. Please contact me with any questions you may have at [phone numbers and e-mail address].

Sincerely,
Ruth Wylie, CPA, CGFM

c: Sam Abraham (Chancery Clerk and County Administrator)
Enclosures

The enclosures gave many details and showed just how bad internal controls were in the justice court clerk's office. It was noted that no monthly cash journal was maintained for the clearing account and indicated that although numerous records were maintained no one record showed the actual cash balance. Wylie had attempted to arrive at a cash balance by using the balance on a June cutoff bank statement, deducting checks written in May, none of which had cleared, and taking into consideration the June deposits that were for monies due to be paid to others. In so doing, she came up with a shortage of $14,118. Although the county was paying an accounting firm to do bank reconciliations, the bank account for the clearing account was not being reconciled because there was no record that maintained a cash balance or a listing of all checks issued.

The Investigations Division of the OSA received a referral from Ed Yarborough in early August 2000 and assigned investigator Louise A. Stewart to the case. In June of 2001, Stewart reviewed justice court clerk records and interviewed persons who were supposed to have received garnishment payments. Stewart determined that some checks received by the justice court clerk's office for garnishment payments were inappropriately deposited to the Leflore County Justice Court Criminal Account to replace cash that had been misappropriated from the criminal account. The checks for the garnishments should have been deposited to the Leflore County Justice Court Clerk's Clearing Account from which garnishment payments are remitted to the appropriate parties. Stewart also determined that the justice court clerk's records associated with garnishments were often incorrect.

In February 2002, OSA Special Agents Louise Stewart and Denver Smith interviewed accountant Marlee Williams Golden. Golden had worked for the accounting firm Killebrew and Moss in Greenwood, which had been engaged to reconcile the bank statements of the justice court clerk's office, and she had accomplished the reconciliations. Stewart's report on the interview revealed that sometimes what is called a reconciliation may not really be a reconciliation. The report included the following:

> Mrs. Golden said that the reconciliations for the Justice Court were different from the other clients in that she did not have a balance to reconcile with. She prepared the reconciliations from the records Mrs. Baker [Longstreet—she had been married three times and used her married and maiden names at different times throughout her life] provided: check stubs, yellow copies of deposit slips, and the bank statements. When Mrs. Golden questioned not having a figure to tie back to, Mrs. Baker said that the reconciliation as prepared by Mrs. Golden, "is all I need." Mrs. Golden said, "I did not feel comfortable with the reconciliations, but I did the best I could with what I had. Alberta was not paying us to audit her work, just to reconcile the bank accounts." When asked if she suspected Mrs. Baker of stealing money, Mrs. Golden said, "No."

Because garnishment monies that should have been deposited into the clerk's clearing account were being stolen, the clerk was not making payments to the plaintiffs in a timely manner. Thus, plaintiffs often did not get their money and the defendants were not credited with payments that had been taken from their paychecks. For example, in a 1996 case, a Viking Range Corporation employee's pay was garnisheed, Viking sent the payment to the justice court clerk, no receipt was written, and the check was substituted for cash in a deposit to the criminal account. Collection Services issued a second garnishment in 1999. When the employee complained and Viking produced copies of the original check, the justice court clerk's office stopped the second garnishment in November of 2001.

OSA Special Agents Stewart and Smith and IRS Special Agents Phillip Hull and Christina Blakely interviewed Alberta Longstreet on June 12, 2002, about funds missing from the Leflore County Justice Court Clerk's Office. Several things came to light during this interview including the following:

(a) Longstreet resided with her three sons; one son was disabled and the other two were employed. Although the disabled son received some money from the state, they were pressed with medical expenses.

(b) Longstreet claimed that a friend, whom she refused to name, did her income tax for free, but she personally signed and mailed her income tax return.

(c) She had two homes remodeled during the time covered by the investigation, and in one case she borrowed $30,000 to do so.

(d) Longstreet admitted that she gambled, but "not a lot."

(e) Longstreet said that she would require the assistance of a lawyer in answering questions about the conditions under which she resigned her position as justice court clerk and other questions pertaining to embezzled funds.

On June 19, 2002, OSA Special Agent Louise Stewart and IRS Special Agent Christina Blakely interviewed Leflore County Deputy Justice Court Clerk Jan Rias, who had worked for Longstreet. The interview revealed several warning signs often associated with embezzlements. Included in a memorandum of the interview were the following statements by Rias:

(a) Longstreet would not participate in the daily office responsibilities, but would rarely, if ever, allow the deputy clerks to make daily deposits. Deposit books were kept in a cabinet in Longstreet's office, and deputy clerks did not have access to them. Longstreet prepared the deposits in her office and made the deposits daily about 1 P.M.

(b) Longstreet was subject to extreme mood changes.

(c) Longstreet almost always retrieved and distributed the daily mail.

(d) Longstreet rarely took time off from work.

(e) On several occasions it appeared that Longstreet had been drinking prior to coming to work.

(f) The justice court clerk's office regularly received complaints about the mishandling of funds. Longstreet generally handled the complaints. Complaints had tapered off since Longstreet resigned.

(g) Longstreet was not concerned with proper record keeping.

Rias also explained how the nonsufficient fund check procedures employed in the clerk's office almost created an invitation to steal. Defendants would pay the "bad check" amount plus a service fee of $150, all in cash. No receipt would be made out. The bad check would be returned to the defendant, and the amount of the check would be paid to the original payee. The $150 service fee should be deposited as operating income to the county. However, since there was no actual accounting for the $150 cash received for the service fee, it could easily be misappropriated.

On the same day this interview took place, Stewart and Blakely also interviewed Larresia Hunt, a deputy justice court clerk. In the interview, Hunt basically confirmed everything that Rias had said in her interview.

Leland H. Jones III served as legal counsel for Longstreet and advised her to cooperate with the investigators. In subsequent meetings with IRS and OSA investigators, Longstreet reviewed a worksheet showing the details of the missing funds and admitted taking the money. She could not confirm or dispute the actual amount since she kept no records. Longstreet also reviewed her federal income tax returns and admitted not claiming the stolen money as income.

Longstreet's attorney was himself soon in hot water. Leland H. Jones III, who was the attorney for the town of North Carrollton, had previously served as attorney for the Carroll County Board of Supervisors. In November of 2003, Jones pled guilty in U.S. District Court in Oxford to bankruptcy fraud. Jones deposited $100,000 in a trust account for his client, Daniel Murrell, during a 2001 bankruptcy case. In doing so, he failed to disclose $10,000 of that amount in papers filed in U.S. Bankruptcy Court of the Northern District of Mississippi in Aberdeen. In February 2004, U.S. District Judge Neal Biggers sentenced Jones to five years' probation, fined him $10,000, and required him to pay restitution of $8,681. The Mississippi Supreme Court disbarred Jones in December 2004.

On January 7, 2004, based on a December 16, 2003, plea agreement with U.S. Attorney Dunn Lampton, Alberta Baker Longstreet waived indictment and pled guilty to a one-count bill of information charging income tax evasion. In U.S. District Court in Greenville, Longstreet admitted that she claimed 1998 taxable income of $11,701 and tax due of $1,759 when her actual taxable income was $62,999 and tax due was approximately $11,628. U.S. District Court documents show that Longstreet actually admitted embezzling monies from the Leflore County Justice Court beginning in 1995, that she did not declare the embezzled funds as taxable income, and that the tax loss suffered by the government from 1995 through 2000 was $45,176. Longstreet was sentenced to a year and a day in prison, and ordered to pay $20,349 in restitution to the IRS. She was also required to serve three years' probation after being released from incarceration. Longstreet was to report to prison in Marianna, Florida, on May 17, 2004.

In May of 2004, under a plea agreement with District Attorney Joyce Chiles, Alberta Baker (Longstreet) pled guilty to one count of embezzlement in Leflore County Circuit Court. Circuit Court Judge Ashley Hinds sentenced the former justice court clerk to four years in prison with one year and one day to serve and three years' probation. This state sentence was to run concurrently with her federal sentence. Longstreet was also ordered to pay $211,033 in restitution to Leflore County, $129,145 interest to Leflore County, $62,286 to the OSA for investigative costs, $250 in court costs, and attorney's fees of $300. On August 9, 2005, the OSA received a $50,000 check from an insurance company that bonded Longstreet.

Georgia Faye Moss, Rankin County Justice Court Clerk

On February 10, 2000, the Investigations Division of the OSA began investigating Rankin County Justice Court Clerk Georgia Faye Moss based on a referral from the county audit section alleging embezzlement. There appeared to be shortages in the criminal, civil, and special clearing accounts of the Rankin County Justice Court. The clerk's office received monies that were supposed to be deposited into several different accounts depending on the source. OSA Special Agent Earl Smith was assigned to the case.

OSA investigators subsequently documented several circumstances and practices in the justice court clerk's office that provided opportunities for extracting cash and covering up the shortages at least for a while, including the following:

(a) Cash deposits were not always made on a daily basis.
(b) Cash deposits were not totally reconciled to duplicate copies of cash receipts daily.
(c) Checks received were sometimes not deposited in the bank but cashed for change.
(d) Faye Moss prepared some receipts and usually prepared all deposit slips and made all bank deposits.
(e) Cash deposits were sometimes split to avoid the paperwork associated with cash deposits exceeding $10,000.
(f) Faye Moss frequently worked after hours and on weekends and holidays.
(g) Receipts for monies that were supposed to be deposited in the criminal and civil accounts were computer generated, and checks received as pay-

ments were usually stamped for deposit only to the appropriate account by employees receiving the payments. However, Moss had instructed at least one employee not to stamp "for deposit only" on checks received for civil payments because she might have to cash a civil check to get change.

(h) Special clearing account receipts were handwritten.

(i) Faye Moss kept a ledger in which she recorded receipts for the special clearing account. She was the only one who had access to this ledger book. Many checks that should have been deposited to the special clearing account came in the mail, and Moss prepared receipts for those payments.

These conditions allowed Faye Moss to embezzle more than $100,000 from 1996 to 2000. A few examples demonstrate how Moss was able to embezzle cash and cover her actions temporarily.

A A A Bonding Company check 2435 dated April 30, 1997, payable to Rankin County Justice Court for $1,000, was deposited in the criminal account. The check was originally endorsed for deposit only to the Justice Court Clerk Special Clearing Account, but this had been crossed out and "Rankin Co Justice Court For Dep only A/C 3282993-01" had been written on the back of the check. Moss was obviously using a payment that should have gone to the clearing account, for which she had not established accountability in her handwritten system, to cover thefts of cash that should have gone to the criminal account, for which accountability had been established by the computerized system.

In May 2001, a doctor's office called Chief Deputy Clerk Kristie Pyles to ask about a garnishment payment they should have received. Pyles's research showed that the $874 cashier's check the clerk's office received in payment was deposited in the Justice Court Criminal Account on May 17, 2001. The check should have been deposited in the special clearing account, but Pyles found that no special clearing account receipt had been issued for the check. Review of the case file showed that the defendant had not been given credit for the payment. Thus, no accountability had been established for the $874. Pyles requested and received a copy of the deposit ticket from the bank and compared it to the retained copy of the deposit ticket. The two differed. Pyles said that Moss had instituted a practice of having the deputy clerk initial deposit tickets to verify that deposited amounts equaled receipts for the day. Her initials, "KP," were on the retained copy but not the bank copy. Deposited checks were listed by receipt number on the retained copy, and the $874 check was not listed. The bank deposit did not have the checks itemized. The amount of currency and coin on the bank deposit slip was $2,705.01, while the amount of currency and coin on the retained deposit slip was $3,579.01, a difference of $874. Moss obviously extracted $874 in cash that should have gone to the criminal account and covered the embezzlement with the $874 check that should have gone to the special fees account. This particular embezzlement was brazen, because Moss had to know her actions were being scrutinized, since she had been interviewed by OSA investigators as far back as April 2000.

The clerk's office maintained a bank account for the Victim's Impact Response Seminar. Judges often ordered defendants to pay $25 that should be deposited in this account. Kristie Pyles became suspicious when she noted that deposits for May 2001 totaled only $550 for a month during which she thought the clerk's office had collected substantially more. She summed the receipts, and the total exceeded $1,200. Pyles then requested bank statements from January 2001 and found in excess of $2,000 in receipts had not been deposited. Deputy clerks receipted the funds, but Faye Moss maintained the account and made the deposits. Again, Moss had continued her chicanery while the investigation was in progress.

The investigators' work papers showed that from 1996 to 2000 deposits to the special clearing account exceeded receipts for the account by $58,862. Moss obviously prepared receipts only for selected items. Despite Moss's attempts to cover thefts from the criminal and civil accounts for which accountability was better established, investigators' work papers showed that from 1996 to 2000 receipts exceeded deposits by $24,734 in the criminal account and $71,116 in the civil account. Moss had a lot of juggling to do!

Former Rankin County Justice Court Clerk Georgia Faye Moss pled guilty to embezzling $110,000 in Rankin County Circuit Court on August 9, 2001. Moss, who had served as justice court clerk for seventeen years, took the money between January 1996 and May 2001. Sentencing was set for September 14. Based on a plea bargain, Moss could be required to pay restitution and serve up to ten years in prison. However, if she complied with terms of the plea, actual prison time could be suspended.

After the plea agreement, State Auditor Phil Bryant said, "It is always difficult to discover public corruption in any form. However, such actions will not be tolerated whether in Rankin County or any other in the state. We will now aggressively pursue and recover these embezzled funds in order to return them to the Rankin County Justice Court." District Attorney Rick Mitchell, who had struck the plea agreement with Moss, said, "While I'm disappointed that such a resolution was warranted, I'm also happy that this matter has been resolved." Rankin County Administrator Jeff Goodwin said, "This is a very regrettable situation. This was an expedient remedy of justice in this case. We look forward to getting these funds returned to Rankin County."

In September 2001, Rankin County Circuit Court Judge Samac Richardson approved the plea agreement, gave Moss a suspended ten-year sentence, and ordered her to pay full restitution.

This light punishment for so many felonious acts should be an affront to the citizens of Mississippi. Georgia Faye Moss was a brazen criminal who planned and executed sophisticated schemes to steal from the citizens of Rankin County. As noted above, Moss served as justice court clerk for seventeen years. The charges against her covered only five years.

The *Clarion-Ledger* editorialized on September 19, 2001:

> Rankin County court officials have redefined "justice" in sentencing one of their own, a former Justice Court clerk.
>
> Georgia Faye Moss, who embezzled $110,000 in taxpayers' money, won't serve a day in jail under the recommendation of Rankin County District Attorney Rick Mitchell. Rankin County Circuit Court Judge Samac Richardson OK'd the deal Friday, giving her a 10-year suspended sentence.
>
> This big kiss was based on Mitchell's excuse that: "We were never able to locate where that money went to." By that reasoning, when someone robs a bank and spends it, the robber should go free if he spends it all.
>
> Moss is supposed to pay back the money she stole, but even here honest, law-abiding people are victimized. Some $50,000 of the restitution will be paid by the company that issued her the bond required of all who handle public money. Or put another way, other public employees required to obtain a bond may have to pay more for one. This is justice?
>
> Shouldn't public officials be held to a higher standard?
>
> Under this standard of "justice," all thieves and robbers can just tell the Rankin County DA and judge they're really sorry and will pay the money back. It appears the standard of justice is slipping in Rankin County at least for public officials who get caught stealing.

On September 10, 2001, State Auditor Phil Bryant issued a formal demand to Faye Moss for repayment of $110,000. Bryant closed the case on August 28, 2002, because full restitution had been made, $50,000 by Moss's bonding company and $60,000 by Moss.

As reported in the preface, the light punishment meted out to Moss led Phil

Bryant to ask the legislature to enact a law calling for a mandatory jail sentence for anyone convicted of embezzling $10,000 or more of public money. Bryant's efforts were successful.

Jesse Bingham, director of the OSA's Investigations Division, commented on this case as follows:

> This case was very frustrating because no one in county government believed that Ms. Moss was capable of embezzling funds. Agent Smith and I approached Rankin County officials one year before the arrest was made requesting that they move her to another position pending the outcome of our investigation. Finally, after a very stern letter from me to the board attorney, Moss was removed as Justice Court Clerk. Shortly thereafter, she was arrested, indicted, and got her "slap on the hand."

Cassandra Price, Jefferson Davis County Justice Court Clerk

While working on Jefferson Davis County's fiscal year 1997 audit, Cary Hartfield of the OSA's county audit section noted a situation that indicated county money was missing. Disbursements had been made from the justice court clerk's clearing account to the clerk's criminal account. It appeared that checks were being written to the criminal account to make up for cash that had been embezzled from receipts associated with criminal charges. The potential problem was referred to the Investigations Division of the OSA in August 1998, and investigator Scott Womack was assigned to the case.

Cassandra Price, who had been hired as a deputy justice court clerk in 1987 and became justice court clerk in 1993, wrote and signed the following sworn statement on August 18, 1998.

> I, Cassandra Price, Justice Court Clerk of Jefferson Davis County, reviewed the CASH Journal Clearing Account of the Jefferson Davis Justice Court Clerk's Office after having been read my Miranda Rights in the presence of District Attorney Investigator Bobby Reed, State Audit County Auditor Carey [Cary] Hartfield and State Audit Investigator Scott Womack. I indicated to these three men which checks I wrote and deposited in the criminal account for cash that I took and converted to my own personal use, which was taken into my office. I started taking money in 1996, but some may have been taken prior to 1996.

By making this statement, I am taking full responsibility for my actions and am now taking steps to right these wrongful actions.

Price immediately resigned her position and turned over the keys to the office to one of the deputy justice court clerks, Judy Cole. Price had called District Attorney Richard Douglas on August 17 and insisted that he come to her home, where she confessed to embezzling funds from the justice court's accounts. Before signing the August 18 statement, Price admitted to using the money she stole to buy clothes and jewelry and to pay bills. She also claimed that no one else was involved in the thefts and that all of the money she had stolen was gone.

OSA investigator Scott Womack's September 1, 1998, report contains the following paragraphs that explain what he found early in the investigation.

During the following week, boxes of envelopes were found from individuals who had received traffic citations in Jefferson Davis County who had sent in money orders and personal checks to pay their traffic fines. The envelope, the violator's copy of the traffic citation, and a photocopy of the check or money order, which had been placed in the envelope, were found in a closet behind Mrs. Price's desk. Upon checking the affidavit files for which these individuals should have been posted as having paid their fines, each account checked for which a copy of the violator's check or money order had been found, each affidavit file indicated that the money received for the fine had not been posted, nor could a receipt for the funds be located. This indicates that these checks and money orders were probably used to deposit into the criminal account, which would allow Mrs. Price to take cash in an amount equal to the amount of checks and money orders deposited which had not been receipted.

Garnishment checks were received from employers of persons who have had garnishments levied against them and wages withheld which were mailed to the Justice Court Office have also been found to have been deposited into the Criminal Account without a receipt generated which should have only been deposited in the Clearing Account or Civil Account. By depositing these garnishment checks into the Criminal Account without generating a receipt, cash in the amount of the garnishment check could be taken. Therefore three separate methods of embezzling public funds have been discovered thus far, and the investigation continues.

On September 3, 1998, OSA agents and representatives from the district attorney's office interviewed Price again. Price admitted manipulating records of persons who paid traffic fines with checks or money orders to make sure they were not notified that they still owed the money. She also admitted handling garnishment and restitution checks in a similar manner. Price admitted to taking cash received in payments for traffic tickets that had not yet been received from the law officers and, when the actual tickets were received, not recording the tickets in the computer system, thus never establishing accountability. She also admitted taking cash for "fixing" DUI citations for two people by never putting the tickets into the computer system. Price claimed that she did not steal money for a trip her family took to Orlando. She claimed to have borrowed the money for that trip.

After Price's resignation, Justice Court Judge Jerry Dyess had to dismiss several traffic violation charges because it was not possible to determine how much if any the defendants had paid on their fines. For example, in March 1999, the charges against Donell Baylous were dismissed. Baylous had been charged with DUI, obstruction of a highway, speeding, resisting arrest, reckless driving, improper passing, failure to yield to blue lights, disorderly conduct, running a stop sign, running a red light, improper equipment, not having a driver's license, following too closely, and no tag. Baylous had been fined more than $3,500 and could produce receipts for $1,300 that he had paid Price as justice court clerk. The judge indicated that it could not be proven that Baylous had not paid the entire amount assessed on these old violations, and, because the defendant had not been given a speedy trial, the charges should be dismissed.

The Jefferson Davis County grand jury indicted Cassandra Price on five counts of embezzlement March 16, 1999. Count one charged Price with embezzling $96,821 of mail-in fines and costs from various individuals between September 1988 and August 1998. Count two accused her of embezzling $77,922 of funds paid into the county prior to disposition of pending criminal or civil actions. Count three alleged that she embezzled $15,485 of monies paid to the justice court where the individuals were given receipts from a private receipt book maintained by Price. Count four alleged that she embezzled $8,623 from criminal cases and jail assessments between July 1995 and March 1997. Count five accused Price of embezzling $5,561 from garnishments between January 1998 and August 1998. The former justice court clerk faced up to twenty years in prison on each charge, a total of one hundred years.

On September 27, 1999, thirty-five-year-old Cassandra Price pled guilty to five counts of embezzlement before Circuit Court Judge Michael Eubanks. Sentencing was set for December 10. Judge Eubanks sentenced Price to five years in prison with four years suspended on each of the five counts. Price was also required to serve four years' probation and to pay court costs of $2,250 at the rate of $50 per month after release from incarceration. No restitution was imposed by the court. There was a flaw in the sentencing order because a new law, which required more prison time, had become effective when one of the five offenses charged was committed. The sentencing order was clarified in January 2001 by Judge Eubanks. Cassandra Price was released from prison on December 11, 2002, having served the required 22.2 months. She immediately began serving four years of probation.

On September 27, 1999, the OSA issued a demand to Cassandra Price and the company that bonded her, Western Surety Company, for payment of $417,841. The total demanded consisted of the principal amount embezzled, interest at 1 percent per month from the date of loss, and costs of recovery. The bonding company paid Jefferson Davis County $260,219.61 in 2000 and secured a judgment against Price for that amount September 29, 2000. The OSA closed the case on November 15, 2002.

4. City Clerks

Officials of Mississippi cities are required to establish accountability for and protect all monies that flow into their cities. They are also required to account for disbursements properly and to ensure the legality of disbursements. Annual audits are required for each of the state's incorporated municipalities. These audits are usually performed by CPA firms. In fact, the OSA is prohibited by statute from auditing a municipality unless a complaint has been filed with it alleging wrongdoing, or a strong indication of wrongdoing has been discovered in another manner. Section 7-7-211(7) of the Mississippi Code is relevant to this matter:

> [The OSA has the authority] [t]o post-audit and, when deemed necessary, pre-audit and investigate the financial affairs of the levee boards; agencies created by the Legislature or by executive order of the Governor; profit or nonprofit business entities administering programs financed by funds flowing through the State Treasury or through any of the agencies of the state, or its subdivisions; and all other public bodies supported by funds derived in part or wholly from public funds, *except municipalities which annually submit an audit prepared by a qualified certified public accountant using methods and procedures prescribed by the department* . . . (emphasis added).

Shirley Ferrell, Belzoni Deputy City Clerk

Thomas N. Turner, Jr., served as alderman of the city of Belzoni for seventeen years before being elected mayor. He had served seventeen years in the part-time position of mayor when he discovered a problem in the city's water department in 1998. Turner, who was also the city's computer operator, discovered the problem while converting the water department records from a manual card system to a computerized data base system in late February 1998. During the conversion process, Turner compared the total monies received for service deposits from approximately twenty-two hundred new customers to the total recorded in the city's accounts for customer deposits. The total received for deposits was $72,896, but the total deposited into the city's account for customer deposits was only $36,578, a difference of $36,318. Turner advised the board of aldermen of the situation and contacted the Horne CPA Group to request an audit of the customer deposit account.

The Horne Group's audit determined that bank deposits to the customer deposits account were not made in a timely manner. Bank deposits were made at three-, four-, and six-month intervals. That is, deposits were only made when a box in which deposits were accumulated filled up! The audit also revealed that two receipt books were missing from fiscal year 1994 and that the only receipt book used in 1998 was missing. The auditors noted that the instances of funds not being deposited into the bank account increased during the Christmas season. The Horne Group's audit showed that, for the total period reviewed, funds received by the city for water deposits exceeded the amount deposited to the bank account by $29,450. Shirley Ferrell, deputy city clerk and water clerk, was the only person who made bank deposits to the city's water service customer deposits account.

The Public Integrity Division of the Mississippi Attorney General's Office began an investigation of the missing funds. AG investigators Tony Shelbourn and Joey Turnage interviewed Mayor Turner and the Horne Group's Andrea Kimbrell on April 1, 1998. The interview revealed that Shirley Ferrell had been "loaning" water department funds to two city employees, Dona Rush, city clerk, and bookkeeper Vergie Hayes. Turner told the investigators that on March 1, 1998, while he was working in city hall converting the water department's records to a computer system, he found two personal checks in the cash box. There was a May 1997 check from Dona Rush for $500 and a November 1997 check from Vergie Hayes for $300. On March 2, Turner told both Rush and Hayes that the checks should be deposited into the city's account immediately. However, the Horne Group's audit revealed that the checks had not been deposited. When Turner inquired as to why the checks had not been deposited, he was informed that Rush and Hayes had replaced the checks with cash.

Turner and Kimbrell explained to the investigators that money had been taken from the water department's cash box and the personal checks used to replace it. The checks were kept in the cash box for an extended period as they were passed over by Ferrell in making bank deposits. This practice resulted in illegal loans of city monies being made to city employees. Turner and Kimbrell also noted that they did not know and could not prove whether the two checks in question were ever actually replaced with cash and the cash deposited in the bank account.

Mayor Turner outlined to the investigators another concern about the integrity of Shirley Ferrell. The mayor reported that, after an early March board meeting, Aldermen Carol Ivy told him about a questionable act. Ivy's husband owned an automotive repair shop in Belzoni, and during 1993 and 1994, Shirley Ferrell's husband, Ronnie Farrell, had run up a debt to the repair shop and was not making payments on the outstanding balance. Carol Ivy said that Shirley Ferrell approached her and offered to pay Ivy's water bill instead of making payments on the debt to the repair shop. This was prior to Ivy being elected alderman, and she agreed to the deal. Shirley Ferrell would send Carol Ivy a water bill stamped PAID each month, and Ivy then recorded this paid amount and credited the amount to Ronnie Ferrell's account at the repair shop. Ronnie Ferrell's account ledger at Ivy's repair shop showed numerous credit entries as "paid on account per Shirley."

During the morning of April 16, 1998, attorney general investigators Tony Shelbourn and Joey Turnage interviewed Shirley Ferrell, who had been employed by the city of Belzoni for approximately twenty-five years. Ferrell explained how the money that came into the city clerk's office for water deposits was receipted and deposited. She stated that a number of people had access to cash received from water deposits and the records pertaining to such receipts. According to Ferrell, Mayor Turner, city clerk Dona Rush, and bookkeeper Vergie Hayes sometimes cashed personal checks using water department cash. Ferrell said she always deposited the mayor's checks because she knew they were good. She also said Rush and Hayes would sometimes ask her to hold their checks because they did not have funds in the bank to cover them. Ferrell acknowledged that she was responsible for making bank deposits but denied having any knowledge of the missing receipt books. The city did not have a polygraph policy, and Ferrell refused to submit to a polygraph test.

On April 16, 1998, the AG investigators interviewed Belzoni City Clerk Dona Rush, who was Shirley Ferrell's immediate supervisor. Rush said that Ferrell was supposed to deposit water department funds to the bank every day. She admitted that she asked Ferrell to hold her May 1997 personal check, but claimed that she asked her to hold it only until the end of the month. She also stated that she didn't know the check had not been deposited until she was told by Ferrell in February 1998. She conceded that placing a worthless check in the city's cash box and receiving cash constituted a loan from the city to her. Rush claimed that she handed Ferrell the cash to replace the May

1997 personal check on March 2, 1998. Rush agreed to a polygraph examination and denied that she had any knowledge of the missing receipt books.

On April 16, 1998, AG investigators also interviewed Vergie Hayes, bookkeeper for the city of Belzoni. Hayes admitted that her November 1997 personal check found in the cash box was not any good and stated that she was behind on everything she owed. She also admitted writing checks and taking cash on four other occasions and acknowledged that she was, in fact, borrowing from the city. She claimed that Shirley Ferrell had helped her when she needed money by telling her to write a check and put it in the cash box and that Ferrell would hold it until it was replaced with cash or Hayes had the money in the bank to cover it. She said that when the mayor found her November 1997 check, she went to a loan shark and borrowed the money and put it in the box and removed her check. Hayes claimed to have counted out the money to Shirley Ferrell before it was placed in the cash drawer. Hayes also said that she would sometimes run a cash register tape (of receipts), sign it, and take cash out of the cash box. She claimed that she only did this for small amounts of $15 or $20 and said if she was going to take a larger amount like $100 she would write a check. She claimed to have always replaced the money she had "borrowed." Hayes denied having any knowledge of the missing receipt books, and she agreed to submit to a polygraph test.

Attorney general investigators Tony Shelbourn and Joey Turnage interviewed Shirley Ferrell a second time on the afternoon of April 16, 1998. During the interview Ferrell said that she would not deposit personal checks from Dona Rush and Vergie Hayes when they informed her that they did not have the money in the bank to cover the checks. Ferrell said that after the mayor told her to deposit the checks from Rush and Hayes, the two women brought in cash and put it in the money box and took out their checks. Ferrell said that she did not verify the amount of cash put in the box to replace the personal checks. She admitted that she had withdrawn cash from the money box and replaced it with her own personal checks but claimed that she always deposited her checks to the proper city bank account. Ferrell also admitted that she knew Dona Rush did not have enough money in the bank when she wrote the May 1997 personal check that was found in the money box. Ferrell claimed that she did not know whether Hayes's November 1997 personal check was good or bad when it was written. She did say that Hayes had asked her not to deposit the check. Ferrell claimed that she personally had not taken any money. During this interview, Ferrell agreed to take a polygraph test.

Shirley Ferrell failed the polygraph test and was interviewed again on April 21, 1998, by Tony Shelbourn. Captain Gail Mills of the Mississippi Bureau of Narcotics also participated in the interview. During this interview, Ferrell admitted that she stole about $100 each month over a period of approximately three years. She claimed that she only took money when there were "overages" in daily receipts. She admitted that consistent "overages" would only occur if receipts were not documented properly.

The OSA received a referral from the Mississippi Attorney General's Office on May 13, 1998, against Shirley Ferrell, deputy city clerk of Belzoni. The OSA opened an investigation and assigned investigator Walt Drane to the case. Drane was asked to assist Tony Shelbourn to determine whether money was missing from the Belzoni water department, and, if so, how much. The OSA investigation, which covered the period from March 9, 1994, through October 3, 1997, determined that $26,793 was collected for water receipts but not deposited in the bank. Ferrell offered to repay $6,000 but District Attorney James Powell promptly rejected the offer.

Shirley Ferrell was indicted on a charge of embezzlement on November 13, 1998. OSA investigators Walt Drane and O. T. McAlpin arrested her on December 1, 1998. This was the first arrest made by OSA agents after the state legislature gave the agency arrest authority during its 1998 session.

District Attorney Powell worked out an agreement with Ferrell under which she pled guilty to an embezzlement charge and was placed in a pretrial intervention program for one year. The agreement called for Ferrell to make full restitution to the city of Belzoni in the amount of $37,660, pay court costs, and pay the DA's office $1,500 for expenses associated with the pretrial program. If Ferrell successfully completed the intervention program and was not charged with a felony offense within five years from the effective date of the agreement, the indictment would be dismissed. The agreement was made effective in an order signed by Circuit Court Judge Jannie Davis on June 25, 1999.

In June 1999, Shirley Ferrell paid the district attorney's office $39,365. This total was composed of $26,793 principal, $8,237 interest, $206 court costs, $1,500 program fees, and $2,629 in OSA investigation costs. The OSA closed the case July 8, 1999.

The fraud triangle emerges again. Ferrell's family obviously had financial pressures. The auto repair bill that they had trouble paying reflects this. The lack of internal controls in the water department, especially lack of supervision by the city clerk and lack of segregation of duties in handling and accounting for cash receipts, provided ample opportunity for embezzlement. Ferrell worked to rationalize her actions. In the April 12 interview with Tony Shelbourn and Captain Gail Mills, she claimed to have discontinued her thefts in October 1997. In that interview, Ferrell said, "I guess the good Lord was telling me that what I was doing was wrong because a couple of, about a couple of months before, right before Christmas, I stopped doing it. I said this is not right, so I started leaving the money in the drawer. And then this all happened."

Larry Niewoehner, Long Beach Municipal Court Clerk

Larry Gene Niewoehner resigned his position of municipal court clerk for the city of Long Beach, Mississippi, on October 31, 1997. Niewoehner had been employed by the city since May 1, 1994. On December 1, 1998, the fifty-three-year-old retired army veteran and former clerk committed suicide. Harrison County Coroner Gary Hargrove ruled that the cause of death was asphyxia due to carbon monoxide poisoning. During 1998, a CPA firm and OSA and FBI investigators unfolded a convoluted tale of embezzlement that took place while Niewoehner was municipal court clerk.

Robert Bass, a CPA, became mayor of Long Beach on July 7, 1997, and his first year was a very eventful one. The day he took office a lightning bolt knocked out the electronics in the city's main water system. Water pressure fell and by late that day three-fourths of the city was without running water. During the year, two policemen were shot and killed, and another one was wounded. The city of seventeen thousand residents also suffered from two floods and a financial crisis. The financial crisis was caused by poor management during the previous administration. Within a month of taking office, the new mayor and aldermen had to cut services, raise taxes slightly, and raise water rates substantially. One of the money-saving measures was to cut off about half of the city's streetlights. The former administrator's excessive spending had depleted the city's resources and left it heavily in debt.

A June 19, 1998, letter to the mayor and aldermen of the city of Long Beach from Stephen P. Theobald, CPA with the firm of Piltz, Williams & LaRosa, contained the following paragraphs:

> During our regular audit of the City of Long Beach, we detected what we believe to be missing funds from the office of the Municipal Court Clerk. We informed the Mayor and City Clerk who in turn informed Long Beach Police Sergeant Kenny Allen. In March of 1998, I was contacted by the City Clerk and was informed that I was to be engaged to perform a detailed inspection and reconciliation of the Municipal Court Clerk's receipts in order to determine if in fact

there were missing funds and if so to document the amount of the loss. After meeting with Sergeant Allen to discuss the case, I informed the City Clerk of the documents that we would need to perform the examination.

We began our examination in May and on June 8, 1998, after having met with investigators from the Office of the State Auditor, decided to issue our report documenting the amount of funds that we had thus far determined to be missing, and then turn the investigation over to the State Auditor's Office. We have recommended to them several areas and periods of time where additional procedures should be applied. These additional procedures may in fact result in the detection of additional missing funds.

Based on our examination, the results of which are summarized on the attached "Accounting Summary of Missing Funds," during the period August 1, 1995, through October 1, 1997, $88,037.30 was systematically embezzled from the Office of the Municipal Court Clerk. Generally, the method used was to simply receive the funds and not deposit them.

Not only had money been stolen, but money had also been spent and the expenditures not recorded in the city's accounting records. On June 21, 1998, the *Sun Herald* published a story outlining the results of an audit by CPAs Piltz, Williams & LaRosa and Van Loon, Sloan, Levens & Farve. The audit report revealed the previous administration had overspent revenues by $441,919, which wiped out a $301,233 balance carried over from the previous year. Mississippi cities are prohibited by state law from deficient spending. The auditors identified more than two hundred instances between 1995 and 1997 in which expenditures were simply not recorded.

The Investigations Division of the OSA opened an investigation on June 17, 1998, and assigned supervisor Ben Norris and investigator Patrick Dendy to the case. The auditors contacted Assistant U.S. Attorney Ruth Morgan, who had received the case from the Long Beach Police Department. Morgan suggested that the auditors coordinate their investigation with that of FBI Special Agent Gerald Peralta, who had been assigned the case. On June 24, Dendy met with Peralta and two members of the Harrison County District Attorney's Office, Beau Stewart and Rufus Alldredge, to discuss how to coordinate the investigation.

On June 30, 1998, OSA investigator Dendy and FBI Special Agent Peralta interviewed Niewoehner in the former clerk's home. Niewoehner explained that the city clerk's office received fine monies and bond fees from the Harrison County Sheriff's Office, receipted and recorded the receipts, and deposited those monies. He and one other employee handled all of the duties of

the office. Niewoehner claimed that he had a problem only one time in reconciling the records to the deposits. He said there was an overage because one
day's receipt copies had been lost. This problem was said to have been solved
based on information in the computer system.

Dendy's report on the interview contained the following paragraphs:

> I told Mr. Niewoehner that a review of several days' activity revealed that there
> were some days' collections for which a deposit was never made, and asked if
> he had any idea as to how this could have happened. He said that all the money
> should have been accounted for. I asked Mr. Niewoehner directly if there was
> ever a time when he took monies out of the collections at the office. He said
> this never happened.
>
> When asked again about problems in the office, Mr. Niewoehner requested
> that I turn the tape recorder off. After I did so, Mr. Niewoehner told us about
> an instance in which he said that he caught the Deputy Municipal Court Clerk,
> Ms. Trisha Dubuisson, short in her collections back in June 1996. He had found
> a receipt in which an individual had paid some money to the office, and this
> money was not on hand and had not been deposited. Mr. Niewoehner said
> that when he confronted her about this problem, Ms. Dubuisson repaid the
> moneys to the office and promised that she would never take money again.
> Mr. Niewoehner provided us with copies of the documentation that he had
> about this problem.

OSA investigator Dendy and FBI Special Agent Gerald Peralta interviewed
Trisha Dubuisson July 7, 1998. Dubuisson had become municipal court clerk
after Niewoehner resigned in October 1997. In his report on the interview,
Dendy wrote that its purpose was "to obtain information from Ms. Dubuisson about operations of the office and determine whether she had any knowledge of discrepancies that may have taken place in the office." The interview revealed serious problems with internal control over cash receipts and
deposits that could have been taken advantage of by either Niewoehner or
Dubuisson.

> We asked Ms. Dubuisson about how the office was generally managed when
> both she and Mr. Niewoehner were employed there. She would collect a ma-
> jority of the monies paid to the office herself, and that on occasions when she
> was not present, Mr. Niewoehner would collect monies from the public. These
> monies would be put into a drawer in the office in which cash was stored.
> When checks were collected, they would also be put into the drawer and then

listed individually on the deposit slips at the time of collection. This collection method was done the same way regardless of who was collecting the money. Mr. Niewoehner was the individual who would normally fill out the remainder of the deposit slips and make the deposits to the bank, which was not done on a daily basis. Ms. Dubuisson would go to lunch the hour before Mr. Niewoehner, and when she returned from lunch he would have the deposits compiled and ready to go to the bank on the days that deposits were made.

Ms. Dubuisson told us how she would check deposits when she made them to be sure that all items were properly included. She said that she would get the receipts from each day's collections, which were put together in bundles. She would then total these and put this amount in the grand total space on the deposit slip. She would then put the total for the checks collected in that box on the deposit slip. The difference in these two amounts would be the cash necessary to make the whole deposit, which should be on hand in the drawer. When asked, Ms. Dubuisson could not remember a time in which there was trouble in assembling a deposit.

We asked Ms. Dubuisson about the allegation that she had once been caught attempting to embezzle money from the Municipal Court Clerk's Office. She admitted that in May, 1996, she had tried to take some money from the office and Mr. Niewoehner caught her and confronted her with it. She said that she repaid the money, which was approximately four hundred dollars, and she had written manual receipts for the collection of these funds. Mr. Niewoehner did not tell anyone with the City of Long Beach that this had happened. Ms. Dubuisson said that she has never on any other occasion tried to take money from the office.

OSA investigator Dendy made a thorough analysis of the records of the city of Long Beach municipal court clerk's office to tie down more specifically the identified shortages, to determine whether other monies were missing, and to determine who was responsible. A paragraph in Dendy's report of January 14, 1999, reads as follows:

For the period May 1994 through November 1997 the receipts and deposits for the Municipal Court Clerk's Office were compared to determine amounts collected and not properly deposited. From May 1994 through August 1995, there was more money deposited into the Clerk's Office bank account than was receipted on the computer system in the office. This can be explained by the fact that often times, manual receipts were issued to individuals making payments to the office, and not posted to the computer system. It appears that these

manual receipts were discarded, and there is no effective reliable way to determine what these payments were. For this reason a calculation of what, if any,
shortage existed in the Municipal Court Clerk's Office prior to September 1995
would not be feasible. It appears that beginning in September 1995, the money
collected in the Clerk's Office was receipted on the computer system.

Dendy's analysis of receipts and deposits from September 1995 until October 1998 revealed a shortage of $88,330.

On February 19, 1999, Phil Bryant issued a demand on the estate of Larry
Niewoehner and his bonding company, St. Paul Fire & Marine Insurance
Company, in the amount of $128,264. The demand was broken down as fol-
lows: failure to deposit collections—$88,330; interest (1 percent per month
from the date of the loss)—$26,063; cost of recovery (hourly rate for staff
work)—$13,871. The bonding company paid the entire amount of the demand
to the OSA by check May 14, 1999. In late May 1999, the OSA closed the case
and repaid the city of Long Beach $114,393, which represented the amount
missing and the interest.

In discussing the recovery with the media, OSA spokesman Langston
Moore said, "Some $88,000 was not properly deposited during [Niewoeh-
ner's] term and he was responsible for the money." He noted that officials
couldn't say that Niewoehner embezzled the money. "That would have been
up to the district attorney or the attorney general to decide," Moore said, but
"the money came up missing during his watch."

Betty Sisco, Brookhaven Municipal Court Clerk

Verbalee Watts, CPA, audited the city of Brookhaven's municipal court records for the fiscal year that ended September 30, 1997. Watts, who completed
the audit November 5, 1997, was unable to trace approximately $25,000 of re-
ceipts to bank deposits. When Municipal Court Clerk Betty Sisco was confronted with the problem, she admitted taking the money and agreed to repay the shortage. The CPA notified Mayor W. W. Godbold, who placed Sisco
and her deputy, Phyllis Watkins, on leave November 19, 1997. Sisco engaged
attorney Jack Price to represent her in this matter.

At a November 21 city board of alderman meeting, city attorney John A.
Fernald informed the board that Price had a check made payable to the city
in the amount of the identified loss, $24,645. Fernald recommended that the
board accept the check with the condition that Ms. Sisco be held responsible

for any additional funds that were discovered missing. Ben Norris of the OSA attended the board meeting, and the board requested that the state auditors review fiscal years 1995 and 1996 pertaining to court fine monies. The board voted to terminate Betty Sisco and to reinstate Phyllis Watkins. The city attorney later advised Price to hold the check until the investigation was completed.

OSA investigator Walt Drane was assigned to the case on November 25, 1997. Drane reviewed receipts of municipal court fines for the period October 1994 through November 1997 and found additional shortages of $3,013, bringing the total to $27,658. When interest of $2,961 and investigative costs of $2,901 were added, the OSA computed a total exception against Sisco of $33,520.

In its January 1988 session, the grand jury of the Fourteenth Judicial District of Mississippi indicted forty-eight-year-old Betty Sisco on a charge of embezzling $27,658. Sisco had served as city clerk from June 1994 to November 1997. The indictment alleged that she willfully, unlawfully, feloniously, and fraudulently received money for fines and court costs, failed to deposit the money in the bank account of the city of Brookhaven, and unlawfully converted it to her own use.

On January 14, 1998, Betty Sisco pled guilty to one count of embezzlement by a public employee before Circuit Court Judge Keith Starrett. Sisco was sentenced to eight years in prison, fined $2,500, and ordered to pay restitution of $38,441 and court costs of $246. Sisco was also required to perform 250 hours of community service. She paid $24,645 directly to the city the day of her pleading, and she was to pay the remainder within two years at 8 percent interest.

Instead of actually going to prison for eight years, Sisco was placed in an intensive supervision program (ISP), or house arrest, as provided for under state law. The sentence was conditioned on Sisco's agreeing to and complying with all of the conditions in an ISP Agreement. Failing to complete the program would lead to immediate imprisonment by the Mississippi Department of Corrections. If the program was completed, the Department of Corrections was to notify the court, and the court was to order the defendant placed on supervised probation for a period to be determined by the court, or until the court altered, extended, terminated, or directed execution of the eight-year prison sentence. Commenting on the sentence, Assistant District Attorney Jerry Rushing said, "This is not a light sentence. If she messes up in any way, she'll go straight to Parchman."

Betty Sisco successfully completed the ISP in July of 1998, and ISP Officer

Tish B. Case recommended that she be released from the program. The court immediately suspended the remainder of her sentence and placed her on probation for five years. The probation order signed by Judge Starrett on July 14, 1988, contained eighteen specific requirements that Sisco had to abide by during the period of her probation.

The money trail associated with Sisco's restitution became convoluted. As noted above, on January 14, 1998, Sisco paid $24,645 directly to the city of Brookhaven. On October 19, 1998, a demand was placed on Sisco and her bonding company, RLI Insurance, by the state auditor in the amount of $14,791 (principal $8,929, interest $2,961, and investigative costs $2,901). The demand was transmitted to the attorney general on December 1, 1998. On January 13, 1999, RLI Insurance paid the city of Brookhaven $11,890, e.g., all but the investigative costs of $2,901. In the meantime, Cisco continued making payments to the court. The payments totaled $41,187. The circuit clerk's office paid the city $2,946. In November of 2001, the circuit court clerk remitted $11,846 to the OSA. The OSA retained the investigative charge of $2,901, remitted the balance of $8,944 to the bonding company, and closed the case on November 6, 2001.

Walt Drane, now retired from the OSA, commented in April of 2004: "Here we go again. This could have been prevented with a separation of duties. I recall that the same person wrote the receipt, made the bank deposits, and reconciled the statements . . . This was a labor intensive investigation due to the number of transactions involved."

Beverly Taylor, Corinth Deputy City Clerk

In November 1994, the CPA firm Dobbins and Brawner began its annual audit of the city of Corinth. When cash receipts of the police department were reviewed, it was noted that the receipt books were missing. City Clerk Jim Billingsley and other city employees attempted to locate the missing receipt books but were unable to do so. Brad Brawner then attempted to reconstruct what had happened using ledger sheets on which cash receipts were supposed to be recorded. The CPA found several discrepancies between bank deposits and what was recorded on the ledger sheets. Brawner found that during the period October 1993 through September 1994, cash receipts exceeded deposits by more than $20,000. After several unsuccessful attempts, Brawner and Billingsley discussed this matter with Deputy City Clerk Beverly Taylor, who claimed she did not know what they were talking about.

In February 1995, Billingsley and Brawner went to Jackson and discussed the matter with Deputy State Auditor Tommy Dyson. This led to a request by Corinth Mayor Jerry Latch that the OSA investigate the matter. OSA assigned investigator Burt Haney to the case.

Haney's discussions with Billingsley and employees of his office revealed how monies coming into the police department were supposed to be handled. Police dispatchers located in the city hall received the money, prepared receipts, accumulated the receipts and money and periodically recorded the receipt number, fine/bond amount paid, and the person writing the receipt on a specially designed envelope, placed the money in the envelope, and transferred the envelope and its contents to the clerk's office. Deputy clerks would verify the money, sign as having received the envelope and its contents, and deposit the money in the bank. Bank deposits would be made to the city court clearing account and recorded in the ledger book. Beverly Taylor, Dorothy (Dot) Wyatt, and Paula Horton were the deputy clerks handling such transactions. Horton and Wyatt indicated that they had little involvement with monies coming into the clerk's office in this manner and that Beverly Taylor usually handled it. During the previous three years nearly all of the entries in the ledger were in Beverly Taylor's handwriting.

OSA investigator Haney compared receipts for fines to deposits using the ledger for the period August 3, 1993, through February 6, 1995. He found forty-three collections of fine money totaling $37,037 that had not been accounted for properly. In four of the instances, more money was deposited than receipted. In seven instances valid receipts had either been voided or were missing from the ledger. In these seven instances, two of the people who paid the money still had the receipts, and in all seven instances court accounting records showed that the money had been paid. These seven receipts amounted to $1,325, bringing the total cash unaccounted for to $38,362. Using similar procedures, Haney determined that $4,844 was missing from the bond money during the same time period. He noted that Taylor had borrowed court records during the latter part of 1994 to "catch up on her posting" prior to an audit. Those records had not been returned to the court. Haney found that each time a receipt was not deposited, the corresponding envelope in which the money was delivered to the clerk's office was missing.

In the summer of 1994, Beverly Taylor resigned her full-time position as deputy city clerk to attend nursing school at Northeast Mississippi Community College. She was to continue as a part-time employee and be paid a full salary until her accrued vacation time was exhausted. After the vacation time was used, she was to be paid an hourly rate. OSA investigator Haney found that a question had arisen about a machine-produced payroll check that Taylor had written to herself in March of 1995 with a gross of $5,524.80 and a net of $3,967.19. The board of aldermen never approved the check nor was the check signed by Mayor Latch or City Clerk James Billingsley, both of whom signed checks for the city. Mayor Latch said he asked Taylor to document the time and that all the information he received was given to the board attorney. On April 1, 1995, Beverly Taylor, who had worked for the city of Corinth since April 15, 1981, resigned her part-time position as deputy city clerk.

OSA investigator Bob Woods administered polygraph tests to City Clerk James Billingsley, two of his deputies, Paula Horton and Dorothy Wyatt, and Deputy City Tax Collector Vickie Roach. Beverly Taylor did not show up for her scheduled polygraph test.

When OSA investigator Haney contacted Taylor and requested an interview, she said she had nothing to add to what others in city hall had already told him. On January 3, 1996, Taylor returned a call from Haney that had been left on her answering machine. During the telephone conversation, Taylor said she had told the CPA, Brad Brawner, everything she knew and had nothing to add. She claimed to know nothing about the missing money and said that she was in school a lot of the time covered by the investigation. She attempted to explain the fact that her handwriting was on all of the records by saying that she was always helping out by doing paperwork for other people.

A warrant was issued for Taylor's arrest on October 9, 1996, and she was arrested and charged with embezzlement on October 23, 1996. In December of 1997, Taylor was indicted on five counts of embezzlement. Count one charged her with unlawfully converting $1,430 of city money to her own use on August 5, 1993. Count two alleged that on October 3, 1994, she unlawfully converted $2,225 of city money to her own use. Count three charged that on November 14, 1994, Taylor embezzled $1,325 of the city of Corinth's money. Count four alleged that on November 21, 1994, she embezzled another $2,975 of the city's money. Count five charged that between August 19, 1993, and January 29, 1995 (excluding the dates related to the other four counts), Taylor embezzled $36,151 from the city of Corinth.

The district attorney's office offered to recommend that the court sentence Taylor to probation rather than prison if Taylor would plead guilty. She turned the deal down and chose to take her chances in court. Taylor went to trial before a jury and Circuit Court Judge Frank Russell in Corinth on February 10, 1998. Assistant District Attorney Arch Bullard prosecuted the case, and Tupelo attorney Brian Neely represented the defendant.

In his opening statement, Bullard told the jury that the state "intends to prove through a series of witnesses that Taylor embezzled $43,206 in cash over a 17 or 18 month period." City Clerk Jim Billingsley was the first witness for the prosecution. He identified Taylor's "neat and pretty" signature and testified concerning documents presented by the prosecution and procedures used in the clerk's office. He noted that the documents showed that money had been received by Taylor and never deposited into the proper accounts. The prosecutor pointed out receipts that had been voided by Taylor and asked the witness whether the voids were in order. Billingsley said that Taylor did not have the authority to void receipts "unless there was an obvious error and a memorandum was attached." Testifying about ledger sheets placed into evidence, Billingsley said the names of several individuals who had paid bond money to the Corinth Police Department had been scratched out. He also said that "zero" appeared in the ledger sheets by the names of individuals who had paid money to the city.

Under cross-examination from defense attorney Neely, Billingsley said that he had never had to take any disciplinary action against Taylor during the thirteen years she had worked with him. Billingsley also testified that Taylor had taken on additional duties since Billingsley became city clerk. Billingsley also agreed that only three envelopes (in which the money came to the clerk's office from the police department) for the dates in question could be found and were available as evidence. Neely pointed out that the three envelopes entered as evidence by the state "didn't even total to $2,500" and indicated that there should be "hundreds" and "boxes of envelopes to total $43,206."

During further questioning, prosecutor Bullard pointed out that Billingsley had "made a diligent search for a number of missing envelopes." Bullard pointed out that the ledger and receipt book showed that Taylor received the funds and that they were missing.

Prosecution witnesses City Court Clerk Diane Johnson, Deputy Clerk Dot Wyatt, and former police department dispatcher Janice Crayton testified concerning the procedures in place to handle bond money during the period of time in question. OSA investigative auditor Burt Haney was the fifth witness for the prosecution. Haney testified that a receipt book from October 1993 to December 1994 was missing, as was a ledger from the prior year. The auditor said he used a ledger from the Corinth Police Department along with an available receipt book for "reconstruction" during his investigation. Haney testified that he found seventeen instances where "deposited funds failed to make it to the bank" and twenty-six instances where "fine money showed deficiencies."

Thirty-nine-year-old Beverly Taylor testified in her own defense. Defense attorney Brian Neely asked Taylor to describe the accounting system for cash receipts that was in place during her employment with the city. Taylor testified that when she received envelopes containing money from the police department she was often busy and would not count the money when she received it. She testified that because she was so busy, she would sometimes take the envelopes and initial the receipt books, "so that the dispatchers could go back downstairs to their jobs. They were as busy as I was." Taylor claimed it was not unusual for one clerk to sign the receipt book and take the envelopes and another clerk to count the money and prepare the deposits. She also noted that on occasions other deputy clerks volunteered to make bank deposits. She told the jury, "We worked as a team on that account. We all had other major jobs and helped each other out."

Taylor claimed not to know what happened to the missing records, including the envelopes that she said were kept in a file drawer. Defense attorney Neely asked Taylor, "Have you taken $43,000 from the city of Corinth?" She replied, "No, I have not." "Have you taken any money from Corinth?" asked Neeley. "No, I have not," Taylor replied. Taylor testified that she resigned from the city of Corinth to pursue her dream of becoming a nurse.

During cross-examination of Taylor by prosecutor Bullard, the witness was asked why her handwriting and signatures were on certain documents admitted into evidence. The documents pertained to twenty-six instances where there was deficiency involving fine money and seventeen instances where funds that were supposed to be deposited never made it to the bank. Taylor replied that she often did not control all aspects of the transactions described, such as signing as having received the money, counting the money, making out the deposit slip, and depositing the money in the bank.

When the defense rested its case after calling only Taylor herself to the witness stand, the prosecution recalled deputy clerks Paula Horton and Dot Wyatt to rebut Taylor's testimony. Both deputy clerks testified that they never signed the receipt book accepting money from a police dispatcher and then let another clerk count the money, make out the deposit slip, or carry the deposit to the bank. They said whoever initialed the receipt book accepting the money from the police department was responsible for all of the duties involved until the money was in the bank. Prosecutor Bullard asked Horton if she had ever seen Taylor put the envelopes anywhere besides the drawer once the money was removed. Horton said that she had seen Taylor throw the envelopes in the trash.

Beverly Taylor was found guilty of counts two, three, and four of the indictment on February 12, 1998. She was found not guilty on counts one and five. Taylor faced a possible maximum sentence of sixty years in prison and fines of $15,000. Prior to the verdict being read in open court, the judge told spectators that any outburst that displayed pleasure or displeasure would result in the person being jailed. It appears that the reason the jury did not convict Taylor on counts one and five related to the lack of complete paper trails. That is, because some of the records could never be located, complete paper trails tying her to each incident in the two counts were lacking.

Circuit Court Judge Frank Russell pronounced sentence on February 13, 1998. Speaking at the sentencing hearing in her own behalf, Taylor said, "I pray and hope you will let me return home with my family. [So] I can continue working hard in the community and doing the good will of God; working hard on my job at Magnolia Regional Health Center and working hard at UNA [University of North Alabama.]" Despite recommendations and requests from friends and acquaintances of the now-convicted felon, the sentence included time in prison. Taylor was sentenced to ten years' imprisonment with seven years suspended on each count. The sentences were to run concurrently, leaving only three of the thirty years to be served in prison. Under the law in effect at the time the felonies were committed, Taylor would have to serve at least 25 percent of the three years actually in jail. She was required to serve five years' probation after being released from incarceration. She was also required to pay court costs of $448 and restitution of $5,625 to the city of Corinth.

The *Daily Corinthian* described Judge Russell's address to Taylor at sentencing as follows:

Noting that character witnesses had indicated she had been an asset to the community, Russell told Taylor, "I hate you have blemished that image with your conduct at city hall." Telling Taylor that charges against her were more serious than those of a private business, Russell reminded Taylor she had been dealing with public funds. "All stealing is bad. Stealing a cookie out of a cookie jar is not a bad thing. Stealing money from a private business is bad," said Russell. "The worst type of stealing is stealing from the church and public who trusted you." Indicating the assistant district attorney had offered Taylor probation in exchange of a guilty plea prior to the case coming to court, Russell told Taylor he was not at liberty to offer her probation after she had been convicted by a jury. "There was an offer made to you to get exactly what you asked for this morning—probation," Russell said. "You chose to roll the dice, so to speak, and play all. When you gamble by nature, sometimes you win, sometimes you lose."

Referring to Taylor's seven-year-old daughter and 19-year-old son, Russell said, "It's sad when parents make choices to hurt children." Recalling other cases in Alcorn Chancery and Circuit Courts where individuals pled guilty and received probation, Russell told Taylor, "You've gone through trial and refused to admit your guilt, which is perfectly your right. (But) one of the first steps to being forgiven is to admit you have sinned."

Taylor appealed the circuit court's decision to the Mississippi Supreme Court but lost the appeal. She reported to prison on January 25, 2000.

In February of 1998, while her case was under appeal, Taylor wrote a letter to OSA investigator Burt Haney, who had testified against her in circuit court. Taylor claimed that justice had not been served because Haney had not gotten the complete story behind his schedule of missing funds. She claimed to have been set up and framed by others working in city hall. She accused the auditor of getting joy from her sentence and asked how he could sleep knowing that he had helped hurt an innocent person. She said the city had a long history of problems with the court fines and that the problems had continued since she left. She also claimed that the two deputy clerks who testified against her, Dorothy Wyatt and Paula Horton, had not told the truth. She claimed the clerks worked as a team, and although she usually signed the receipt books, she was not always the one who would count the money and make bank deposits. She closed her letter by asking Haney for his help and saying that she was writing to everybody she could think of to help her out of her situation. This letter was written by the same woman who consistently refused to talk to auditors and investigators working on the case and refused to take a polygraph test.

In 1996 the OSA made a demand on Taylor and her bonding company for $74,086. This total comprised the amount of fine and bond payments that were recorded on ledgers but not deposited and the amount of an unauthorized paycheck issued to Taylor while she was deputy city clerk of the city of Corinth. In 1999, the Office of the Attorney General settled with the bonding company for $53,000. Beverly Taylor filed for Chapter 13 Bankruptcy on July 21, 1999, in federal court. The OSA received the bonding company's check in the fall of 1999 and presented the money to the city of Corinth on October 11, 1999. The OSA closed the case February 15, 2000.

5. Schools

Officials of public school districts, community colleges, and universities are required by law to establish accountability for and protect all monies that flow into their units. These officials must also ensure that all disbursements made by their units are legal, properly documented, and that the accounting for each disbursement is proper. The OSA has audit authority for public school districts and their various subunits, community colleges, and universities. This section describes four embezzlements from public high schools, one from a community college, and four from universities.

Sharon Morgan, Columbus Municipal School District Bookkeeper

The OSA received a complaint on October 21, 1997, from Kenneth Hughes, business manager of the Columbus Municipal School District Office. Hughes alleged that Sharon Morgan, the district's activity funds bookkeeper, had altered activity fund checks and kept the money for herself. Morgan was suspended without pay October 3 and terminated October 7, 1997. Hughes said that Morgan admitted taking the money and agreed to pay it back. Hughes also referred the matter to the Columbus Police Department. OSA assigned investigator Lewis Johnson to the case on October 21, 1997.

Hughes discovered the embezzlement when the athletic department "came up short." Hughes then notified the bank to start sending the bank statement to his attention. Prior to this, Morgan received the athletic fund bank statements and kept them in a locked filing cabinet. During the time Morgan was alleged to have been embezzling money, the fund was kept afloat by gate and concession receipts and other athletic department revenues.

Investigator Johnson's report, dated February 20, 1998, contains the following paragraph that outlines events surrounding the discovery of the embezzlement.

In September 1997, Kenneth Hughes, according to his statement, was checking the athletic petty cash fund bank statements when he discovered several checks were written in the name of Sharon Morgan. Checking further, more bank records revealed that she had written checks also in her husband's name, Richard Morgan. Mr. Hughes stated that he began to total up the checks and discovered that the checks totaled over $30,000. Mr. Hughes called Sharon Morgan in his office October 3, 1997, and confronted her about the checks. According to Kenneth Hughes' statement, Sharon Morgan told him that she and her husband had split up in the summer of 1995, and she could not make ends meet and needed extra money. After she admitted taking the money, Mr. Hughes contacted Assistant Superintendent John Zerangue and notified him of what was discovered. Sharon was suspended and later fired. In talking with Mr. Hughes, he informed me that Mrs. Morgan had total control over the bank account and kept it under lock and key, and no one had access to this account. On October 9, 1997, the School District turned the matter over to the Columbus Police Department's Captain [Corporal] Rick Jones. Sharon Morgan was arrested and charged with embezzlement by Captain [Corporal] Rick Jones on November 3, 1997.

The following is taken from a transcript of an interview with Sharon Morgan conducted by Corporal Rick Jones of the Columbus Police Department on November 3, 1997.

RICK JONES: And you're saying that you were needing the money to maintain two separate households and that was, a, as a result of a separation or divorce or . . .

SHARON MORGAN: Separation that lasted two years. Um . . .

RICK JONES: Were you paying. . . ? Now your husband's name is Richard Morgan.

SHARON MORGAN: Yes.

RICK JONES: And Richard Morgan's name is on the face of some of these checks. Did Richard have any knowledge that you were putting his name on this or did he receive any proceeds from this check?

SHARON MORGAN: No. He had no idea. Um, that's one of the things about, you know, he always let, what, like with the petty cash account, I maintained the checking counter and the bank statements in reference to, you know, to making sure the bills got paid even though we were separated. He, because his check is direct deposited, so, you know, he never went to the bank. He didn't do that kind of stuff. Um . . .

R I C K   J O N E S : And the money you were using, uh, it was to help hold your household during the separation.

S H A R O N   M O R G A N : Yes.

R I C K   J O N E S : And then when y'all got back together, you continued to do this, and, uh, the money still went into the household.

S H A R O N   M O R G A N : To, yes, it went into the household. We were still having, of course, I mean, we incurred major expenditures and debts during the time that we were separated. Um, and then even after we got back together, there were still problems. Uh, Richard ended up in the hospital and off of work for a month and a half, and uh, you know, I guess just, just problems in general in terms of having been separated for so long in that of trying to get back together, um, and um, we were just having a hard time. And, and, he still didn't have, you know, any idea to what was going on until I actually told him after I got, you know, after everything was found out in the office. Um, and working with the, uh, athletic petty cash account, we write checks for different things on, sometimes every day of the month, especially during football season, um, and in writing those checks, like you said, I, I wrote the checks. I maintained the bank statement and checkbook. And, um, what I did was, I wrote the original check which was the check that was needed by the athletic department for whatever purpose that check was for and got it signed by one of the three administrators and actually sent out the original check to the school for the, for what, for their purposes. And then I duplicated that check and got it signed by a different administrator and then I would take the second check and if the amount needed to be changed, changed the amount and then also changed who the check was made out to. And so that I could use it for my own purposes.

R I C K   J O N E S : And you would take this check and deposit it into your account.

S H A R O N   M O R G A N : Yes.

A more detailed explanation of how Morgan was able to extract money from the school system appeared later in the Columbus *Commercial Dispatch*:

Four different employees—but not Morgan—were authorized to sign athletic department petty cash fund checks.

Morgan prepared the checks to pay game officials, etc. She admitted preparing duplicate sets of checks to pay game officials and having each set of checks signed by a different person. Morgan would then forward one set of signed checks to pay the game officials and alter the other set for her own use.

She said she placed the set of checks she planned to divert to her own use back through the typewriter and erased the name by typing back over it with the eraser part of the typewriter. She would then type in her name or her husband's name and alter the dollar amount by adding one digit.

The OSA's investigation revealed that between November 1991 and September 1997, Sharon Morgan wrote 136 checks to herself and her husband. These checks, which totaled $72,862, were deposited into Sharon and Richard Morgan's bank account. The OSA issued a demand against Sharon Morgan and United States Fidelity and Guaranty Co. on October 2, 1998. The demand totaled $94,040 ($64,862 embezzled, $26,935 interest, and $2,243 cost of recovery). Morgan had already repaid the school system $8,000, which had reduced the principal amount of this demand.

On February 6, 1998, Sharon Morgan was indicted by the Lowndes County grand jury on charges of embezzlement. The forty-one-year-old Morgan entered an open plea of guilty on December 1, 1998, with the state making no recommendation as to sentence. Circuit Court Judge Mickey Montgomery sentenced Morgan on February 25, 1999. She was sentenced to ten years in custody of the Mississippi Department of Corrections but actually placed in an intensive supervision/house arrest program for one year. Upon completion of the year's house arrest, the remaining nine years of her sentence were to be suspended, and she was to serve four years' probation. Morgan was also ordered to pay all court costs, a $10,000 fine, and restitution of $50,105. By the time this sentence was imposed, Morgan had been credited with $35,000 in restitution. The restitution included $37,862 principal, $2,243 investigative costs, and $10,000 interest. Restitution was to be paid at the rate of $1,000 per month beginning April 15, 1999.

Referring to the required restitution, Judge Montgomery told Morgan, "If you do not make the payments, I am not going to have any reservations about sending you to jail." The judge said he was hesitant to sentence her to house arrest, but if she were incarcerated there would be no way for her to make the restitution payments. Columbus school superintendent Owen Bush, who had told the court, "I believe that some time should be served and restitution made," indicated that house arrest was acceptable to him if it facilitated restitution.

In September 2002, Phil Bryant presented a check to the Columbus school district for $43,935. The money came from Morgan's bonding company. The

OSA closed the case November 15, 2002. By March 2003, Morgan had paid the entire amount of restitution, $50,105.

Gerilyn Murphy, South Jones High School Bookkeeper

On April 23, 2002, Robert Murphy, principal of South Jones High School in Ellisville, went to Jones County Superintendent of Education Thomas Prine to report that money had been embezzled from the school's club and activities funds. Accompanying Murphy was Cecilia Arnold, an attorney and friend of Murphy's wife, Gerilyn. They had the unpleasant duty of reporting to the superintendent that the money had been embezzled by Gerilyn E. (Geri) Murphy, who was the South Jones High School bookkeeper. Robert Murphy said he first learned of the embezzlement on April 22, 2002, when Gerilyn told him she had taken money from the South Jones High School club account. After admitting embezzling school funds, Gerilyn appeared suicidal, and her husband did not leave her side until she was admitted to the psychiatric ward of St. Dominic Hospital in Jackson.

Superintendent Prine advised Scott Lewis, Jones County schools business manager, and Dr. Edna Thomas, Gerilyn Murphy's supervisor. Lewis met with Thomas to secure and catalog documents that might be pertinent to any investigation. Prine met with Terry Caves, attorney for the Jones County School Board, who suggested that the records be moved to his law office and that the school board be informed of the situation. The records were moved to Caves's office; Prine removed Gerilyn Murphy's computer to his office, and reported the problem to the Jones County School Board on April 30, 2002. The board advised Prine to report the incident to the OSA, and he did so on May 6, 2002. The OSA opened an investigation May 7 and assigned Special Agent George Blue to the case.

OSA Special Agents George Blue and David Hollingsworth interviewed Robert Murphy at the OSA office in Ellisville on May 7, 2002. Robert Murphy claimed he had no knowledge of embezzlement until Gerilyn confessed to him on April 22. He then explained to the agents his understanding of how monies were taken from the school's club funds based on what his wife had told him. Robert indicated that Gerilyn told him about her actions because she just could not live with it any longer. However, Robert indicated that her confession might have been caused by Scott Lewis's announcement about two months previously that he was going to start doing spot audits on various accounts, such as club accounts.

Gerilyn Murphy was hired by John T. Bryant, former principal of South Jones High School, as office manager/bookkeeper on June 9, 1999. According to Robert Murphy, Gerilyn admitted that she started embezzling money soon after taking the job. Robert Murphy said that when he became principal he wanted Gerilyn to quit the bookkeeping job but that she begged him and Bryant to allow her to stay. During her tenure as bookkeeper, Gerilyn Murphy took only one vacation, and that was during the summer break from school in 2001. Robert Murphy said Gerilyn claimed to have taken the money from the high school club account that had never been audited. Funds in this account came from the Beta Club, FFA, SSA, and vending machine money.

Robert Murphy said that his wife had handled all their personal finances for about twenty years. When Gerilyn's actions came to light, Robert was surprised to learn some bills had not been paid for three or four months, that there was no money in their savings account, and that they had maxed out on credit cards. Robert claimed that Gerilyn had never used drugs and that when they went to casinos she would put only about ten dollars in the machines. He also said she never went to casinos alone. Robert Murphy submitted to a polygraph test on June 20, 2002, and passed the test, indicating that he had no knowledge of his wife's illegal activities.

George Blue interviewed Gerilyn Murphy on May 21, 2002, in the office of the Jones County district attorney. Murphy's attorneys, Anthony Buckley and Cecilia Arnold, were present during the interview, which was audiotaped. During the interview, Murphy admitted stealing between $50,000 and $100,000 over about a three-year period and explained how she was able to take the money. She claimed to have used the stolen money to pay bills and to have given much of it to her two daughters, one in Texas and one attending Mississippi State University. Murphy said, "I'm the type of person who likes to please everyone. And when my family wanted something, I was going to make sure they got it, even though I knew it was wrong. OK. And that's what happened."

Gerilyn Murphy's embezzlement scheme was very simple. It involved writing forty-nine checks to her husband Robert Murphy (sometimes Bobby) on the club account maintained by South Jones High School at the Community Bank in Ellisville, Mississippi. She forged the signatures of Aaron Heidelberg or John T. Bryant, who had signature authority for the account. Then she deposited the checks into a personal account that she and her husband maintained at another bank.

On February 5, 2003, Jones County District Attorney Grant Hedgepeth and State Auditor Phil Bryant announced the indictment and arrest of Gerilyn

Murphy. Murphy was indicted on forty-nine counts of forgery by the Jones County grand jury. Murphy was charged with forging checks for a total of $108,491 on an account that belonged to South Jones High School. She was released on a $100,000 bond.

On February 5, 2003, Phil Bryant issued a demand on Murphy and her bonding company for $146,235. The total included principal, interest, and recovery costs. The demand for repayment was transmitted to the Office of the Attorney General for collection on March 5, 2003.

Forty-seven-year-old Gerilyn Lynn Murphy pled guilty to forty-nine counts of forgery on December 16, 2003. She was sentenced to ten years in prison with the first five years to be served on house arrest. While under house arrest, Murphy was to participate in the 18th Circuit Court Community Service Program. If she successfully completed the house arrest, the remaining five years were to be suspended. She was also ordered to repay $146,235, $108,491 of which was to be paid to the OSA on the date of the plea. Another $29,950, the amount of interest charged, was to be paid to the OSA within thirty days of the plea. She was also ordered to pay the OSA recovery costs of $7,795, and she was fined $2,000 and ordered to pay court costs of $222. This final $10,017 was to be paid at the rate of $170 per month until paid in full. If Murphy failed to make the $29,950 payment as ordered, or failed to successfully complete the house arrest part of her sentence, she would be required to serve the remaining part of the ten-year sentence in prison.

Murphy's lawyer, Cecilia Arnold, made the required $108,491 payment by check on December 17, 2003. As of the end of January 2004, Murphy had repaid a total of $138,445, and the OSA had returned these funds to Jones County Superintendent of Education Thomas Prine. Murphy was paying off the remainder monthly at the rate of $170.

Superintendent Prine noted that the case had been prosecuted rapidly and said it was a tribute to the agencies involved. According to Prine, "This is almost unheard of. So many agencies were involved in this, the Jones County District Attorney's Office, the State Auditor's Office, the State Attorney General, and others. For it to take only a few months is really phenomenal." Prine went on to say, "Our main concern was the students who worked so hard to raise the money for trips and activities wouldn't suffer. It was unfortunate we had an employee who chose to do this. We have made additional changes to the bookkeeping processes at the school as a result of this incident, but the fact remains if someone wants to embezzle money bad enough, they will find a way to get away with it—for a while anyway." Prine indicated that the severity of the sentence meted out to Murphy should be heeded. "The result of this case sends a couple of messages," he said. "The first is that you will eventually get caught, and the second is that you will be prosecuted to the fullest extent of the law."

Mary Nelson, Moss Point High School Bookkeeper

An employee of the Moss Point School District registered a complaint with the OSA on August 21, 2002, alleging that Mary Nelson, a former bookkeeper at Moss Point High School, had embezzled at least $10,000. The OSA immediately opened an investigation and assigned Special Agent Earl Smith to the case. Mary Nelson, who had held the bookkeeper position for three school years, resigned in June 2002 and was replaced by Ruth McDowell, who discovered the alleged embezzlement.

When McDowell became bookkeeper, Nelson stayed on for a week to help with the transition. McDowell immediately noted a problem because there didn't appear to be any records. Nelson told McDowell that she had wiped out all her records from the computer but assured McDowell that "everything balanced." The school had two main funds for which the bookkeeper was responsible, the school activity fund and the principal's activity fund. Monies received from vending machines, parking permits, fines, textbook store sales, etc., went into the principal's activity fund, and monies received by clubs and fund-raising projects went into the school activity fund.

The bookkeeper received monies from students, parents, teachers, and other parties, prepared deposit reports, noting which fund the deposit was to be credited to, and forwarded the reports to the CFO's office. The reports, which were signed by the bookkeeper and the principal, were sent to the school district office, where Pat Keenan was responsible for making sure they were credited to the proper fund. The bookkeeper did not write checks on the funds. Paperwork supporting disbursements was prepared by the bookkeeper and sent to the district office, where Keenan issued the necessary checks.

OSA Special Agent Earl Smith's report, dated September 11, 2002, included the following paragraphs.

> Ms. McDowell stated that she found items that were questionable soon after she started the job. These items included checks being deposited for which no receipt was issued, cash receipted for, but not deposited, and unaccounted for

money from fundraisers. Some of the areas Ms. McDowell identified as having potential problems were parking permits, summer school, school store sales, a petty cash fund, candy fundraisers, yearbook sales, school pictures, transcripts, fines, sale of graduation cords, junior class prom, and cheerleader uniforms. Ms. McDowell stated that she also discovered that receipts were not issued consistently for funds received by Mary Nelson, the former bookkeeper. Ms. McDowell stated that any funds received in her office amounting to One Dollar ($1.00) or more is receipted.

Ms. McDowell described Mary Nelson's actions as suspicious during the period Ms. McDowell was working with Ms. Nelson to take over the office. Ms. McDowell stated that Ms. Nelson would not let Ms. McDowell go behind her desk and when Ms. Nelson went to lunch she would lock her door so that Ms. McDowell could not get into the office. Ms. McDowell stated that she noticed a substantial difference in funds she had collected since she took over as compared to the same funds that Mary Nelson receipted.

Ms. McDowell stated that during the time Mary Nelson was the bookkeeper, Ms. Nelson prepared the deposit tickets and made deposits of activity fund money. Ms. McDowell also stated that she discovered where Ms. Nelson had requested Pat Keenan to pay invoices out of funds that were from the Moss Point School District's account. Ms. McDowell stated that there were several invoices received after she arrived and that money had to be taken from different activity funds to pay these invoices causing certain funds to start the new school year with a negative balance.

Ms. McDowell stated that she inquired of Pat Keenan regarding how some funds were being handled. Ms. McDowell stated that Pat Keenan kept changing the accounts that Ms. McDowell . . . was to apply funds to. Ms. McDowell said that when she told Pat Keenan that there appeared to be a problem with missing funds, Ms. Keenan told her not to tell the Principal, Mr. Goings, because Ms. McDowell would be opening up a can of worms. Ms. McDowell stated that Pat Keenan made a comment, "if they don't like the way we are handling things, they can the whole bunch." [Willie Goings was a new principal at Moss Point High School having moved up from the position of assistant principal to replace Larry Fry.]

Ms. McDowell stated that several teachers and others have stated that they gave Mary Nelson large sums of cash for various activities and did not receive a receipt. Ms. McDowell stated that these people later realized they did not get credit for the funds they turned into Ms. Nelson.

Ms. McDowell stated that several people had made comments about Mary

Nelson wearing expensive jewelry, purchasing at least two new vehicles, and purchasing seadoos, while she was employed as bookkeeper.

Ms. McDowell said that in addition to Mary Nelson deleting all records on her computer, hard copies of records were missing.

The OSA's investigation revealed that Mary Nelson had embezzled at least $23,000 from the funds she received that should have gone to the principal's fund or the activity fund. Nelson had not prepared receipts for some checks and had not deposited some checks for which she had prepared receipts. Nelson often prepared deposit tickets and substituted unreceipted checks in the deposit for cash and removed the same amount of cash from the deposit. To determine the amount of missing money, investigators analyzed deposit records secured from Merchants and Marine Bank and records available in the bookkeeper's office.

Three examples illustrate how Nelson was able to steal cash and cover her actions for a while. The school rented reserved parking spaces to students. Records showed that for school year 2001–2002, 192 spaces were rented for a total of $1,900. Nelson reported renting only 48 spaces for $480 and extracted $1,420 in cash. Nelson controlled the candy sale fund-raiser for the yearbook. Records showed that 10,530 candy bars had been purchased, to be sold at $1 per bar. When McDowell became bookkeeper, she received 524 candy bars from Nelson, leaving 10,006 to be accounted for at $1 each. Nelson had reported sales of $4,753 and deposited that amount to the proper account. Nelson apparently pocketed $5,253 from candy sales. Nelson was also responsible for summer school receipts. For the 2002 summer school, she reported and deposited receipts of $5,515 in cash and $4,915 in checks. Records showed that the total amount collected for summer school was at least $11,880, indicating that Nelson had shorted deposits by at least $1,440.

At the request of Jackson County District Attorney Keith Miller, Mary Nelson was indicted by a Jackson County grand jury on three counts of embezzlement on October 9, 2003. Count one charged embezzlement of $704 from Moss Point High School between August 19, 1999, and June 13, 2000. Count two charged embezzlement of $6,151 between August 2, 2000, and June 23, 2001. Count three alleged embezzlement of $704 from July 5, 2001, to June 14, 2002. Nelson surrendered to the Jackson County sheriff's department on November 20, 2003, posted a $7,500 bond, and was released. The forty-two-year-old former bookkeeper faced up to ten years in prison and a $10,000 fine.

In a letter dated November 19, 2003, the OSA demanded that Nelson and her bonding company, St. Paul Fire and Marine, pay a total of $38,356. The total was the sum of the amount embezzled ($23,041), interest at 1 percent per month from the date of the loss ($4,556), and cost of recovery ($10,759). In December 2003, the OSA received a check for $22,541 from Nelson's bonding company. Phil Bryant presented Moss Point High School the recovered funds in January of 2004.

Based on a plea agreement, Nelson pled guilty to embezzlement in the Jackson County Circuit Court on August 31, 2004. She was sentenced by Circuit Court Judge Kathy Jackson to six years in the Mississippi Department of Corrections, with the first year to be served in the intensive supervision program (house arrest). If she successfully completed the house arrest, she was to be placed on postrelease supervision for five years. Failure to successfully complete the house arrest would result in immediate imprisonment for the remainder of the sentence. Because the offenses were committed prior to July 1, 2002, the law that requires at least one year of jail time for anyone convicted of embezzling $10,000 or more of public money was not in effect. Nelson was also ordered to pay court costs, fined $1,000, and ordered to pay restitution in the amount of $14,815. Payments were to be made at the rate of $50 per month beginning in October 2004. At this rate it would take Nelson nearly twenty-five years to pay the restitution required.

Bennie Tillman, Yazoo City Schools Athletic Director

On June 11, 1999, M. James Chaney, Jr., attorney for the board of trustees of the Yazoo City School District, faxed a letter to the OSA saying the board had received information about possible misappropriation of funds and other financial irregularities in the district's athletic department. Attached to the letter was a narrative written by Ardis Russell, a parent of a Yazoo City High School student. Mr. Russell, who is a practicing CPA, based his narrative on personal knowledge and "what I heard on the street from friends I trusted." The narrative outlined several alleged problems with the way money was spent by the athletic department. The OSA opened an investigation on June 14, 1999, and assigned Special Agent Earl Smith to the case.

The ensuing investigation revealed that a substantial amount of money had been embezzled or misused by members of the school system's athletic department. The following paragraphs are from a November 1, 1999, "Synopsis Report" written by OSA investigator Earl Smith.

The problem area was that of reimbursement for meals for ball teams. Bonnie Smith, Business Manager, Yazoo City Municipal School District, explained the process for reimbursement of meals. Prior to the spring of 1999, the Athletic Director [and Head Football Coach], Bennie Tillman, submitted a requisition for funds for meals. This requisition was submitted to Bonnie Smith to determine if the funds were available to pay for the meals. Bonnie Smith then submitted the requisition to the Superintendent for approval. Once approved, the invoice was submitted to the accounts payable clerk for payment. A check was made payable to Bennie Tillman. Bennie Tillman then cashed the check and provided money to coaches to purchase meals. Once the meals were purchased, Bennie Tillman was responsible for returning a receipt, along with any funds left over, to the business office. In fact, on September 5, 1995, Bonnie Smith provided a memorandum to Bennie Tillman stating the requirements for receipts. Beginning in the spring of 1999, the checks were made payable to each individual coach and that coach was responsible for returning receipts and any excess funds to the business office.

Based on the results of the investigation, it was determined that Bennie Tillman failed to provide receipts to the business office for meals and provided false receipts. On three occasions, Bennie Tillman admitted in interviews that he solicited and obtained false receipts which he turned in to the business office. Bennie Tillman stated that when he did not have a receipt, he would go to a business, such as Wendy's, McDonald's, Shoney's, Bumpers,' etc., and obtain blank receipts and complete the receipt and submit it to the business office.

By comparing purchase requisitions, cancelled checks, and receipts for school years 1996–1997, 1997–1998, and 1998–1999, investigators were able to identify disbursements to athletic director Bennie Tillman that were not properly supported. They classified the disbursements as follows: payments for meals for which no receipts were submitted—$8,168; payments for meals that were supported by receipts made up by Tillman (supposedly because individual coaches responsible did not provide him receipts) and excess payments when there was a failure to return to the business office excess funds when receipts turned in totaled less than the total amount requisitioned—$5,392; payments for meals that were supported by false receipts. This category included payments for meals where the responsible coaches submitted receipts for less than the amount of the requisition, and Tillman prepared false receipts for the difference. It also included payments supported by bogus receipts prepared by Tillman for meals associated with games that were neither scheduled nor played—$3,494.

The auditors' work on this case included several interviews with those having knowledge of conditions in the Yazoo City Schools Athletic Department and extensive analysis of records. Those interviewed included the parent who first registered the complaint, school officials, accounting personnel, coaches, and persons doing business with the athletic department. The investigation revealed an almost complete lack of internal control in the athletic department, and allegations of wrongdoing included the following:

(a) Payments had been made for baseball uniforms and baseballs that were never delivered. When the baseball coach discovered this, he informed the Yazoo City school system's superintendent of education, Arthur Cartlidge. The coach said he was subsequently pressured by the vendor to order the items after the fact. Cartlidge said he later contacted the vendor, and the school system was reimbursed for the uniforms not delivered. (Cartlidge resigned his position with the Yazoo City schools in June 1999 and accepted a similar position with the Greenville school system.)

(b) A $500 check was accidentally deposited into a booster club bank account that the club did not know existed. Cartlidge said that, when he became aware of this account, he told Tillman to close it.

(c) Many athletes apparently never received trophies that were due them.

(d) Security guards (off-duty city police officers) were hired for athletic events and were paid in cash. The checks for such payments were actually made out to the security guards, and the Form 1099s they received at the end of the year for tax purposes were for the amount of the checks and for more than they claimed to have received in cash. This caused at least two of the guards problems with the IRS. Bonnie Smith, director of finance for the school system, said the security guard arrangements involved a deal that had been worked out by the former police chief, Jimmie Fleming, and the officers. Smith said that she understood the guards wanted the money when they worked and that Fleming paid them in cash. Supposedly the guards later endorsed their checks over to Fleming. In order to get the officers to work the games, Fleming claimed he had to pay the officers in cash, but checks would not be issued until the Tuesday after the games. Fleming said that the officers would then endorse the checks, or if they were not available, he would endorse the checks. Fleming claimed that, on many occasions, he paid the officers more than the checks and that he showed the officers exactly what the records indicated they made.

(e) Coaches often received less in cash from Tillman than the business office disbursed to him in payment for various things.

(f) The athletic department was said to have purchased a set of golf clubs every year from 1993 to 1999. The school did not have a golf team until 1998, and that was a one-man team. Bonnie Smith said that golf clubs were only purchased during the 1994–1995 and 1998–1999 school years. Superintendent Cartlidge said that Tillman told him the athletic department had sufficient golf clubs on hand for a team and that he stopped the purchase of any additional golf clubs.

(g) The manager of a local McDonald's restaurant was reported to have "run off" a football coach who had been in the restaurant requesting customers' food receipts.

(h) The coach of the baseball team, Steve Ramsey, and the coach of the track team, Andrew Gates, identified instances in which more meal money was disbursed for their teams than they received or paid. They also identified instances in which money was paid for meals for events when no meals were provided and instances where their signatures on receipts appeared to have been forged.

(i) Tillman controlled ticket and concession sales for all football and basketball games. When tickets were sold and the buyer presented them for entrance to a game, the whole ticket was taken up instead of being torn in half and given to the purchaser. Cartlidge said that when he became aware of this situation he made some changes that included removing control of ticket sales from Tillman and giving it to the school principals.

The following paragraphs are taken from a report written by OSA investigator Earl Smith. There are several similar reports that deal with interviews of others involved with the athletic program.

On Friday, July 2, 1999, I interviewed Steve Ramsey, Baseball Coach at Yazoo City High School, and Ardis Russell, CPA.

Ramsey stated, in regard to an invoice from Judge Little Company for baseball equipment, that he did not receive baseball uniforms, baseballs or the 3 dozen caps and supporters. Ramsey stated that Tillman provided baseballs to him, however, they were not Diamond baseballs. The baseballs provided by Tillman were Wilson baseballs.

Receipts for reimbursement for baseball players' meals were reviewed. Ramsey stated that the baseball players are not provided meals for home games. Ramsey stated that the baseball team has not eaten at Wendy's in Yazoo City since he has been baseball coach. Ramsey said that the only meals provided were for away games and these meals would be at out of town locations.

Ramsey reviewed a claim for reimbursement for meals for the Capital Classic in Jackson. The reimbursement is for 5 games. Ramsey stated that the baseball team only played three games. The requisition also showed meals for 30 players, 4 coaches, and 4 managers. Ramsey stated that for these games there were 9 players and 4 coaches. Ramsey stated that the copy of the two receipts attached to the requisition for Wendy's store #1201411 appeared to be correct, however, the other receipts do not represent expenditures for meals for the baseball team. Ramsey stated that the most players he has ever had would have been twelve. Ramsey said that he did not even have 30 uniforms.

Ramsey stated that the requisition for meals of 30 players, 4 coaches, and 4 managers for the Cleveland game was not correct. Ramsey stated that he would have had 9 players and 4 coaches. Ramsey stated that the team did not eat at Wendy's.

Ramsey stated that the requisition for meals for 30 players, 4 coaches, and 4 managers for the Humphrey County game on March 24, 1997, was completely false. Ramsey stated that the baseball team was not given anything for meals for this game and that the team did not eat a meal.

Ramsey stated that the requisition for meals for 30 players, 4 coaches, and 4 managers for the game at Kosciusko on March 28, 1997, was inflated also. Ramsey stated that the baseball team did not eat at Wendy's, and the signature on the receipt is not his signature.

Ramsey stated that the requisition for meals for 30 players, 4 coaches, and 4 managers for the game at Clarksdale High on April 3, 1998, was inflated in regard to the players and managers. Ramsey stated that the baseball team did not eat at Wendy's. Ramsey stated that the team ate at Burger King. Ramsey stated that the signature on the receipt was not his signature.

Ramsey stated that the requisition for meals for the baseball team in [for the] Capital Classic on March 8–10, 1999, was not correct. Ramsey said the number of players was around 12. Ramsey said they participated two days in the tournament.

The following paragraphs are taken from OSA investigator Earl Smith's August 23, 1999, report. It is based on an interview with Dr. Arthur Cartlidge, who was at this time superintendent of the Greenville school system.

Dr. Cartlidge stated that on one or two occasions, his business manager [Bonnie Smith] came to him and discussed the fact that there was a problem with receipts. Dr. Cartlidge stated that he discussed this with Coach Tillman and in turn Coach Tillman discussed this with the other coaches. Dr. Cartlidge stated that one or two times he was aware that the receipts did not quite add up to whatever they had issued in the beginning. Dr. Cartlidge stated that Ms. Smith had spoken to him on one or two occasions about not receiving receipts from Coach Tillman. Dr. Cartlidge stated that he sat down and talked with Coach Tillman and told him that they had to have receipts. Dr. Cartlidge stated that it was about that time that Coach Tillman started requiring individual coaches to submit receipts. Dr. Cartlidge stated that at the same time Ms. Smith made him aware of the fact that some receipts looked questionable. Dr. Cartlidge stated that each time Ms. Smith brought it to his attention [that] there was a problem with receipts, he talked to Coach Tillman about it. Dr. Cartlidge stated that each time he spoke to Coach Tillman he indicated that the receipts were authentic. Dr. Cartlidge stated on each occasion he talked to Coach Tillman, he never got anything from him to indicate that there was any wrongdoing. Dr. Cartlidge stated that his business manager showed him one or two of the receipts that were questionable. Dr. Cartlidge stated that he could not recall reviewing any receipts from Wendy's.

Dr. Cartlidge stated that he could not recall either Ms. Smith or Ms. Washington [accounts payable clerk] telling him that they could not issue a check for meals because Coach Tillman had failed to turn in a receipt for a prior game. Dr. Cartlidge stated that he could not recall Coach Tillman coming to him and complaining about not being able to get a check for meals. Dr. Cartlidge stated that he did not give Ms. Smith or Ms. Washington specific instructions to issue a check to Coach Tillman. Dr. Cartlidge stated that he can not recall giving any specific instructions to the accounts payable clerk. Dr. Cartlidge stated that he never told Coach Tillman that it would be okay for him to submit bogus receipts to get funds for other activities.

Dr. Cartlidge stated that Coach Tillman never gave him any money or gratuities in any form. Dr. Cartlidge stated that Coach Tillman did not make any payments to him or on his behalf.

In an interview with OSA investigators, Bennie Tillman claimed he never diverted any funds from ticket or concession sales to himself. However, he admitted turning in Wendy's receipts that he prepared to cover amounts on purchase orders that had been used to support advancing him money for team meals. There were many such Wendy's receipts, and they were a type that Wendy's used only when their cash registers were down, which was rare. Tillman claimed he made up the receipts because coaches failed to turn in to him receipts as required. Tillman also admitted asking for and receiving blank, signed receipts from an employee of the local Wendy's. Tillman also admitted that he sometimes received advances of $80 for out-of-town meals for the cross-country team, gave only $60 to Coach Gates, and kept $20 to pay for his own meal and gasoline for his trip. He covered the $20 difference with phony Wendy's receipts.

In April 2000, the OSA issued a letter to Bennie Tillman demanding that he pay $32,191 ($16,735 principal, $4,830 interest, and $10,626 investigative costs). The OSA closed the case on November 15, 2002. As of June 30, 2003, Tillman had repaid all but $6,588 of the OSA's demand.

Bennie Tillman was indicted by the Yazoo County grand jury on February 29, 2000. He was charged with one count of embezzlement of approximately $16,719. Tillman was arrested and released on a $2,500 bond. He faced maximum punishment of ten years in prison and a fine of $10,000. On July 17, 2000, Circuit Court Judge Jannie Lewis Davis ordered that Tillman be admitted to the district attorney's pretrial intervention program. If Tillman successfully completed the program, he would not be prosecuted on the indictment.

Scott Blouin, Pearl River Community College Remote Sensing Education and Training Coordinator

On October 27, 2003, the OSA received an allegation that the director of remote sensing education and training coordinator at Pearl River Community College (PRCC) and his wife might have set up a bogus company and received funds from the college. The OSA opened an investigation into the allegations against Scott Blouin and his wife, Janet Wagner Blouin, and assigned Special Agent Louise Stewart to the case on October 28, 2003. The director of adult services at PRCC, Mrs. Sharron Bellew, had questioned the legitimacy of a company that had invoiced the college for services and books.

Agent Louise Stewart and Senior Special Agent Ben Norris met with PRCC's business manager, Roger Knight, on November 3, 2003, to secure documents and learn more about the allegation. Knight provided the agents copies of all checks, invoices, and purchase orders pertaining to Statewide Educational Consultants, a company thought to be owned by Janet Wagner Blouin. Knight also provided a copy of a letter to PRCC from Amanda Wagner, owner of the company. The letter stated that the company was a single source vendor for specialized geospatial books including geographic information systems and remote sensing lessons used for research, teaching, and geographic learning. Knight noted that the letter, dated October 6, 2003, contained three discrepancies: the tax identification number was invalid; the company's address was a mailbox, not a suite as indicated on the letterhead; and the telephone number was invalid.

OSA agents Stewart and Norris discussed the case with Lamar County Assistant District Attorney Kathy Sones on November 3, 2003, and disclosed to Sones evidence accumulated to date. Numerous invoices had been submitted to PRCC from Statewide Educational Consultants for geographic information systems books for prices ranging from $150 to $285. Norris confirmed by a telephone conversation with Cheryl Buckley, a county employee, that Marion County had paid PRCC for "Educational Supplies for ESRI ArcGIS I class March 18–19, 2003," for six students at $150 each. An Internet search showed that the Environmental Systems Research Institute, Inc., published and held the copyright to the books listed on invoices from Statewide Educational Consultants, and that the books could be bought for less from the Institute. According to PRCC paperwork, Scott Blouin had purchased the books from Statewide because the Institute would not sell them to him. The Institute would only sell the books to teachers it had certified, and only certified teachers were authorized to sell the books to students. Sones noted that the evidence justified a search of both the residence and the work sites of the Blouins. Since Scott Blouin's office and the couple's Lamar County residence were in Hattiesburg, Sones referred the agents to Forrest County Assistant District Attorney Ben Saucier.

On November 3, 2003, Stewart and Norris discussed the case with Saucier. The assistant district attorney asked the agents to prepare an Underlying Facts and Circumstances document and agreed to prepare an Affidavit for Search Warrants for Scott Blouin's office at PRCC, Janet Wagner Blouin's office at Jones County Junior College (JCJC) in Ellisville, and for the couple's home. Saucier also agreed to subpoena the couple's bank records. Stewart and Norris subsequently prepared the Underlying Facts and Circumstances document, which showed that invoices submitted by Statewide to PRCC from April 2001 through October 2003 totaled $73,250.

Having obtained the search warrants, OSA agents and Hattiesburg police detective Mark Ogden searched the Blouins' residence on November 4, 2003. Several items were seized and an inventory of the items removed was left with Scott Blouin. The same day, OSA agents searched Janet Blouin's office at JCJC, where nothing of interest was found, and Scott Blouin's office at PRCC, where several items were seized.

During the search of the Blouins' residence, keys were found to two post office boxes. A search warrant was obtained and the contents of the boxes were examined. The contents included bank statements from Hancock Bank and Trustmark National Bank and state and federal papers associated with the formation of Statewide Educational Consultants.

In a supplemental report of November 11, 2003, Louise Stewart wrote:

Friday, November 7, 2003, at 9:00 a.m., Senior Special Agent Ben Norris and I, Louise Stewart, met with Scott Blouin's attorney, Ray Price, in his office at 214 West Pine Street, located in downtown Hattiesburg, Mississippi. Mr. Price also identified himself as the Public Defender.

Mr. Price said that he represented both Scott and Janet Wagner Blouin. Mr. Price said that they were guilty, but what they did was just stupid. According to Price, there were problems within the Workforce Development Center at Pearl River Community College. When funding cuts by the state caused several other programs to be discontinued, Mr. Blouin's supervisor, Ed Felsher, instructed Mr. Blouin to do what he had to do to make the program work. Mr. Blouin tried to hire his wife to assist with the program, but politics interfered and "somebody's cousin" got the job.

Mr. Blouin personally purchased Ten Thousand Dollars ($10,000) worth of books because Pearl River Community College would not approve book purchases in a timely manner. Mr. and Mrs. Blouin can provide documents where work was performed by Mrs. Blouin under the name of Statewide Educational Consultants. Mrs. Blouin wrote grant requests, wrote programs, conducted research and ran errands for the Workforce Development Center. Since she was at Jones Junior College only on a part-time basis, she was able to spend substantial time working for the Workforce Development Center.

Senior Special Agent Norris and I reviewed documents provided by Mr. and Mrs. Blouin. They appeared to be documentation to support Mrs. Blouin's research, including hand written notes and magazines.

Mr. Price said that he would inventory all items and deliver them to Assistant District Attorney Ben Saucier who agreed to make copies for the Office of the State Auditor. At our request, Mr. Price will recommend the Blouins provide bank records for our review. It was noted that no bank records were found at the residence.

The OSA files contain a confidential synopsis of the investigation used to support grand jury testimony that reads as follows:

Evidence developed in this investigation will show that SCOTT M. BLOUIN and his wife JANET WAGNER BLOUIN did willfully accept funds from Pearl

River Community College for invoices they generated for alleged services. Using the name Amanda Wagner, d.b.a. Statewide Educational Consultants, invoices were submitted between April 2001 and October 2003.

As the Remote Sensing Education & Training Coordinator of Pearl River Community College Workforce Development Center, Scott Blouin conducted Remote Sensing Projects. He scheduled and coordinated instructors and classes on Remote Sensing including geographic information systems (GIS). The funds that were embezzled from Pearl River Community College were funds received from businesses, government agencies, or individuals as payments for Remote Sensing classes in the Workforce Development Center.

During a search of the Blouin residence, a check book, deposit books, and a "Statewide Educational Consultants for Deposit Only" stamp were discovered. Investigation revealed a bank account was opened in April 2001 at Lamar Bank in Hattiesburg, Mississippi. The account was styled *Janet W. Blouin, D.B.A. Statewide Educational Consultants,* Post Office Box 18392, Hattiesburg, Mississippi 39404. During the embezzlement period, a merger changed Lamar Bank to Hancock Bank. There were no other changes to this account.

Invoices totaling Seventy-Three Thousand One Hundred and Fifty-Three Dollars ($73,153) were prepared by Scott and Janet Wagner Blouin and submitted to the Workforce Development Center where Mr. Blouin had approval authority. The majority of these invoices were for textbooks. Pearl River Community College checks were payable to either Amanda Wagner, d.b.a. Statewide Educational Consultants or Statewide Educational Consultants. Two checks totaling Two Thousand Seven Hundred Twenty-Five Dollars ($2,725) were not cashed. Alert PRCC personnel began questioning the number of textbooks purchased and the legality of Statewide Educational Consultants. They did not release two additional payments totaling Four Thousand Two Hundred Dollars ($4,200). The net total for these transactions for which checks were issued was Sixty-Six thousand Two Hundred Twenty-Eight Dollars ($66,228).

Correspondence between ESRI (Educational Systems Research, Inc.) and Scott Blouin advised [that] only Authorized Training Instructors could purchase textbooks for GSI classes. Blouin was not authorized and had received numerous warnings about purchasing ESRI textbooks. Credit card statements provided by Scott Blouin reflected he purchased textbooks on several occasions for a grand total of Eight Thousand One Hundred Seventy-Three Dollars and Seventy-Six Cents ($8,173.76). ESRI confirmed these purchases and payments. This total was deducted from the amount Pearl River Community College paid to Statewide Educational Consultants.

Invoices submitted by Educational Consultants included ones totaling Five Thousand Dollars ($5,000) for research on the Southern Pine Beetle. Further investigation revealed Mr. Blouin, in his role as coordinator of Remote Sensing Projects, applied for a NASA Space Grant Program through the University of Mississippi. Pearl River Community College received this grant in the amount of Five Thousand Dollars ($5,000). Documentation confirmed that research was done by either Scott or Janet Blouin. No exception was taken on these invoices.

The amount which Scott Blouin retained for himself was Fifty-Three Thousand Fifty-Four Dollars and Twenty-Four Cents ($53,054.24). This amount consists of Sixty-Six Thousand Two Hundred Twenty-Eight Dollars ($66,228) which he actually received, less the amount which he remitted to ESRI, Eight Thousand One Hundred Seventy-Three Dollars and Seventy-Six Cents ($8,173.76) and Five Thousand Dollars ($5,000) for Pine Beetle Research.

CONCLUSION

Based on the evidence developed in this investigation, SCOTT AND JANET BLOUIN did willfully and intentionally embezzle funds from Pearl River Community College. The scheme was accomplished by the Blouins creating a fraudulent company for the sole purpose of submitting false invoices to Mr. Blouin's employer, Pearl River Community College.

Scott and Janet Blouin were indicted on three counts by a Forrest County grand jury on November 19, 2004. Count one charged the Blouins with conspiring to defraud Pearl River Community College by creating a fraudulent company for the purpose of submitting false invoices to Scott Blouin's employer. Count two charged them with defrauding Pearl River Community College by submitting invalid invoices for $73,153. Count three charged the Blouins with fraudulently converting (embezzling) $53,054 of Pearl River Community College's money to their own use.

As the results of a plea agreement worked out by District Attorney Jon Mark Weathers and the Blouins' attorney, Ray Price, Scott Blouin entered a plea of guilty to counts one and two of the indictment November 23, 2004, before Circuit Court Judge Bob Helfrich in Hattiesburg. In an Order of Nonadjudication, Judge Helfrich deferred acceptance of Blouin's plea for five years and put the defendant on probation for that time period. Numerous conditions were imposed by Judge Helfrich, including that Blouin pay a fine, assessment, OSA investigative costs, and restitution. The total, which was to be paid immediately, came to $74,905. The order also prohibited Blouin from handling any state monies or other assets during the time of probation. Count three of the indictment was passed to the inactive files. Upon successful completion of the probation requirements, the defendant was to be automatically discharged.

The arrangement worked out by the district attorney with Scott Blouin, which resulted in Blouin's guilty plea, included a provision that all three charges in the indictment against Janet Blouin would be dropped. In a January 7, 2005, Order Passing Cause to the Files, Judge Helfrich wrote:

> On this day this Cause came on to be heard upon Motion of the State of Mississippi, *ore tenus*, to pass the above styled and numbered matter to the inactive files for the reason that Co-Defendant,Scott M. Blouin, has accepted full responsibility for the crimes set forth in the Indictment and was thereafter sentenced by the Court following the entry of a guilty plea; that Defendant apparently did not actually participate in the commission of the crimes alleged in the Indictment; and that justice would be served by passing this matter to the inactive docket as to Defendant Janet M. Blouin.
>
> It is therefore, ordered, and adjudged that this case be and the same is hereby passed to the inactive files, without prejudice as to Defendant Janet M. Blouin.

In December 2004, the OSA received a check for $8,815 from the Forrest County circuit clerk for investigative costs that Scott Blouin had been ordered to pay. Noting all of the circuit court's actions, the OSA closed this case February 7, 2005.

As noted above, count three of the indictment against Scott Blouin was passed to the inactive files. This count charged embezzlement of $53,054 of public monies. Since 2002, Mississippi law has required that anyone convicted of embezzling $10,000 or more of public money be sentenced to at least one year in jail. The plea agreement seems to have been designed to circumvent this law. Also, Janet Blouin was obviously complicit in her husband's actions, and she received no penalty at all. Perhaps District Attorney Jon Mark Weathers's comments after Scott Blouin was sentenced explain the authorities' thinking. According to the *Hattiesburg American*, Weathers said, "In a case like this, it's a non-violent crime, and the penitentiary is full of people, we've got to move the cases, and I felt like the important thing to do was get full restitution to the public entity that's our money."

James Hilton, Manager, Aquarium Admissions Office and Gift Shop, J. L. Scott Marine Education Center and Aquarium, University of Southern Mississippi

The J. L. Scott Marine Education Center and Aquarium in Biloxi is a subsidiary of the University of Southern Mississippi (USM). When Cathy Gemmill came to work at the Center on May 15, 2000, she discovered that money was missing from two cash registers. May 15 was a Monday, and James Hilton, the manager of the aquarium admissions office and the gift shop was off that day. Hilton had worked alone the previous Saturday. Both cash registers had been "Xed" out (subtotaled) but not "Zed" out (totaled) as was required when a register was closed out for the day. When Gemmill totaled the registers, she found that the total of the admissions register was greater than the subtotal. When she counted the money in the registers, she found that it equaled the subtotals plus the $100 change fund for each register. The $200 difference between the total and subtotal in the admissions register was missing. Gemmill immediately reported what she found to Johnette Bosarge, who reported it to Howard Walters, assistant administrator and coordinator of educational programs. Walters called Dr. Sharon Walker, a USM associate dean of outreach administration, and reported that something was wrong with the admissions cash register tape. This call started a process that eventually resulted in an audit exception of more than $200,000 and a federal felony conviction.

On May 15, 2000, Dr. Sharon Walker received a telephone call reporting a questionable refund of $200 on the admissions cash register at J. L. Scott Marine Education Center and Aquarium. The "detailed tape" for May 13 indicated a refund for fifty adults at $5 ($250). The admissions register indicated only sixty-eight adult admissions that day, and the amount paid by the largest group admitted was only $28. A large refund was also shown on the gift shop register for May 13. Walker suggested that James Hilton be called and asked to come in, because she was sure that he could explain the error. Hilton came to the Center, and Johnette Bosarge showed him the large refunds on the cash register tapes. Hilton worked with Cathy Gemmill and tried to explain the refunds. He indicated that he really didn't see a problem because the totals matched what was in the registers. Hilton was gone when Walker went to the gift shop. She left a message for him to see her that afternoon or early the next day.

Walker, Hilton, Johnette Bosarge, and administrative assistant Howard Walters met in Walker's office May 16, 2000. Walker asked Hilton if he could explain the $200 refund, and he could not. He said he did not remember giving anyone a $200 refund. Hilton claimed he had not left the register open and that no one had access to the money except him on the prior Saturday. According to Walker, Hilton seemed extremely nervous during this meeting. Walker asked Hilton to bring all the cash register tapes to her office, and a short time later Hilton brought in three boxes of tapes. During this time, Hilton was so nervous that he was unable to open the cash register. Later in the day, Walker learned that Hilton had taken off without proper approval. Walker left another note for Hilton to see her.

Hilton called in sick the next day. Walker left Hilton another note requesting that he see her on Thursday morning, May 18, 2000. Walker saw Hilton in the lobby on the morning of May 18 and told him she did not appreciate his leaving without approval. She also asked Hilton to bring all the 1999 and 2000 cash register tapes to her office. Walker also told Hilton that from then on she wanted two people to "check out" the registers in the afternoon. Hilton brought Walker his resignation and requested to leave the center at that time. Walker told Hilton to go through the "check-out" procedure first. He did so and immediately left the premises. Walker later learned that, shortly after the large refunds were discovered, Hilton had taken some boxes to the dumpster.

In April 2000, Walker had requested that Jennifer Spring, Gulf Coast Research Laboratory Technical Liaison, copy all the gift shop computer files because three of the Center's employees had mentioned that Hilton was spending a lot of time on the computer. Hilton was also suspected of forging the initials of Sylvia Covacevich on items received by the center. According to Walker, Hilton ordered merchandise and Sylvia Covacevich was to check the merchandise in.

During the time they were trying to determine what the large refunds were for, Walker learned that Kris Fulton, assistant director for business and finance at Gulf Coast Research Laboratory, had told Hilton to stop placing orders for merchandise because the Center was "in the red." Hilton had not stopped ordering merchandise, and Walker learned that he had about $168,000 in gift shop inventory.

USM's internal auditor, Dana Keith, was notified, and Vijay M. Patel, senior internal auditor, began work on the case. Patel concluded that embezzlement in the Center had begun about September 1996 and that it amounted to approximately $122,930. Patel noted a pattern of large refunds for adult admissions to the aquarium and refunds from the gift shop being recorded on cash register tapes at the end of the day. The money collected at the Center was sent by courier to the Gulf Coast Research Laboratory, which made all the bank deposits. Patel discovered that large and questionable refunds appeared to have been made when Hilton was working and that they stopped when he was on vacation. Refunds were made with no documentation. Internal controls should have required that refunds be approved by a supervisor of the person making the refunds and that recipients of refunds sign a document acknowledging receipt. Other employees said Hilton told them that, when he was not there to close, they should subtotal ("X") but not total ("Z") the registers. Patel also learned that some of the cash register tapes had been destroyed and that sometimes a security guard operated the gift shop register when other employees were at lunch. According to Patel, the admissions register for May 13 showed a $200 refund and only $268 for adult admissions. There were no large groups of adults admitted to the Center that day.

Patel also learned about the potential problem that involved gift shop inventory. He noted that there was an unusually large volume of inventory and that annual physical inventories had not been taken until 1998. Hilton was said to object to having to take physical inventories. Patel noted there were no questionable refunds during the time an inventory was being taken. The auditor thought Hilton might have sold some of the merchandise on eBay, an Internet auction.

Dana Keith reported the suspected embezzlement to the OSA in June 2000. OSA Special Agent George D. Blue was assigned to the case June 13, 2000. On June 27, 2000, Blue and Senior Special Agent Ben Norris interviewed James Hilton in his home in the presence of his wife, Carol Lynn Hilton. Hilton's father also showed up at the residence late in the interview. Blue's report on this interview made the following points:

(a) James Hilton had worked at the J. L. Scott Marine Education Center and Aquarium for thirteen years.
(b) Hilton said Sylvia Covacevich, Cathy Gemmil, and Cheryl Dimetry worked at the Center, and indicated that they had access to the cash registers as did he himself. Hilton also indicated that Dr. Walker and Johnette Bosarge had access to the registers. He said all who had access to the registers except Dr. Walker could close them out.
(c) Hilton said daily register closing involved getting a "Z" (final) total, and putting the money in a locked bank bag along with the "Z" tape. The bag would be sent to the USM Gulf Coast Research Laboratory by courier daily. He claimed not to know what happened to the money when it reached the lab. The lab would send the bag and a handwritten receipt back to the Center.

(d) Hilton claimed that cash register receipts were maintained at the Center except for some that had been water damaged about two years earlier.

(e) According to Hilton, the registers could be "Xed," or subtotaled, if there was a problem. Potential problems included: senior citizens getting refunds for full-priced adult tickets; refunds requested on small concession purchases; and large group refunds for admissions that had been rung up on the cash register but were actually to be paid for based on a purchase order to be handled by the lab.

(f) Hilton said that refunds were usually made shortly after the sales had been entered into the cash registers and that in the gift shop they usually ran from $10 to $30 a day.

(g) Hilton said whoever was working was responsible for closing out the register and usually no other person was present when the register was closed out.

(h) Hilton said that if there were a number of $200 refunds shown on register tapes it would surprise him. He also said that if there was a subtotal "X" on a register tape, then a refund, then a total "Z" on a tape, it would surprise him.

The OSA agents told Hilton that money was missing from both the gift shop and admissions and that it seemed that money was missing from as far back as 1996.

When asked why he left employment at the Center, Hilton said that Dr. Walker told him there was a problem with the register the day before he left. Hilton said he asked Walker if she were setting him up for a downfall. He claimed she had been "on my case forever," and if he were being set up for a fall he would just resign. He said that he told Walker, "I haven't taken a dime from this place." Hilton said he intended to retire from his work at USM.

During July 2000, OSA Special Agent Blue interviewed several administrators and employees of the J. L. Scott Marine Education Center and Aquarium. The interviews revealed the following:

(a) Walters, Covacevich, Gemmill, Brown, Bosarge, and Dimetry had keys to the Center.

(b) There were no security alarms on the building.

(c) There was no after-hours sign-in register.

(d) Profits in the gift shop had increased dramatically after Hilton's resignation.

(e) Hilton always got nervous when Dr. Walker came around.

(f) Another Center employee, Dick Vermeulen, sometimes operated a cash register when Hilton went to lunch, but he never closed out the register.

(g) Hilton went to the casinos frequently and often bragged about his winnings. He did not say much about his losses. He talked so much about his winnings that he was nicknamed "Diamond Jim."

(h) Vermeulen also visited the casinos, but he didn't seem to win like Hilton.

(i) Hilton seemed to spend a lot of time on the computer.

(j) Covacevich received merchandise coming to the gift shop, and she noted that sometimes merchandise arrived that was not on the list that Hilton had given her.

(k) Dimetry had also received merchandise for the gift shop, and she had heard a vendor offer to send something to Hilton's home if the vendor received an order.

(l) Hilton and his wife, Carol Lynn, took the physical inventory. She was a singer at a casino.

(m) Two Center employees saw Hilton put some boxes in a dumpster on May 16.

(n) Hilton had recently bought a $30,000 boat, a house, and a used car for his wife.

(o) Keith Brown, a security guard, would sometimes operate the gift shop cash register to relieve regular operators who had gone to lunch, the restroom, or out for a smoke.

(p) Hilton told a couple of employees who could close out the registers to ring up a "sale" for any overage and a "refund" for any shortage.

(q) Walker had admonished Hilton because he was often late for work.

(r) Hilton took long lunch breaks, often carried a large quantity of cash on his person, and refused to put bar codes on inventory items to establish a perpetual inventory record.

The case was discussed with the local district attorney, who denied the OSA's request to subpoena needed records. Subsequently, in November 2000, the OSA asked the FBI to enter the case. FBI Special Agent Steve Callender worked with OSA investigator George Blue and USM internal auditor Vijay Patel to tie down the facts in the case.

In late October 2003, forty-four-year-old James (Jim) Robert Hilton, now a resident of Bokeelia, Florida, was indicted on three federal charges alleging embezzlement. The J. L. Scott Marine Education Center and Aquarium operated by the Gulf Coast Research Laboratory of the University of Southern Mississippi received more than $10,000 of federal funds annually, making the crimes federal offenses. Hilton was charged with embezzling more than $5,000 during each of the years 1998, 1999, and 2000. On November 21, 2003, the FBI and the OSA jointly announced that Hilton had been arrested at his home in Florida on November 17, 2003. He was to be returned to Gulfport to be arraigned.

On February 3, 2004, Hilton and his attorney, Fredrick J. Lusk, Jr., appeared before U.S. District Judge Walter Gex III in Gulfport, and Hilton pled guilty to count one of the indictment. Gex ordered a presentence investigation and set sentencing for May 4, 2004. On May 3, 2004, the OSA presented a schedule of exception totaling $211,063 (the amount embezzled—$158,725, interest—$44,837, and the cost of recovery—$7,501). Judge Gex sentenced Hilton to fifteen months in prison and three years' probation, ordered him to pay restitution of $100,000, and assessed him a $100 court fee. He was to report to prison September 7, 2004. Counts two and three of the indictment were dismissed.

USM internal auditor Vijay Patel noted in April of 2005 that internal controls had been put in place to safeguard assets at the aquarium admissions operation and gift shop. According to Patel, inventory in the gift shop had been reduced from about $168,000 to about $34,000, and admissions revenue was up.

Lisa Lindsey, Mississippi State University Print Shop Clerk

A report by OSA Special Agent Burt Haney describes the problems uncovered in the Mississippi State University (MSU) print shop that led to his being assigned to the case on August 10, 2001.

On August 13, 2001, I met with University Auditor Eileen Hayes on the campus of Mississippi State University to discuss some concerns she had on deposits from the university print shop. Hayes began by showing me one particular deposit from May 2, 2001. The documents prepared at the print shop, a cash receipt voucher, showed a total deposit of $4,881.15, with .06 of this in cash. There are approximately 19 daily cash detail receipts attached to the voucher as backup which shows the date, ticket number, voucher (receipt) number, and amounts. The total of these backups equals the total on the voucher. The problem starts when a review of the actual receipts shows at least a total of $483.74 of the receipts were marked as being in cash. There is an additional amount of $1,063.84 which is not marked on the receipt as either cash or check. The total checks per the receipts shown on the cash detail sheets total $3,333.58. On initial review it would seem that there is $484.68 in cash missing. The bank provided a list-ing of what made up this deposit which shows account numbers and amounts of each check used to make up this same deposit. On this particular deposit, the bank shows a total of 46 checks which were used to make up this deposit. A comparison of this list to the checks shown on the print shop detail sheet indicates there are only 24 checks which match up for a total of $871.99. This suggests that there are some $2,461.59 in checks the bank has that we do not have any receipt on.

We are in the process of trying to get the backup on other deposits. The cashier's office has researched and produced the deposits themselves, but they have very few of the daily cash sheets. These are supposedly located in the print shop somewhere, but at this time only a few have been located. We will continue to look for these, and at the same time a comparison of total receipts for outside sales will be done to total deposits. The deposits received from the cashier's office for a one year period indicate no cash deposited, only checks. A determination must be made of (1) the amount of cash collected, and (2) the amount of checks the bank has in deposits that were not receipted at the print shop. We will continue to work on this and reports will be filed as appropriate. There will probably be documentation that will have to be obtained from the bank, but this will be worked out as the case progresses.

Haney and Hayes met with Lisa Lindsey, former MSU print shop clerk, on October 1, 2001, at the Oktibbeha County Courthouse to discuss operations at the university print shop. Lindsey claimed that she had always been uncom-fortable about everyone having access to the cash box that was maintained at the office. Lindsey said that she did the deposits for the shop, but claimed that all shop employees opened the incoming mail. She noted that the shop was supposed to have converted to the university's accounts receivable ban-ner system but that it had not happened. The print shop still handled a lot of billings and received payments. Lindsey was unable to explain why there was no cash in a majority of the bank deposits, why some checks sent to the shop were never processed, or why checks in deposits were often not the same as those listed as making up the deposits. Lindsey consistently denied knowing why things were done the way they were. Haney quickly concluded that she was not going to cooperate, and he terminated the interview.

On February 16, 2002, Haney and Hayes met with Lisa Lindsey and her hus-band, Vic Lindsey, in Hayes's office. The meeting had been scheduled at Lisa Lindsey's request. She said her husband now knew what happened and that she wanted to do whatever she needed to do to straighten this out. Haney's report, dated February 18, 2002, outlined what happened at this meeting:

Lindsey was informed that this was a noncustodial meeting (she was not under arrest), and she read and signed an advice of rights form.

Lindsey was asked to describe in her own words what had happened, and all she would say was that she took the money that was missing. She claimed not to remember when she started taking money and blamed her behavior on job-related stress.

When shown a list of checks payable to MSU that had been deposited in her personal account, Lindsey agreed that they were all intended for the university. She also confirmed that they were all checks she had taken, but said she did not remember that there were that many.

When asked how much she had stolen, Lindsey claimed to have no idea. She admitted stealing cash and checks but said that not much cash came into the print shop. She said that she started working in the print shop in May of 1999 and that she thought it wasn't until 2000 that she started taking money.

According to Lindsey, no one else was involved with her embezzlements, and no one else was aware of what was going on.

When she was asked what she would do with the invoices when she decided to take a check or cash, she indicated that she would sometimes throw them away and sometimes she would let them go through. Since she was the person making most of the deposits, she could make the deposits match with the underlying paperwork. She said deposits were made once a week or once every two weeks.

Lindsey was shown deposit slips to her personal bank account that indicated she had received cash back several times in amounts of $500 to $1000. She was asked if anyone at the bank was involved, and, after hesitating, she said no one else was involved. She said she was taking responsibility, that she was not going to name names, and that she just wanted to get it out of the way.

When asked how the bank let her deposit checks made out to MSU to her personal checking account, Lindsey said that she didn't know and that the bank never questioned her. She said she came up with a name to endorse on the checks, but she didn't remember what it was. Haney noted that she had made deposits at two or three branches and that the deposits were handled by different tellers.

Lindsey said that Karon McKamson ran things at the print shop and that the man who was the director was seldom around the office.

Haney informed Lindsey of how his investigation would proceed and that he would be discussing the case with the district attorney.

After the interview, Lisa Lindsey wrote and signed the following sworn statement:

> I, Lisa Lindsey, have looked over the papers set before me and do not disagree with the evidence of the money I took from Mississippi State University. I admite [*sic*] fault in this matter [.] I did take what is listed as best I remember. I do not know of a certain dollar amount. But I will do all I can to help resolve this matter as quickly as possible. As best I remember I deposited all money into my personal checking account.

As the investigation progressed, MSU provided OSA agent Haney a printout showing the total of cash sales at the print shop and the total deposited in the bank during Lisa Lindsey's employment as clerk at the print shop. The list showed that receipts exceeded bank deposits by more than $31,000. Haney obtained Lindsey's personal bank records and determined that there were numerous checks deposited to her account that should have been deposited in MSU's account. In doing so, Haney determined that approximately another $11,000 of MSU's money had been deposited into Lindsey's personal bank account.

Having completed their investigation, OSA agent Haney and MSU internal auditor Hayes met with Lisa Lindsey again on October 17, 2002. Haney showed Lindsey a copy of the financial summary in the case and explained how the numbers had been derived. Lindsey was informed that she would get a demand letter from the OSA and that she would be given a specified time period in which to respond. She was also told that failure to respond during the established time period would result in the case being turned over to the Mississippi Attorney General's Office. Haney also informed Lindsey that a copy of the file would be delivered to the district attorney's office, which would make a determination on whether to prosecute. Haney noted that the OSA would make no recommendation concerning prosecution to the district attorney's office. At this meeting, Haney once again asked Lindsey if there had been anyone else involved in taking the money. Lindsey said she did not have proof that anyone else was involved so there was no reason to name names.

In addition to Lindsey's depositing cash and checks belonging to MSU into her personal bank account, Haney found that she had deposited an MSU check payable to a terminated employee into her personal account. Lindsey requested the check for unused vacation time in the amount of $867.84. When the check came to the print shop to be issued, Lindsey simply deposited it into her own account. The payee of the check was contacted by Haney, and he was completely unaware of what had happened. Haney secured copies of cashed payroll checks made out to the payee and noted that the endorsements were obviously not the same as that on the check which had been deposited to Lindsey's account.

In January 2003, State Auditor Phil Bryant demanded that Lisa Lindsey repay $59,428, which included $42,909 that she was accused of embezzling, $7,825 interest, and $8,694 in investigative costs. OSA Public Relations Director Pete Smith said that after the investigation by the state auditors, the case was turned over to District Attorney Patricia Faver for prosecution.

An Oktibbeha County grand jury indicted Lisa Lindsey on one count of embezzlement on January 24, 2003. Attorney Mark Williamson worked out a plea bargain, and Lindsey signed a plea agreement on July 31, 2003, in which she agreed to plead guilty to the embezzlement charge. She faced possible penalties of up to ten years in prison and a fine of up to $10,000. The thirty-five-year-old high school graduate and Sturgis resident was scheduled to be sentenced in October of 2003.

W. Daniel Bryant, MSU's chief budget and finance officer, said that the crime was committed over a period of many months. In a victim's impact statement, Bryant said: "It was not an impulse one-time event. It involved deception of those who trusted her with dutifully depositing all the money in the treasury of the institution. The crime reflects negatively on the university and the printing shop supervisors. Perhaps more importantly, it damages the taxpayers in the State of Mississippi at a time when resources are most scarce. The university has zero tolerance for crimes on campus. For the reasons stated, we request the maximum sentence be applied in the case."

Circuit Court Judge Lee Howard sentenced Lisa Lindsey on October 30, 2003. The judge ordered Lindsey to pay full restitution and sentenced her to ten years in prison with five years suspended. This relatively harsh sentence was obviously designed to send a message.

Danny Oswalt, Mississippi State University Housing Business Manager

OSA Special Agent Burt Haney wrote the following offense report on June 5, 2001.

On May 25, 2001, I was told by Senior Special Agent Denver Smith to be in Starkville, Mississippi on May 29th to meet with officials of Mississippi State University about a possible embezzlement they had uncovered. On May 29, 2001, I went to Director of Internal Audit Don Zant's office to determine what kind of problem they had. Mr. Zant explained that Mr. [Danny] Oswalt was the Business Manager of the housing department for the University and, as such, had handled the purchasing for that department. Mr. Zant said the documents they had showed he had requested payment be made to Shivers Painting— William J. Shivers on eight different occasions for a total of $45,846. Mr. Zant said according to people in the maintenance department, Mr. Shivers had never performed any work for the university. Mr. Zant said the paperwork indicates Mr. Oswalt falsified some of the documents for payment, and even endorsements on the checks are different. Mr. Zant said some of the paperwork found in Mr. Oswalt's office indicates it was fictitious billing. Mr. Zant said he found out after the fact that Mr. Oswalt and Mr. Shivers are related.

Mr. Zant said they have also discovered where Mr. Oswalt had set up a bogus company to do business with the university. The company name is University Group, Inc.,[it] is incorporated in Mr. Oswalt's name, and supposedly sells calendars, pens, hats, cups, etc. Mr. Zant said there have been twelve billings from this company since January 2001 with a total billing of $38,126. He said the documents in Mr. Oswalt's office indicate there were no materials delivered to the university, only the billing and the university paying. Mr. Zant said even some of the check stubs from the payments were found in Mr. Oswalt's office.

Another area of some concern to Mr. Zant was Mr. Oswalt handling the funds from housing deposits. They found some instances in his office where they had documents showing where checks, cash, and credit card charges were turned in to Mr. Oswalt, but when it got to the cashier's office there was no cash. I asked Mr. Zant if there would be documents showing how much cash was given to Mr. Oswalt each time, and he said he would have to find out what kind of documentation was passed from one office to the next. (We checked with the cashier's office and were told that over the last year or so there had been little if any cash turned in by Mr. Oswalt.) Mr. Zant said he would get someone working on this area to see what they could find.

There were some other questions which would have to be answered, such as the use of the university charge card, travel, use of the telephone, and computer network use. Mr. Zant said they would check all areas and keep me posted as the investigation proceeded.

Mr. Zant said the University Police Chief, Tom Johnson, had said when I got there he would like to meet with me. I told Mr. Zant to contact me if he wanted to meet, and Chief Johnson said he would be over in a few minutes. Chief Johnson came in with his investigator, Lt. Ken Spencer, who had been doing some preliminary work on the case, and Chief Johnson talked for some time about what needed to be done on the case. I told him I was in the process of obtaining a subpoena for the bank records of University Group, and would let him know as soon as we had the information. Mr. Zant told Chief Johnson that they were going to see if a meeting could be set up with Mr. Oswalt, and Chief Johnson said he nor Lt. Spencer needed to sit in on that meeting because they would have to read him his rights and that might keep him from talking. Chief Johnson said he would like me to be there when he met with Shivers. I told him if he would let me know I would like to be there. The meeting ended, and I told Mr. Zant if they set up a meeting with Mr. Oswalt to let me know, and he said he would.

On May 31, 2001, OSA Special Agent Burt Haney met with Mississippi State University's Director of Internal Audit Don Zant, Vice President for Student Affairs Dr. Roy Ruby, Director of Housing Dr. Ann Bailey, Danny Oswalt, and Oswalt's father, Larry Oswalt, in Ruby's office. The purpose of this meeting was to confront Danny Oswalt with the auditors' findings, which indicated that he had embezzled significant amounts of money from the university. During the meeting, Danny Oswalt was questioned by Zant. Oswalt admitted that as business manager he paid a first cousin, William Shivers, for painting work that was never done, that he kept for himself cash deposits made to his department, that he charged personal purchases to an MSU credit card, and that he set up a bogus company and paid it for materials never delivered to MSU. Oswalt was immediately fired.

Danny Oswalt expressed regret for his actions, and said he wanted to apologize to his family, friends, and coworkers. He said that he had lost his job, his fiancé, and everything, and that he wanted to do whatever was necessary to make it right. When asked why he had stolen money from MSU, Oswalt said he wasn't sure; he guessed he thought material things would make him happy. He said he always wanted his two girls to look up to him, but look what they would think now.

On June 8, 2001, Haney, Zant, and Johnson met with William J. Shivers (Shivers Painting), Mr. Shivers's father, and Mark Williamson, an attorney representing William Shivers. The meeting was scheduled at William Shivers's request to explain what he knew about the Oswalt case. Shivers said that he had worked for MSU's housing department doing painting and other jobs as a student worker during the summers of 1990–94 and in 1998. Shivers said Danny Oswalt, his first cousin, called him and told him he had a way to get some money. According to Shivers, in December 2000, Oswalt asked to use his name for work that was not going to be done. The next month Oswalt approached him again and they billed the university for work not done. Shivers said he thought Oswalt was in some kind of financial bind.

Shivers said that Oswalt had become a different person since he began dating Krystal Hernandez, and that he now seldom talked to Oswalt unless the couple was broken up, which had happened several times. He also said that Oswalt always wanted the best, and that took money. He said he knew that during the prior six months Oswalt bought a Yukon vehicle and a diamond engagement ring. According to Shivers, Oswalt gave Hernandez his Jeep Cherokee, and he thought she still had it. He also said that Oswalt and Hernandez would sometimes go to Philadelphia or Tunica but that Oswalt was not a big gambler. Shivers said the two were dating before Oswalt's divorce, but that Oswalt had told him that Hernandez did not know anything about what was going on at the university.

Shivers said that Oswalt told him about a company he had established and about getting some gift certificates through MSU. Shivers said Oswalt shocked him when he said that he had probably gotten $100,000 from the university. After being shown eight checks made out to Shivers Painting, Shivers admitted that he knew about the first five but denied any knowledge of the last three. He claimed his signature was not on the three and that he had not received any of the money. He said Oswalt gave him the other five checks, and he either took them to the bank and deposited or cashed them. He claimed that Oswalt always got more than half of the money when the checks were cashed. He said he wrote Oswalt checks for his part when the MSU checks were deposited. Shivers admitted he had done no work for the university since 1998 when he worked for the physical plant. Shivers also said he had heard that Oswalt had used an MSU credit card for purchasing personal things, and that he had gotten gift certificates from Cabela's and Wal-Mart.

In late June 2001, the investigators heard that Oswalt was living in Knoxville, Tennessee, and wanted to arrest him before he could skip out completely. Based on information developed by the investigators, District Attorney Forrest Allgood approved an arrest before indictment. MSU Police Chief Johnson obtained four arrest warrants on Oswalt from a justice court judge. The judge set bond at a total of $500,000. Oswalt was contacted and asked to come to a meeting at the MSU Police Department on June 29.

Several of the investigators attended the meeting, and Lt. Kenneth Spencer conducted an interview with Oswalt that was audiotaped. The transcript of this interview is very revealing. Oswalt admitted that he and Shivers billed MSU several times for work never done, and that they personally got the money from checks associated with the billings. He said that he and Shivers engaged in this behavior "just to get money." When asked how he and Shivers came up with the amount to invoice MSU, Oswalt said one of them would say how much money he needed and "they would just go from there." Oswalt also admitted stealing cash deposits, misusing an MSU credit card to buy personal items, and establishing a bogus company that billed MSU for things not delivered. Oswalt repeatedly explained his actions by saying that he "needed the money." Concerning the cash deposits that he took, Oswalt said that if the money was given to him with a deposit slip he would deposit it, but if it was not with a deposit slip, he would keep the cash. Oswalt claimed no one ever checked to see whether the correct amount was being deposited and that he didn't have to account to anyone. The fraudulent activity had taken place over the period January 1999 through May 2001.

Larry Daniel Oswalt wrote the following confession on June 29, 2001.

MISSISSIPPI STATE UNIVERSITY POLICE DEPARTMENT
STATEMENT OF EVENTS
While employed at Miss. State University, I and William Shivers submitted receipts to the University that was for work that was never done. All of these receipts but 2 or 3 were usually split around half by me and Mr. Shivers. There were only the last 2 or 3 receipts he had no knowledge of. We would split the money from these checks. I also made a few purchases using the MSU procurement card for my personal use. I do have these items and I will be giving these items back to the university whenever they would like to recover them. There was also some money from some deposits that I would keep and not deposit. I do not remember the amount of this money. There was no one else that knew about these transactions but myself and Mr. Shivers. There was money made from the University Group that was also for items that were not received by MSU. I was the only person aware of these transactions. I did keep the money from these transactions. To the best of my knowledge, these are the only things that were done that were fraudulent.

Oswalt was arrested on the four warrants immediately after the interview was conducted and the confession was written. He was taken to the Oktibbeha sheriff's department, where he was processed and incarcerated. Bruce Brown, Oswalt's attorney, persuaded the judge to reduce his bond to $20,000. Later, Oswalt bonded out of jail.

The *Starkville Daily News* reported on July 2, 2001, that Larry D. Oswalt, former housing business manager for Mississippi State University Department of Housing and Resident Life, had been arrested and charged with embezzling $117,000 from the university. The university police and the office of internal audit conducted an investigation and worked with the OSA and the district attorney to bring the charge. MSU internal auditor Don Zant said the university had insurance of up to $100,000 per employee against employee dishonesty. MSU officials indicated that they did not believe any other university employees were involved. Zant said that internal controls had been strengthened to guard against subsequent incidents.

The grand jury of Oktibbeha County indicted Danny Oswalt July 23, 2001, on two counts of false pretense, one count of embezzlement, one count of credit card fraud, and one count of conspiracy. The first false pretense count alleged that Oswalt defrauded MSU in excess of $250 by falsely representing to the university that certain work was accomplished by William J. Shivers, doing business as Shivers Painting, and submitting an invoice for the work. In fact, there was no such entity as Shivers Painting, nor had any work been done for the university. The second count of false pretense charged Oswalt with falsely representing to the university department of finance that The University Group, Inc., sold various items to the university and submitted invoices in excess of $250 for these items. In fact, The University Group, Inc., was wholly owned by Oswalt, and it never sold any merchandise to MSU. The third count charged Oswalt with embezzling money of a total value in excess of $250 from MSU. The fourth count alleged that Oswalt purchased for personal use various items of merchandise with a total value in excess of $100 with an MSU credit card he was not authorized to use. The fifth count alleged that Oswalt conspired with William Shivers and another person or persons to obtain money and other property by false pretense.

On August 31, 2001, Phil Bryant issued a demand letter to Larry Daniel "Danny" Oswalt. Bryant demanded payment of $132,636, which included $116,890 in principal, $11,183 interest, and $4,563 of investigative cost.

On February 4, 2002, Oswalt and his attorney, Charles Bruce Brown, signed a Petition to Enter a Plea of Guilty in which Oswalt agreed to plead guilty to one count of embezzlement if the state would retire the other four counts to the file. Based on this plea, Oswalt could be sentenced to up to ten years in prison and fined $1,000. The next day, Oswalt pled guilty to one count of embezzlement before Circuit Court Judge John M. Montgomery, who delayed sentencing and ordered a presentence investigation.

In April 2002, the thirty-one-year-old MSU graduate was sentenced to five years in prison, to be followed by five years of probation. Judge Montgomery also imposed a fine of $1,000 and ordered Oswalt to pay restitution of $116,890 and court costs of $659.

Judge Montgomery approved the district attorney's motion to retire to the files the other four counts on which Oswalt had been indicted. This was accomplished by an order signed by Judge Montgomery on April 29, 2002. In June 2002, MSU's bonding company paid the OSA $100,000, and the OSA paid that amount to Mississippi State University.

In early 2003, William Shivers pled guilty to one charge of false pretense based on a plea agreement that had been worked out with the district attorney. On February 7, 2003, Circuit Court Judge Lee Howard sentenced Shivers to supervised probation for a period of three years, ordered him to pay the Mississippi Department of Corrections $30 per month for the cost of this supervision, fined him $1,000, and ordered him to pay restitution of $16,318. Shivers paid the restitution as required by the order.

Greg Rector, University Emergency Physicians Practice Group Operations Manager, University of Mississippi Medical Center

In early February 1998, the OSA received a complaint alleging that Gregory Neal Rector embezzled funds from the University of Mississippi Medical Center (UMC) in Jackson. The complainant alleged that the missing funds actually belonged to the University Emergency Physicians Practice Group (EPPG), PLLC, and were private, not public, funds. Rector was a state employee and operations manager for EPPG. In addition to his state salary, Rector was compensated by EPPG.

EPPG contracted with UMC to provide medical doctors to staff the hospital's emergency department. Doctors who worked in the emergency room had contracts with UMC, and EPPG supplemented their salaries. There were similar PLLCs and arrangements with physicians who worked in the medical center's other eleven clinical departments. UMC paid EPPG approximately $72,000 per month. Monies received by EPPG were deposited into its private bank account. Dr. Robert Galli, chairman of UMC's emergency department, owned 95 percent of EPPG. Dr. Rick Carlton, another physician in the department, owned the other 5 percent. In addition to the monthly payments from UMC, EPPG received $75,000 to $100,000 monthly from private practice billings to Medicaid, Medicare, and individuals. Dr. Galli controlled all of the monies that came into EPPG, and he and Rector could write checks on EPPG's account. Rector had simply written unauthorized EPPG checks made out to himself.

Greg Rector agreed to a plea bargain worked out by his attorney, John M. Colette, and Assistant U.S. Attorney Robert G. Anderson. In a Memorandum of Understanding dated April 3, 1998, Rector agreed to plead guilty to a two-count information charging embezzlement, "and truthfully and voluntarily and completely disclose to the government and/or Court, if required, all information and knowledge that he has regarding the subject matter and events described in the proposed criminal information against him in this cause and other matters relative there to . . ." The U.S. attorney agreed to recommend a sentence in the lower 25 percent of the applicable sentencing guideline range and to recommend an additional one-level downward adjustment for acceptance of responsibility. The agreement also noted that Rector would pay whatever restitution was deemed appropriate. As part of that restitution, Rector agreed to transfer to EPPG his ownership interest in a piece of real estate, a 1995 Jeep Grand Cherokee (former OSA auditor Denver Smith noted that this Jeep had been purchased from Dr. Galli with money stolen from Dr. Galli), some furniture, and two bank accounts. Rector was prosecuted by the federal government because UMC received federal funds.

Greg Rector appeared for a sentencing hearing before U.S. District Judge Henry T. Wingate in Jackson on July 30, 1998. Dr. Galli testified at this hearing and objected to the proposed light sentence, noting that Rector had earlier convictions. However, in accordance with the plea agreement, Judge Wingate sentenced Rector on September 9, 1998, to twenty-seven months in prison and three years' probation. He was also ordered to pay $406,459 in restitution. Rector was to surrender to the Bureau of Prisons by October 13, 1998, to start serving his sentence. Restitution was to be paid during the period of incarceration with any remaining balance to be paid in 32 monthly payments of not less than $350. The entire amount of restitution had to be paid or arrangements made to pay off the balance before Rector could be released from probation.

The OSA initially assigned Jerry Hardin to the case, but it was transferred to investigators Walt Drane and Denver Smith in September 1998. The auditors were to review the records and determine how much of the money stolen from the EPPG was actually public funds. In an attempt to make this determination, OSA investigators Drane and Smith met with Rector in a motel in Nashville, Tennessee, on September 29, 1998. The interview took place after Rector's sentencing but prior to his incarceration. During the interview, Rector claimed that EPPG's checking account was "run wide open" and that he and several physicians borrowed money from the account. The following is part of Smith and Drane's report on the interview.

"If anyone needed money, they could borrow money. It was not an oddity for a physician's wife to call and say Greg, I can't meet my monthly bills and I need to borrow $5,000 or $10,000, and I would just write them a check and put it in their husband's chair. It was just run wide open, whatever anyone wanted to borrow." Sometimes they would pay it back and sometimes they would not, according to Rector. Rector stated that he knows what he did was wrong; "I borrowed too much; there were no controls; Dr. Galli did not care as long as Dr. Galli was getting his $400,000 or $500,000." Rector said that he told Dr. Galli that he was enrolled in the Masters Program at Tulane, and Dr. Galli said, "I will pay for that for you." Rector said that he was accused of stealing a lot of money that he had actually borrowed from the PLLC with Dr. Galli's permission and knowledge. Rector stated that nothing was ever documented in writing as far as his personal loans and that he knew he took too much but that he never took the $416,000 he was accused of taking. Rector said he actually took about $150,000.00 from the PLLC.

Rector was asked about him skipping a question on an application for employment with the UMC that asked about prior arrests and convictions. Rector said that he did skip the question on one application. Rector was asked if he made a statement to the Director of Human Resources that the reason he skipped the question had something to do with him being convicted concerning something to do with student loans. Rector said he had no idea how that got started that he has never had a student loan. Rector was asked if this was something that just happened or is someone in Human Resources or any other department covering up his past record for him. Rector said, "I think I skipped that block, and I think it skipped through the system. I went through the orientation process and it was mentioned that they do background checks and that scared me to death. At that time I had already been convicted of bank fraud. My conscience bothered me greatly, and I knew that I had not checked that block. I went to my Supervisor and my Supervisor sent me to see Don Seagrove; this is two weeks after I started working for the UMC. I went to see Don Seagrove and told him that I had a conviction and that I had not properly filled out that question on the application. It was just a conversation between Don and I, and he said well his statement was that everyone had skeletons in their past and it is not, those skeletons should not matter, it is what you do from now on is what should matter. He said don't worry about it, just let it go and go on and do a good job and don't worry about it. That, in my opinion, got me and my supervisor off the hook; once we realized that something had been done wrong with institutional policy, we had gone and tried to correct it." "I continued to work there for a year or so when my probation was revoked on August 11th and I had worked the day before, and they threw me in the county jail in Oxford that day. The next morning I called the UMC and talked to my Supervisor and told her what had happened. My thoughts were that I had lost my job and my Supervisor believed so much in me that she went to Dr. Nelson and to Don Seagrove and told them what had happened. A PAR was filled out and I was put on temporary leave, and it had to be signed off by them and they had full knowledge of where I was. When I came back the next May, I went right back to work in the library. I had a meeting with Don Seagrove at that time, and he told me to write a letter about the facts involved and put it in a sealed envelope and it would be put in my personnel file. The envelope was to be addressed to Don Seagrove, and Seagrove said that no one would ever know about my past." "He did not want me to suffer any stigma or repercussions by individuals within the medical center; he wanted me to go on. I did that and gave it to Don Seagrove, and we had a fifteen minute conversation and I assumed it was placed in my personnel file. He did not want other people in Human Resources that had access to files to go in and read that information and find out about my past. Now when I moved to other locations, (jobs), I filled out other applications and I marked 'no' where it asked if I had been convicted of a felony or misdemeanor. The reason I did that was because of the conversation between me and Mr. Seagrove. He told me that you mark 'no'; I have the documentation that is going into your personnel file, I don't want you to be prejudged by another department; I don't want you to be kept from getting another job because you marked it 'yes'. I felt like I had been given a clearance; that is why I marked 'no'." "This is something that I have never been able to explain to anyone before, because they always pulled out that last; in my court proceedings they always pulled out that last employment application that I filled out just for the Department of Energy Management." "Seagrove knew within two weeks of my employment that I had prior convictions, I went to Ms. Seltzer and she said you immediately go to Human Resources and to Don Seagrove, and she felt that at the time as long as I was cleared through Human Resources and through Dr. Nelson that it was fine. Dr. Nelson certainly knew about my past when I was on leave of absence, Ms. Seltzer did talk to Dr. Nelson about it; Ms. Seltzer told me she talked to Dr. Nelson about it."

Rector was asked what the convictions were for [that] he was talking about that [and] he stated "bank fraud." Rector stated he misrepresented information or lied on applications for loans from banks and the loans were signature loans. Rector said that he filed bankruptcy and the banks objected to the loans being written off, and he was charged with bank fraud for making false statements on the applications.

Rector was asked if he acted alone or if someone else may have been involved with him in stealing the money. Rector stated that no one else was involved, he was not blackmailed nor did anyone ask him for anything. "I was just doing what I thought all of the other doctors had the privilege to do." "I let it get out of hand." Rector was again asked about the statement he made to the media, "this is just the tip of the iceberg." Rector again stated that he was referring to the fact that state employees were being paid by the state and the PLLC for working eight hours a day, and he thinks this is against the state law. Rector was asked what his salary was from the state and what he was being paid by the PLLC in addition to the state salary. Rector said he was paid approximately $32,000 by the state when he left, and he was asked what he was being paid by the PLLC legitimately, and he stated approximately another $25,000. Rector stated he was contributing to a profit-sharing plan in the PLLC and received a monthly deposit of $1250 per month after taxes and the contribution to profit sharing was deducted. Rector stated in addition to this, he received a bonus in August and another bonus at Christmas.

Rector also informed us that he was given a form and asked to indicate on the form that he and other employees were working an extra two hours per day, even though they were not. The extra two hours were supposed to represent compensatory time and justify on paper the supplemental salary the various employees received from the clinical PLLCs.

On September 30, 1998, the case was put on hold by the OSA because of the public/private question.

On October 20, 1998, UMC filed a Proof of Loss form with CNA Financial Insurance stating that Rector pled guilty to taking $416,810 from the University Emergency Physicians Practice Group and making false entries in the group's books. Based on an agreement with UMC and the Board of Trustees of the Institutions of Higher Learning (IHL), a minimum of 39.4 percent, or $160,128, of those funds should have been remitted to UMC.

On January 20, 1999, OSA investigators Drane and Smith met with UMC Assistant Vice Chancellor Brenda Melohn to discuss the case and to secure copies of documents related to income and expenses of various doctors for the years 1995 through 1997. The doctors were employees of UMC and were also receiving payments from EPPG. Based on their contracts, the doctors were allowed to earn $140,000 per year after expenses from UMC, EPPG, and the V.A.

hospital. Any overage had to be split with UMC. Review of the documents received from Melohn revealed that the minimum amount UMC should have received if Rector had not embezzled money from EPPG was $160,128.

As a result of the Rector embezzlement, state representative Rita Martinson (R-Madison) asked the Joint Committee on Performance Evaluation and Expenditure Review (PEER) to review the relationships between private practice groups and UMC. In a January 1999 report, PEER recommended that UMC take control of the twelve autonomous groups, handle payroll, and eliminate bonuses to the groups' employees. Salary inequities had developed among UMC employees of the same pay grade. The practice groups associated with the clinical departments were able to pay their employees "bonuses" out of private funds, but such "bonuses" were not available to employees of science departments. The PEER report noted that the accounting firm of Haddox, Reid, Burks and Calhoun knew more about the financial structure of the UMC than did its chancellor or other administrators who "have limited knowledge regarding the finances and management of the plans."

Max Arinder, executive director of PEER, said, "The system that is currently in place is fragmented to the degree that there is simply less accountability from the state's perspective." The groups used UMC staff and space, and UMC received part of the payments made to the practices. According to Arinder, "Management, budgetary, and accounting controls . . . would be much better managed under a multi-specialist group of common governance." Dr. Wallace Conerly, UMC vice chancellor, indicated that he intended to implement PEER's recommendations and that salary and bonus payments would stop immediately. While claiming that it might take two years to make the changes, Conerly said, "This is a good review. It points out issues that should be addressed. We are accepting every recommendation that has been made."

On February 1, 1999, Phil Bryant issued a demand on Gregory Neal Rector and his bonding company, Continental Insurance, for $196,588. This represented UMC's part of the funds that Rector had embezzled ($160,128), interest ($32,632), and the cost of recovery ($3,828). Bryant said, "Mr. Rector violated the trust of the physicians and taxpayers. The sad part about this case is Mr. Rector not only embezzled funds, he harmed the University Emergency Physicians ability to participate in continuing education and to purchase equipment needed to care for the thousands of Mississippians that need emergency medical care." Bryant indicated he was not convinced that Rector would pay the restitution that had been ordered by the court because he had not paid the court-ordered restitution for his previous conviction for bank fraud. Noting that Rector could repay the bonding company if it paid the demand, Bryant said, "We appreciate the court order but we would like to settle this as soon as possible. We don't want to get into a situation with Mr. Rector where he is paying monthly." Because of the complicated interrelationships between UMC and the private EPPG, it had taken the OSA about eight months to determine how much of the embezzled money belonged to UMC. Bryant said, "Certainly we would like to have some method of stricter accountability over these funds." In early July 1999, Phil Bryant announced that the OSA had recovered $191,588 (the amount of the claim less a $5,000 deductible) from Continental Insurance under Rector's bond.

Upon his completion of twenty-seven months in prison, the judgment against Rector was amended January 31, 2001, by Judge Wingate. The amendment added several features to Rector's sentence. Rector was prohibited from incurring any new debt or opening any lines of credit without prior approval from his probation officer. He was to participate in a mental care aftercare program if deemed necessary by his probation officer. He was to secure suitable employment, but if any employment was to involve fiduciary responsibilities, it was to be approved in advance by his probation officer. He was to pay restitution of $389,699, one half to University Emergency Physicians Practice Group, PLLC, and one half to the state of Mississippi in care of State Auditor Phil Bryant. The schedule of restitution payments in the original sentence was maintained. Apparently, Rector had paid approximately $16,000 in restitution while incarcerated. In June of 2002, Rector filed for chapter 7 bankruptcy. However, the state's and the insurance company's claims for restitution were not set aside by the court.

OSA closed the case in April of 2003 after the U.S. District Court issued an Agreed Order to Amend Judgment in a Criminal Case. That order directed the clerk of the court, who was receiving restitution payments from Rector, to pay Continental Insurance Company all receipts from Rector until it recovered $191,588. Any payments after that would go to the state of Mississippi through the OSA. It is highly doubtful that Rector will ever finish paying off the $191,588.

6. Other

While the five cases of embezzlement briefed in this chapter are not easily categorized, Section 7-7-211(F) of the Mississippi Code gives the OSA audit authority over each entity involved. The code section reads as follows:

> [The OSA has the authority] [t]o post-audit and, when deemed necessary, pre-audit and investigate the financial affairs of the levee boards; *agencies created by the Legislature or by executive order of the Governor; profit or nonprofit business entities administering programs financed by funds flowing through the State Treasury or through any of the agencies of the state, or its subdivisions; and all other public bodies supported by funds derived in part or wholly from public funds,* except municipalities which annually submit an audit prepared by a qualified certified public accountant using methods and procedures prescribed by the department . . . (emphasis added).

All of the entities involved received public monies and were bound by law to account for the monies properly, protect the monies, and disburse the monies only for lawful purposes.

Keith Blaylock, Director, Economic Development Partnership of Monroe County

The Monroe County district attorney's office registered a complaint with the OSA on July 24, 1998. The complaint alleged that Keith Blaylock, who had been executive director of the Economic Development Partnership (EDP) of Monroe County since February 1995, had embezzled approximately $40,000 of Amory Railroad Festival funds. Blaylock also held the position of secretary/treasurer of the Amory Railroad Festival. The OSA immediately opened an investigation and assigned Special Agent Burt Haney to the case.

Scott Wiygul, an officer in the National Bank of Commerce (NBC) in

Amory, reviewed a personal loan of Keith Blaylock in mid-July 1998. Wiygul made a computer search that pulled up all accounts that had Blaylock's name associated with them. One of these accounts belonged to the Amory Railroad Festival Committee. Wiygul, a former chairman of the festival and a board member of the Economic Development Partnership, discovered that the account had an unexpectedly low balance. The festival committee maintained this bank account at NBC and a savings account at Amory Federal Savings and Loan. The committee had not received any financial statements from its secretary/treasurer, Keith Blaylock, for quite a while despite the fact that Wiygul had requested financial statements several times.

On July 22, 1998, Wiygul phoned Ed Stanford, another festival committee member, and Raymond Cox, chairman of the EDP, and suggested that they get a copy of the festival's account at Amory Federal to determine how much money was on deposit there. Based on information provided by Blaylock, Wiygul thought there should be more than $50,000 in the savings account. Ed Stanford and Keith Blaylock had signature authority for the festival committee's two accounts. A meeting was arranged at the NBC in Amory. Wiygul, Stanford, and Cox attended the meeting. Ed Stanford brought a statement from Amory Federal showing a balance of only $1,796. Keith Blaylock walked into the meeting, and it soon broke up without further discussion of the matter.

Blaylock went with Wiygul to his office, where he told Wiygul that he had betrayed his trust and taken money from the festival's account. Blaylock went on to explain that he was under pressure from the bank, the state, and suppliers of his Hancock Fabrics store. He claimed that he planned to pay the money back at the rate of $5,000 per month and any remaining balance in December 1998. Blaylock said he planned to ask his father to help pay off a "loan" that was due in December, and he pleaded with Wiygul not to tell anyone.

Cox's office was at the Mississippi Valley Gas Company, and Blaylock showed up there shortly after his meeting with Wiygul. Blaylock told Cox that he had betrayed his trust by stealing approximately $42,000 from the railroad festival account. When asked what he was thinking when he took the money, Blaylock told Cox the same story he had told Wiygul and asked that Cox, Wiygul, and Stanford not tell anyone and allow him to pay the money back.

On July 23, 1998, Wiygul phoned Assistant District Attorney Rob Coleman about the missing funds. The city of Amory had an interest in the matter because the city donated approximately $6,000 a year to the festival. The district attorney's office assigned the case to Brine Chamblee, who arranged a meeting that same day with Wiygul and Cox. Chamblee received written statements from both Wiygul and Cox explaining what had happened.

Chamblee's ensuing investigation revealed how Blaylock had embezzled money that belonged to the Amory Railroad Festival.

Interest on the festival's savings account was being mailed monthly to Blaylock. The festival paid the EDP $200 per month for time spent dealing with festival business. This $200 was usually paid in part by interest on the savings account, with the difference being paid by a festival check issued by Blaylock. For the past several months, Blaylock had paid the entire $200 from the festival's checking account and not used the interest payment from the savings account.

Records for the bank account and the savings account reflected unusual transactions that indicated possible embezzlement. Checks were written for cash and endorsed by Blaylock. Some recorded deposits were net of cash returned to the depositor. The savings account records showed unexplained withdrawals.

On one occasion, the EDP did not receive the monthly payment it expected from the city of Amory. When EDP secretary Eileen Hathcote followed up with the city, she learned that the check had been cashed. When Hathcote confronted Blaylock about the matter, he said that the check must have gotten mixed up with other checks. Blaylock later gave Hathcote a money order for the missing check.

On July 24, 1998, Wiygul, Cox, Stanford, and Amory Mayor Thomas Griffith, who was also a member of the EDP, met with Blaylock at the EDP office to discuss the situation. Blaylock admitted stealing approximately $42,000 from the railroad festival accounts, apologized for his actions, and said he would pay the money back. The EDP members asked for and received Blaylock's resignation from the position of executive director. Blaylock left the meeting but later called and asked if he could retain his position if the money was repaid. Griffith told him that he must resign and that the OSA would determine the amount of restitution. After the meeting, the door locks were changed and all festival documents were taken to the mayor's office.

The *Amory Advertiser*'s July 29, 1998, edition reported that Keith Blaylock had resigned as executive director of the North Monroe County Economic Development Partnership, a position he had held for three years. The newspaper quoted an EDP press release saying, "On the 24th of July 1998, Keith Blaylock, executive director of the EDP, submitted his resignation immediately to pursue private business interest." The article went on to note that Assistant District Attorney Rob Coleman said there was an ongoing investigation into the circumstances surrounding Blaylock's resignation and that the state auditor was involved in the investigation.

Keith Blaylock paid the Amory Railroad Festival $50,000 on July 31, 1998. The document supporting the payment reads as follows:

Receipt of Payment
The Amory Railroad Festival hereby acknowledges receiving $50,000 from Keith Blaylock. These funds will be deposited into the account of Amory Railroad Festival, Inc. at the National Bank of Commerce. This receipt does not acknowledge payment in full until after an audit has been performed by the department of audit.

Funds paid by:
John Blaylock
Keith Blaylock

Funds received by:
Raymond Cox
Scott Wiygul – 7-31-98

OSA investigators established the total amount of the embezzlement at $53,481. In early March 1999, the Monroe County grand jury indicted Keith Blaylock on two counts of embezzlement. Count one charged that, between February 1996 and July 1998, Blaylock embezzled $52,481 from the Amory Railroad Festival. Count two charged that on April 30, 1998, Blaylock embezzled $1,000 from the Amory Railroad Festival. Blaylock faced up to twenty years in prison.

In accordance with a plea agreement worked out between Blaylock's attorney, Tim Pace, and the district attorney's office, Blaylock entered an open plea of guilty to both counts of the indictment in Monroe County Circuit Court on November 19, 1999. In an open plea, the state makes no recommendation as to sentencing. Circuit Court Judge Frank Russell sentenced Blaylock to serve two years of unsupervised probation and required him to pay a fine of $5,000 and court cost of $288. The fine and court cost were to be paid at the rate of $250 per month beginning December 20, 1999. The court withheld adjudication of guilt. Thus, Blaylock could wipe his record clean by living up to all of the requirements of the sentence.

The OSA closed the case January 21, 2000.

Fred J. Heindl, Executive Director, Mississippi Agribusiness Council

The legislature created the Mississippi Agribusiness Council in 1993 to support research involving energy-related agricultural projects. The agency was funded by state appropriations and federal grants. The Council included the chairman and vice-chairman of the senate agriculture committee and five additional members of the senate appointed by the lieutenant governor based on recommendations by the chairman of the agriculture committee. The house was represented by the chairman and vice-chairman of its agriculture committee and five additional members appointed by the house speaker based on recommendations of the chairman of the house agriculture committee. The Council appointed Fred Heindl as its executive director, and he was directly responsible to the Council. In 2001, the legislature quit funding the Council because of its ineffectiveness and the malfeasance of its former executive director.

During the period 1996 through 2001, Fred J. Heindl contracted with Michael Walters for research work under an agreement that required Walters to pay kickbacks to Heindl. Walters was given contracts by the Agribusiness Council to complete research involving energy-related projects. In 1999, Walters also entered into an agreement with Jim Wyatt, assistant director of the Mississippi Agribusiness Council, to pay Wyatt kickbacks on contracts from the Agribusiness Council. While the scheme was functioning, Walters (Agritechnologies, LLC) received $507,430 as the result of the illegal agreements. The payments came in the form of sixty-one checks from the Mississippi Department of Finance and Administration and Alcorn State University. Walters in turn paid kickbacks of $73,175 to Heindl and $9,000 to Wyatt.

In 1999, with the aid of Heindl and Wyatt, Michael Walters received a $320,000 federal grant through the Mississippi Development Authority Energy Division to build a bioreactor designed to purify pig waste. A Mississippi pig farmer donated the land on which the bioreactor was to be housed. Ecosens of Salt Lake City, Utah, owned by Michael Hughes, was to build the bioreactor. The Agribusiness Council also gave contracts to Walters for work related to the bioreactor.

In October 1999, Walters had his company, Agritechnologies, LLC, write a check for $17,200 to Hughes's company, Ecosens, to be used to pay kickbacks to Heindl and Wyatt. Hughes then had Ecosens write a check to a Mississippi mobile home dealer, Flora, Inc., for $7,729 to make the down payment on a mobile home for Heindl. Hughes cashed a check on his company for $7,000 and gave the money to Walters, who gave it to Wyatt. These payments were made while Heindl, Wyatt, and Walters were in Salt Lake City meeting with Hughes about the bioreactor. About two weeks later, Walters paid Wyatt another $2,000, which Wyatt maintained was part of the money left over after the purchase of the bioreactor equipment and payment of expenses related to the project. Walters claimed that both Heindl and Wyatt demanded kickbacks for their part in securing funding for the bioreactor project.

Walters also wrote company checks to Heindl's wife, Dorian Rogers Heindl, totaling $11,537 and Heindl's sister, Pat Klar, totaling $11,601. Walters admitted that these payments were kickbacks to Heindl. Klar indicated that Heindl told her the payments to her were for work that Heindl had done for Walters and that he wanted to hide the money from his former wife. Klar, who did no work for the money, claimed that she simply cashed the checks and gave the proceeds to Heindl.

Glenn Patterson was going through financial difficulties in 1994 when Fred Heindl, the cousin of his former wife, approached him about doing some energy-related contract work for the Agribusiness Council. Heindl made it clear that he expected to be paid kickbacks on any contracts given Patterson by the Council. From 1994 through 1997, Patterson received forty-three payments totaling $108,850 from contracts he made with the Agribusiness Council through Heindl. During this time, he actually worked on only six of the contracts, with a total price of $17,700. Patterson kicked back half of the proceeds of the contracts, $54,425, to Heindl. Heindl would print invoices from a computer at the Agribusiness Council's office and have a check processed to pay Patterson for the invoiced amount. Heindl would then meet with Patterson and give him the check. Patterson would immediately deposit the check in a bank, get cash back, and pay Heindl his kickback.

On May 21, 2002, Heindl waived indictment, and the next day he pled guilty to a criminal information charging embezzlement of $163,383 in Hinds County Circuit Court. He had agreed to cooperate with a state and federal investigation into contract kickbacks. The fifty-four-year-old Heindl told Judge Tomie Green he had awarded state contracts and in return received part of the proceeds from the contractors. Prosecutors said that Heindl received state money between June 1997 and January 1999. Heindl, who told the judge that he had not been promised a deal for his guilty plea, faced up to twenty years in prison. The defendant, who had never been jailed, was freed on a $2,000 bond, which had to be posted within ten days. During the court session, Hinds County Assistant District Attorney John Tully told the judge that Heindl "cheated and defrauded the people of Mississippi."

State Auditor Phil Bryant said, "We are working with special agents of the Internal Revenue Service and anticipate additional state and federal indictments to be forthcoming." Judge Green delayed sentencing until the ongoing investigation was completed. Tom Royals, Heindl's attorney, indicated that the ongoing investigation could take several months. Federal authorities were brought into the cases against Walters, Wyatt, and Patterson. United States law applied because the Mississippi Agribusiness Council received federal money, some of the illegal activities took place in interstate commerce, the federal crime of money laundering was involved, and there were income tax implications associated with the crimes. From 1994 through 1997, the Mississippi Agribusiness Council received at least $514,000 from various federal programs.

On February 6, 2003, Michael Walters and his attorney, John M. Colette, struck a plea agreement with Assistant U.S. Attorney John M. Dowdy, Jr. The memorandum of understanding called for Walters to plead guilty to a one-count information charging conspiracy to launder money in the amount of $82,175. Under the United States Code, the maximum punishment for this crime is twenty years in prison, a term of supervised release of three years, and a fine of not more than $500,000 or twice the value of the property involved, whichever was greater. The prosecutor agreed to recommend a sentence within the lower 25 percent of the applicable sentencing guidelines range as determined by the court.

Glenn Patterson, his attorney, Davey L. Tucker, and Assistant U.S. Attorney John M. Dowdy, Jr., made a plea agreement January 6, 2004. The memorandum of understanding called for Patterson to plead guilty to a one-count indictment charging conspiracy to launder money in the amount of not more than $54,000. The terms of the understanding were basically the same as those agreed to by Walters about a year earlier. Under terms of the plea agreement, on January 8, 2004, Patterson pled guilty before U.S. District Judge Henry T. Wingate. The conspiracy involved some forty contracts that Heindl approved as head of the Mississippi Agribusiness Council. According to the indictment, Patterson paid kickbacks of $54,000 to Heindl on contracts worth $108,000. Patterson faced maximum penalties of twenty years in prison and a fine of up to $500,000. Assistant U. S. Attorney John Dowdy, Jr., said, "He readily admitted his involvement in this scheme. He said he knew what he and Mr. Heindl did was wrong, but he needed the money." Judge Wingate released Patterson on a $10,000 bond and set sentencing for March 19, 2004.

On January 10, 2004, Michael Walters and Jimmy R. Wyatt were in federal court. Both pled guilty to one count of conspiracy to launder money.

Walters paid Heindl about $73,000 and Wyatt $9,000 in kickbacks on contracts with the Mississippi Agribusiness Council. Wyatt claimed to be a marketing specialist with the agency, but prosecutors initially said he was assistant director. Assistant U. S. Attorney John Dowdy, Jr., indicated that Walters told investigators that he knew he was wrong and added, "But he said he was told on the front end by Fred Heindl that it has to be part of the deal if he wanted contracts."

Phil Bryant noted that an investigation was started in May of 2001 when a field auditor noticed Heindl's handwritten note on a document indicating that an invoice needed to be created. The auditor thought it was odd that the agency would be creating an invoice to bill itself. The note to his administrative assistant read: "Stacey – Develop an invoice & payment to Agritechnologies LLC for 'Development of information on a Waste System for a college campus in a rural area using biotechnology and producing electricity,' $2,100.00." This was a classic example of what auditors call a "red flag" indicating that something improper was probably happening. As noted above, Heindl would often have fictitious invoices created on the agency's computer. According to Bryant, "Heindl entered into a conspiracy to actually defraud taxpayers out of 50 percent of every contract issued. It was a classic kickback scheme." Heindl was clearly the mastermind behind the whole scheme.

On April 5, 2004, nearly two years after Heindl's guilty plea, Judge Green sentenced him to three years. One year was to be served in jail on weekends, one year was to be served on supervised probation, and the final year was suspended. Heindl was also ordered to pay restitution of $163,383. The year-long weekend sentence was to be served from 6:30 P.M. Friday to 6:30 P.M. Sunday in the Hinds County Detention Center. The light penalties imposed for Heindl's egregious crimes probably reflect his cooperation with the authorities' investigations of Patterson, Walters, and Wyatt.

State Auditor Phil Bryant said, "Fred Heindl not only betrayed the trust of the taxpayers, but his criminal behavior destroyed the Mississippi Agribusiness Council and by extension harmed the entire agribusiness community of this state."

U.S. District Judge Henry T. Wingate did not actually sentence Michael Walters, Glenn Patterson, and Jimmy Wyatt until late March 2005. Walters was sentenced to eighteen months in prison and ordered to pay $82,164 in restitution to the state. Patterson was sentenced to eighteen months in prison and ordered to pay $36,736 in restitution to the state. Wyatt was sentenced to a year in prison and ordered to pay the state $9,000 in restitution. U.S. Attorney Dunn Lampton and State Auditor Phil Bryant described the $9,000 that Wyatt received as part of the scheme as "hush money" to keep him quiet. Wyatt and Walters still faced similar state charges.

Jesse Bingham, director of the OSA's investigative division, said, "These convictions should send a strong message to those who attempt to profit at the taxpayers' expense. This agency will use any legal means available to us to bring them to justice." Bingham indicated that the OSA's lengthy and costly investigation "was particularly frustrating because the Agribusiness Council could have benefited citizens of this state. Because of a few corrupt individuals, [their activities] led to it being abolished."

Sandy Johnson, Director, Mississippi Firefighters Memorial Burn Association

In December 2002, Attorney General Mike Moore's office began investigating H. S. "Sandy" Johnson, director of Mississippi Firefighters Memorial Burn Association (MFMBA), and his daughter, Tisha Cole, who served as office manager and kept the association's books. The sixteen-bed Mississippi Firefighters Memorial Burn Center was part of the Delta Regional Medical Center (DRMC) in Greenville. It was the only such facility in the state and the only comprehensive burn center between Georgia and Texas. The association raised money for the burn center and was a separate not-for-profit entity. The association sought contributions through fund-raisers held by individuals and organizations around the state. Also, all levels of government (state, county, and city) regularly contributed to the center. During 2002, the center treated 231 patients, of whom 211 were from Mississippi. The others came from Louisiana, Arkansas, Texas, and Illinois.

The MFMBA's board fired both Johnson and his daughter on December 18, 2002. Johnson, whose salary was $82,990, had headed the association for twenty-seven years, and Cole had handled the association's books for thirteen years. The board of directors of the MFMBA and the board of trustees of the Delta Regional Medical Center issued a press release on January 16, 2003, noting the terminations and stating that the state attorney general's office was conducting an investigation of the possible misuse of private donations. The press release, which came nearly a month after the firings, noted that Greenville resident and MFMBA board member James Karr had been named interim director.

When the firings and related investigation were revealed, Ray Humphreys, CEO of the DRMC, said that the MFMBA was a fine organization with outstanding people and that these events were tragic for the cause of the entity served. Humphreys said, "We hope and pray that these events will not do anything to disrupt the very fine and excellent healthcare services provided by the burn center, which is unique to the area. Most patients of the burn center cannot afford the level of healthcare the center provides and donations are needed."

The Jackson *Clarion-Ledger* reported on September 7, 2003, that Mississippi authorities planned to seek charges in connection with allegations that the director of the state burn center's fund-raising organization and his daughter embezzled about $100,000. Special Assistant Attorney General Lee Martin indicated that the investigation was complete and said, "We will begin the process of pursuing charges as a result of our investigation." The association's board president, Bobby Allen, said, "What happened is bad, it's terrible. It's taken away from a lot of people. The state needs this burn center."

Documents obtained by the *Clarion-Ledger* showed that, as the newspaper put it, "Johnson and Cole sometimes paid themselves early and often." For example, in November 2002, the day before a pay period ended, Johnson received his biweekly paycheck for $2,682 and another check for $1,341. The newspaper noted that, based on his biweekly pay, Johnson would have been paid $69,738 annually, but IRS records show in 2001 he was paid $82,990, which did not include $12,875 in benefits.

The investigation, which included a "sting" operation, pursued allegations that Johnson and Cole kept some cash donations and used some of the money to gamble at casinos. In conducting the sting, investigators gave Johnson contributions to the burn center in the form of checks and marked money. Johnson deposited the checks to the proper accounts but kept the cash. Private donations to the association reported by Johnson dropped from about $500,000 in 1998 to about $350,000 in 2002. Government support of the burn center rose from about $1 million to about $1.2 million during the same period.

In 1996 a controversy had surrounded the association over alleged fund-raising improprieties and nepotism. The MFMBA's three employees were Johnson, his daughter, Tisha Cole, and his mother-in-law. During a 1997 audit, Cole had been caught stealing $4,500 from the association. She repaid the money, and the association allowed her to continue as bookkeeper. This brings into question whether the board took seriously its fiduciary responsibility and whether it was competent.

In a 1996 series of reports, the *Clarion-Ledger* had raised questions about both fund-raising and spending by the association. The paper noted that the association employed Johnson's daughter and mother-in-law. The director maintained, "It's all legal. It's all above board." It was also reported that Johnson had been paid about $120,000 a year on travel, conferences, conventions, and meetings. Johnson defended the spending, saying that he put about 60,000 miles a year on a car provided by the association. The association made some changes in response to the newspaper series, and travel expenses dropped to a little over $27,000 by 2001.

Robert Owens, a Greenville promoter who raised $115,000 for the center, became concerned about the association's spending in 1996. He began to suspect something was wrong when he learned that Johnson's title was different from what he had originally heard. Owens said, "He told me he was director of the burn center and that he was a county employee. What I found out later was that he was a private fund raiser and not a part of the burn center."

Association board chairman Bobby Allen described the allegations of embezzlement by Johnson as "a total shock to me." Johnson had worked for the association since 1982, and Allen praised his early work. "I know the time Sandy put into the burn association," Allen said. "He was working on weekends. We tried to get Sandy to take a vacation, and he said, 'I don't have the time.'" Allen claimed that he had learned that the board was not informed about some financial matters, and he maintained that had been changed. The board chairman added, "We're trying to put safeguards on everything we do. We've taken every measure we can."

In September 2003, Amanda Williams, executive director since May 2003, vowed, "It's not going to happen again. We have put systems of checks and balances in place so that there's no fear of this happening in the future." Board president Allen indicated that several changes had been made, including choosing a new bank, a different accounting firm, and developing new bylaws. Williams had been traveling the state assuring officials that things were fine with one of the state's favorite charities. She said that when she first met with the Washington County Board of Supervisors they were the ones assuring her. "Everyone has been very positive," she said. "They still realize it's a worthwhile charity and that we still need the money. At the end of the year the burn center will face a $1.8 million deficit."

Board president Allen assured potential contributors that their money was safe and that it would be used to directly aid the burn center. Government contributions go to a separate account and can only be used for indigent care. Carol Chady, vice president of the Ladies Auxiliary of the Knights of Columbus of Mississippi, said that she had faith that the problems had been corrected and that her organization would continue to give to the center. "You can't stop donating and hurt the people it's benefiting," Chady said.

Ray Humphreys, CEO of the medical center, said, "We are in full support of the board of directors and Amanda Williams, executive director of the Mississippi Firefighters Memorial Burn Association, as they move forward to address the need of burn patients who rely on the generosity of citizens throughout the state. We have confidence in the integrity of their future fund-raising efforts, which are so vital for the burn center to continue operations."

In December 2003, a Washington County grand jury indicted Sandy Johnson on six counts of embezzlement and his daughter, Tisha Cole, on four counts of embezzlement. Each of the charges against Johnson and Cole carried maximum penalties of ten years in prison and a fine of $10,000. No trial date was set.

Count one charged Johnson with embezzling $2,000, the proceeds of the spring festival held March 29, 2001. Count two charged Johnson with embezzling $358, the proceeds of the Stinky Jim's Trail Ride held October 16, 2002. Count three involved the embezzlement of $500, the proceeds of a 2002 October festival. Count four charged embezzlement of $615 from an October 29, 2002, donation from a private citizen. Count five charged that Johnson embezzled $400 of the state of Mississippi's money that was given to him to benefit the burn center in a "sting" operation. Count six charged Johnson with embezzling $52,606 that belonged to the burn center. In total, the six counts charged Johnson with embezzling $56,479 from his employer.

The four counts against Cole charged her with embezzling $27,272 from the Mississippi Firefighters Memorial Burn Association. The embezzlements were said to have taken place between January 2001 and December 2002. Cole was alleged to have embezzled $250 in proceeds from a 2001 motor sports fund-raiser, $600 from money given to her for the burn center in a sting operation, $970 from fraudulent checks, and $25,942 from writing fraudulent payroll checks.

Special Assistant Attorney General Lee Martin said the father and daughter embezzled money in two ways. They took money from fund-raisers designed to generate support for the burn center. Martin also noted that as part of a sting Johnson was given money for the association and that he used it to gamble at a casino. The attorney general's investigation involved two different undercover stings in which a person took donations in the form of cash and checks to the burn center. The investigators observed Johnson and Cole leaving the burn center and spending the cash at a casino. They also took money from various checking accounts. Martin said, "They were writing extra paychecks or just cashing [petty cash fund] checks."

On August 23, 2004, Sandy Johnson pled guilty to count six of the indictment, and the state agreed not to prosecute on the other five counts. The same day Tisha Cole pled guilty to embezzling more than $27,000. At the time of the pleading, Johnson had repaid $36,645, and Cole had repaid $17,645.

On September 8, 2004, Circuit Court Judge Margaret Carey-McCray sentenced the sixty-year-old Johnson to six years' imprisonment with three years suspended and three years of supervised probation. Johnson was also ordered to pay court costs and $31,059 in restitution. A payment of $10,000 was to be made the day of sentencing, and the remainder was to be paid at the rate of $750 per month. Cole was also sentenced to six years' imprisonment with three years suspended and three years of supervised probation. She, too, was ordered to pay restitution.

Richard Alcott of Greenville spent seventeen days in the burn center as a patient in 2002. Alcott commented on the embezzlements, "If it were any other organization other than the burn center, I wouldn't be so upset. But after being there and seeing what goes on and knowing what they do for people, I can't believe anyone would do such a thing. The burn center does a wonderful job and they need every dime they can get."

Amanda Williams said she regretted the circumstances surrounding the convictions. She indicated that the association had taken steps to assure that all contributions were safeguarded from the possibility of future malfeasance. Saying that the association would only grow stronger with time, she promised to continue its twenty-eight-year tradition and mission of providing critical burn care.

The OSA became involved in this case in December 2002 when it received a complaint alleging that Sandy Johnson had embezzled money from the Mississippi Firefighters Memorial Burn Association. The OSA coordinated its very limited work on this case with the Public Integrity Division of the Mississippi Attorney General's Office, which actually did the investigation. The OSA closed the case September 9, 2004.

In May of 2005, the *Clarion-Ledger* reported that the Mississippi Firefighters Memorial Burn Center had reduced its bed capacity from sixteen beds to six. The center had a cash flow problem and was in danger of being closed. Amanda Williams Fontaine, executive director of the Mississippi Firefighters Memorial Burn Association, the fund-raising group associated with the center, indicated that lack of beds could cause time-consuming transfers of burn victims out of state. Fontaine said, "You are really risking lives by not having a burn center in the state." In a letter to medical officials in Mississippi and neighboring states, Ray Humphreys, CEO of the Delta Regional Medical Center, wrote, "The burn center lacks a solid funding stream to continue its mission in attracting top-quality physicians and professional staff to practice medicine, maintain facilities, and upgrade equipment." Terri Land, a spokeswoman for the regional medical center, indicated that the burn center's supporters were seeking $3.8 million per year in addition to the $1.3 million the association had been providing, and that federal state and private sources had been contacted.

The *Clarion-Ledger* editorialized on May 18, 2005:

> News that the Mississippi Firefighters' Memorial Burn Center at Greenville might be forced to close by the end of the month should concern state lawmakers. However, the remedy is not to continue the center at Greenville, but transfer operations—state paid, and not by donation—to University Medical Center in Jackson.
>
> The facility, part of the Delta Regional Medical Center in Greenville, has been operating under a cloud for some time. Last year, Sandy Johnson, the former director of the center's fundraising arm, Mississippi Firefighters' Memorial Burn Center Association, and his daughter, Tisha J. Cole, pleaded guilty to embezzling more than $84,000. Its funding through volunteer donations had been declining.
>
> But the center, now operating with only six beds, due to a lack of revenue and the failure to attract qualified physicians, and no longer accepting critical pediatric patients, remains the only comprehensive burn center between Galveston, Texas, and Augusta, Georgia. Mississippians need this trauma care, and UMC— as a teaching hospital and being centrally located—is the logical location.
>
> It should have strict state oversight and stable funding, not requiring donations.

The Mississippi Firefighters Memorial Burn Center stopped accepting new patients on May 31, 2005. Ray Humphreys said that the burn center's resources would be devoted to critical care and surgical patients at the hospital. Humphreys had contacted the governor, members of Congress, and private sector sources in hopes of securing funds to save the center. Meanwhile, the University Medical Center was exploring the possibility of opening a burn center at its Jackson campus.

Efforts were made in late May and early June 2005 to add the burn center funding to the agendas of two special sessions of the legislature called by

Governor Haley Barbour to deal with economic development matters. The efforts failed, but supporters of the center began a two-month campaign to raise $5 million annually to save the center. Ray Humphreys wrote a letter saying that "the public reaction has been so strong that our legislative representatives have requested that we extend our efforts to save the burn center." Humphreys said that because of the "very heartfelt outcry and reaction to the closure," the board had developed a new plan. He went on to say, "The board feels this approach will provide additional time for legislators to find and develop alternate strategies to address the urgent burn center issues of funding and recruitment." In early June 2005, Governor Barbour appointed a special panel to make recommendations about how to handle the care of burn victims in the state.

Deidre Ann Marshall, Bookkeeper/Accounting Audit Technician, Allied Enterprises of Harrison County, Mississippi Department of Rehabilitation Services

Allied Enterprises of Harrison County, operated by the Mississippi Department of Rehabilitation Services (DRS), provides training and employment for people with disabilities (clients). Clients employed by Allied work on contract for such things as food and janitorial services. When not enough clients are available to meet contract demands, Allied employs other persons (nonclients) to do the work. Both clients and nonclients are paid hourly wages.

Kevin R. Bishop, facility administrator of Allied at its Long Beach location, learned of a discrepancy on August 8, 1996, when Nancy Crocker, production manager, attempted to reconcile Allied's bank statement. The check stub for a paycheck made out to Allen Gray showed $59.83, but the cashed check returned by the bank was actually for $593.83. A review of payroll records by Bishop revealed that Gray had not worked during the time period covered by the payroll check. Comparisons of the endorsement on the check to the signatures on checks for periods when payroll records showed that Gray actually worked revealed notable differences. Bishop then went to the Pineville Road branch of Hancock Bank and showed Lonnie Sirworth, assistant vice president, two checks made out to Allen Gray with different endorsements. Bishop asked if he could view surveillance tapes for the day and time the $593.83 check was cashed to determine who cashed the check. Sigworth agreed that the endorsements were different and allowed Bishop to view the appropriate tape. The tape showed Deidre (Dee) Ann Marshall, an accounting audit technician for Allied who wrote the checks, standing at the teller window when the check was cashed. Mr. Sigworth said, "This must be Deidre," and added that "she cashes checks for other people all the time."

Further review identified three additional payments to people who did not work during the payroll period covered. These three checks, which totaled $1,531.56, were made out to Brenda Boothe, Yolanda Brown, and Tracey Curry. Comparisons of the endorsements on these checks to signatures on valid paychecks of the employees revealed notable differences. The checks were processed by Deidre Ann Marshall and were signed by Kevin Bishop and Nancy Crocker. Marshall, a forty-five-year-old Pass Christian resident, had worked for the Department of Rehabilitation Services since June 1991.

On August 9, 1996, Bishop and Darrell Vaughn, chief fiscal officer of the DRS, who had come from the agency's headquarters to look into the situation, visited the branch bank. With the aid of Sigworth, they viewed a tape that showed Marshall at the teller's window when one of the other three checks was cashed. Vaughn asked Sigworth how a person could cash someone else's check; Sigworth indicated that other businesses do it all the time. Sigworth said a designated person would bring in a number of checks, cash them all, take the money back to the place of business, and distribute it appropriately. Vaughn and Bishop both said that this practice did not appear to be ethical, and Vaughn asked if Dee Marshall had ever done this. Sigworth indicated that tellers had told him that Marshall had done this. Bishop then told Sigworth that no one from Allied was authorized to cash a check for anyone else.

That same day, Marshall was confronted with the discrepancies by Bishop and Vaughn. According to Vaughn, Marshall initially denied any wrongdoing but later confessed to embezzling the funds in question. Marshall was immediately suspended with pay. Three days later, Marshall revealed that she had written more checks and embezzled the money. Marshall apologized for taking the funds and claimed that she had not taken any other money. She was immediately suspended from her position with the DRS. In a later discussion with Bishop, Marshall claimed that she had gotten behind in her bills due to her sister's illness (cancer). Further review by DRS personnel revealed that from October 1993 through July 19, 1996, more than $70,000 had possibly been embezzled.

The embezzlement was reported to the Long Beach Police Department, where it was assigned to Detective Don Wells. In mid-August 1996, Detective Wells filed a complaint against Marshall with the OSA alleging embezzlement. The OSA assigned investigative auditor James Scott Womack to the case.

Sarah Doloach, assistant attorney general assigned to the Department of

Rehabilitation Services, learned of the suspected embezzlement and contacted the Public Integrity Division of the AG's office. Warren Emfinger, an investigator with the division, was advised of the OSA's involvement and assigned to the case. On August 15, 1996, Emfinger contacted Womack and suggested that they coordinate their investigations.

On August 22, 1996, Bishop, Emfinger, and Womack went to the Pineville Road branch of the Hancock Bank, which is close to Allied's facility. With Lonnie Sigworth's permission, they reviewed surveillance videotapes made at the times stamped on the backs of cashed checks to determine who actually cashed them. They found three instances where Deidre Marshall cashed checks made out to other persons. Check 50364 for $642 was payable to Vanessa York; check 50514 for $190 was payable to Veronica Neal; and check 50622 was payable to Debra Mitchell. In each instance the person whose name was on the check had not worked during the payroll period covered by the paycheck.

OSA investigator Scott Womack phoned security personnel at seven Gulf Coast casinos in late August 1996 in an attempt to determine whether Marshall was gambling heavily. Casino Magic indicated that she was listed as "a rated player" and that they would be glad to assist in the investigation, but a subpoena would be required. The Grand Casino in Gulfport reported that Marshall was a "big player" and that they would cooperate if subpoenaed. The President Casino in Biloxi replied that Marshall had lost approximately $1,200 there, and that they would be glad to respond to a subpoena. The other four casinos contacted stated that they had no information on Marshall.

On August 30, 1996, Lisa P. Miller, an administrative assistant at the DRS, gave the following written statement to OSA investigator Scott Womack:

> On the evening of August 11, 1996, I received a telephone call from Dee Marshall. I had been out of the office since Thursday, August 8, 1996, at 12:00 noon and had not seen or spoken to her until this call. She stated something had happened at work. She stated she had taken some money at work, but not to think she was a bad person. She said her sister, Cassie, had incurred some medical bills that she needed to help pay. She stated, "I would give Mommy money and Mommy would ask where I got the money, and I told her I won the money at the boats [casinos]." She said that she had already apologized to Kevin Bishop for what had happened, but she wanted to call to let me know she wasn't a bad person. I told her I didn't think she was a bad person.
>
> She more or less talked excessively and sort of rambled. She said, "I have already discussed it with my father, but I have not said anything to Mommy."

She stated, " If I have to go to jail, it would just kill Mommy." I told her I knew it would because her mother depended on her to help take care of Cassie. I told her that if she needed anything or just wanted to talk to call me. We then ended our conversation.

On August 30, 1996, Nancy Crocker gave the following written statement to OSA investigator Scott Womack:

On August 10, 1996, at approximately 10:30 a. m., I received a telephone call from Dee Marshall concerning the problems at Allied Enterprises. She stated she was very sorry for hurting me, that she would never cause anyone hurt. Dee stated that with Cassie's bills, she just lost it. That with all the bills, her mother and father would never be able to pay them. Therefore, she needed the funds to help. Dee stated that it was a very foolish mistake and asked that I not hate her.

My response was that I do not hate you, but I do not condone the mistake you made either. Surely there was another way and she responded there was no other way.

During August and September 1996, OSA investigator Scott Womack and AG investigator Warren Emfinger interviewed the following people for whom suspicious Allied payroll checks had been discovered: Lou Ella Scott (four checks for a total of $2,519.19), Sheryl Walton (four checks for a total of $3,067.86), Veronica Neal (two checks for a total of $850), Brenda Boothe (three checks for a total of $1,336.89), Alando Mason (two checks for a total of $841.76), and Leslie Howell (one check for $275.47). All of these people said they never cashed or even received the checks involved. Veronica Neal indicated that although she applied for work at Allied, because of health problems she never actually worked there. Lou Ella Scott said Mary Magee, who also worked for Allied, reported that a paycheck made out to Scott had been returned to Allied's office. The check came to the naval home where they both worked on a day when Scott was not working. It was noted that Scott had not actually worked during the pay period, and the check was returned.

On November 27, 1996, the attorney general's Division of Public Integrity interviewed Marshall. Scott Womack and O. T. McAlpin of the OSA, Lee Martin and Warren Emfinger of the AG's office, Marshall's father, Caesar Marshall, and Marshall's attorney, Donald Rafferty, were present during the interview. Rafferty had objected to going forward with the interview before a plea bargain was worked out with the state. Marshall elected to go forward anyway. The following paragraphs are taken from a transcript of that interview.

LEE MARTIN: Dee, I'm gonna, for the sake of time, and it's gonna get redundant; [inaudible] if you want me to, I can continue to do this, and by this I mean, by killing the checks, showing you the surveillance pictures that we have and of you standing there at the teller cashing these checks. For calendar year 1996, since the 1st, what we've learned our investigation based with too, pulling checks that are in excess for the most part of $500.00. We're basically looking, have done interviews concerning thirty-five (35) different individuals. Checks written up to some different payees, thirty-five (35) different payees; a lot of them have multiple checks issued to them as you've seen some this afternoon. We are dealing with a total of sixty-four (64) checks for the short time period we've been working for 1996. Of those 64 checks, which we believe, the investigators have gone, they've interviewed each of the individuals that the checks were made payable to, people who at one time or another were associated with Allied Industries either as an employee or as a client, who would receive compensation or payment from Allied and shown them each of the checks, asked the individual "Is your signature on the check, the endorsement on the back of the check?" And they say "No." "Have you ever seen this check before today?" "No." You understand what I'm saying? And of date, 64 checks, as I was telling you this morning, I've got a total of 19 of those checks where the surveillance camera in the bank can put you standing there in front of that teller cashing the checks. [Inaudible.] As I showed you, Dianne Carter's check made payable to Dianne Carter and you've got an endorsement on it. You told me that you endorsed it, and I've got a picture of you standing there at the teller cashing the check and receiving the money. And this is all basically for the calendar year 1996. You've been employed at Allied since June of 1991. Is that correct? . . . How did you ever think of doing this thing?

DEIDRE MARSHALL: Um, well, um, it started off with, I'd issue checks, and they'd never come and pick it up. And I kept it myself. And then, um, it just got, uh, so weird. And then there were no internal controls, you know, nobody was watching, you know, to see if I followed the correct procedures. Oh, um, it just got real easy to cash the checks. And then the bank person wouldn't question me, and, um, it just got easy to cash them so.

LEE MARTIN: So initially you're saying that you made out checks to someone who was actually entitled to receive the money for whatever reason, whether an employee or a client or anything like that? So they failed to pick up the check, so you took it upon yourself to cash it and got away with that? And at that point did you think about going back and using a former employee's name? You did that as well, correct?

DEIDRE MARSHALL: Yeah.

LEE MARTIN: Ok. And you talked about no internal controls. As book-keeper, accounting clerk, did you have the responsibility of reconciling the checkbook each month?

DEIDRE MARSHALL: No.

LEE MARTIN: Whose responsibility was that?

DEIDRE MARSHALL: Nancy Crocker.

LEE MARTIN: She was the one who would, say, balance the checkbook each month, right?

DEIDRE MARSHALL: Yes.

LEE MARTIN: Ok, now you [inaudible] checks. You were issuing checks to people; these would be people who were not entitled to receive them. Is that a fair statement?

DEIDRE MARSHALL: [Must have nodded her head/could not hear response.]

LEE MARTIN: Ok. There had to be an adjustment somewhere else, right? Did Nancy Crocker ever come to you and say, "The books aren't balancing; we're off or what have you?

DEIDRE MARSHALL: No. The books [inaudible] were fine.

LEE MARTIN: That's because somebody's documentation had to be manipulated?

DEIDRE MARSHALL: Yes.

From the above it is apparent that the combination of an error in recording the amount of a check and the functioning of one feature of a good internal control system led to Marshall's thefts being discovered. Marshall obviously did not mean to record the $593.83 check to Allen Gray as $59.83 on the check stub. In accord with a basic principle of good internal control, the functions of writing and recording checks and reconciling the monthly bank statements had been segregated. When Crocker attempted to reconcile the bank statement and discovered the discrepancy, Marshall's chicanery began to be revealed. Two essential controls over payroll were missing: budgetary control and the review of payroll time cards for proper authorization. It appears that Marshall's scheme could have continued indefinitely without this one mistake in recording the amount of a check on a check stub.

In a report dated September 17, 1997, OSA investigator Scott Womack noted that he had determined that Deidre Marshall had embezzled a total of $84,449.26 from the DRS during the period October 8, 1993, through August 5, 1996. The thefts involved a total of 191 checks. Payroll withholdings of $8,131.47 associated with the fraud brought the gross amount to $92,580.73. The state's contributions to FICA and Medicare totaled $3,851.62, and its contribution to workmen's compensation totaled $1,862.52. This brought the total principal amount to $98,294.87. The OSA issued a formal demand on Marshall and the surety company ITT Hartford September 29, 1997. The demand, which included the principal, interest, and cost of recovery, totaled $154,783.74.

In December 1997, ITT Hartford paid the DRS $79,449.26 (the $84,449.26 that Marshall actually received less a $5,000 deductible). The IRS refunded $10,352.73 for excess federal withholding taxes. The DRS also expected to recover from the state $3,492.88 (the remaining principal) in excess workmen's compensation payments. This was reported to State Auditor Phil Bryant in a December 18, 1997, letter from DRS Executive Director H. S. "Butch" McMillan. The letter was extremely complimentary of Scott Womack's work on the case. The Mississippi Workers' Compensation Commission later issued a credit to DHS in the amount of $3,492.88.

Special Assistant Attorney General Loni Eustace-McMillan wrote to Phil Bryant on February 19, 1998, and recommended that the case be closed because there was no hope of recovering the balance of the demand from Marshall. The letter noted the recovery mentioned above and stated that, with the help of Scott Womack, the AG's office had determined that Marshall was "judgment proof." This letter also complimented Womack for his work. The interest and cost of the investigation have not been recovered.

In March 1998, a Harrison County grand jury indicted Deidre Ann Marshall on six counts. Count one alleged embezzlement of $98,294.87. Counts two through six alleged forgery of five checks for $690, $642, $593.83, $512.38, and $586. Marshall, who faced maximum prison time of eighty-five years, pled guilty to the charges in April 1999. In September 1999, Circuit Court Judge John Whitfield imposed a sentence of fifteen years, all of which were suspended, and placed Marshall on five years' probation. Whitfield also ordered Marshall to pay restitution at the rate of $300 per month to the state and the insurance company that had bonded her.

At sentencing, Marshall said, "I lived in a dream world. I always thought I could go to the casinos and win the money I took from the state." Marshall's attorney, Donald Rafferty, said that she had a lesson to teach: "No matter what the economic benefits of gambling, there's always going to be a dark side." As a part of Marshall's sentence, Judge Whitfield required her to attend Gamblers Anonymous and banned her from casino properties. Ironically, at the time of sentencing, she worked as a reservationist for the Grand Gulf Casino in Gulfport. Marshall had to look for a new job.

This case presents a classic example of the fraud triangle. Family sickness and gambling losses put much financial pressure on Marshall. Lack of basic internal controls over payroll provided her with a golden opportunity to embezzle. Finally, Marshall apparently had little trouble rationalizing her actions and lying about her motives.

Sandra Allan Stovall, Executive Director, Holly Springs Tourism and Recreational Facilities Bureau

On June 2, 2001, John Crittle, treasurer of the Holly Springs Tourism and Recreational Facilities Bureau, met with Holly Springs Police Chief Jimmie L. Howell and Lt. John C. Norman to report four instances of forgery. Crittle stated that he had received a bank statement for Holly Springs Tourism and noted that his signature had been forged on checks written on that account. Only Crittle and Mabel (Maxine) Hall, the organization's board chairman, had signature authority for the account. Sandra Allan Stovall, the bureau's executive director, was said to have written checks to herself and forged Crittle's signature.

The checks in question were on an account of the Holly Springs Tourism and Recreational Facilities Bureau at the Bank of Holly Springs. The checks were as follows: no. 1180 for $2,500, dated March 5, 2001; no. 1198 for $5,732, dated March 2, 2001; no. 1217 for $1,584, dated April 1, 2001; no. 1219 for $2,700, dated March 30, 2001.

Crittle indicated that there were several thousand dollars more that could not be accounted for and that he would soon submit further information to the authorities. Crittle then signed four counts of uttering forgery against Stovall. An arrest warrant was issued, and Stovall was arrested by Officer Dwight Harris. The fifty-nine-year-old Stovall was transported to the Marshall County jail and retained in the Marshall County Detention Center.

Through an attorney, the Holly Springs Board of Aldermen reported the incident to the OSA. The Holly Springs Tourism and Recreational Facilities Bureau was supported by a local 2 percent food and beverage tax and a 2 percent tax on the gross sales of motels and hotels that had been approved by local and private legislation. On June 6, 2001, OSA Senior Special Agent Denver

Smith informed Jones that the OSA would conduct an investigation as the lead agency in the case. Jones agreed, and OSA Special Agent Johnny Shannon was immediately assigned to the case.

Shannon went to the Marshall County Detention Center to interview Stovall. Saying that she was not going to talk to anyone until she conferred with her attorney, Stovall refused to talk to the OSA agent. The Holly Springs Police Department cooperated with the OSA but continued its own investigation into the matter.

The OSA's investigation revealed thirty-one fraudulent checks written by Stovall between October 20, 2000, and May 22, 2001, for a total of $111,992. The name of either John Crittle or Maxine Hall was forged on all of the checks. Four of the checks were written to Alyse Sykes Ringo, Stovall's daughter. Stovall was the payee on all the other twenty-seven checks.

Shannon's July 18, 2001, report noted:

Stovall prepared financial reports and submitted them to the board but did not include the aforementioned checks. In numerous instances, the board approved the issuance of checks and Hall and Crittle would actually sign them, but Stovall would not send the checks to the payee. Stovall's reporting would include these checks, however. This would make the book balance of the account appear to be in the black, though, at numerous times it was, in fact, overdrawn. It was not until the bank notified the treasurer, Dr. Crittle, that anyone at the tourism office with the exception of Stovall knew the bank account was depleted.

The original amount of the funds that were believed to be misappropriated was $113,577. The difference between this amount and the $111,993 is $1,584. Though Hall and Crittle contend the former amount was correct, an analysis of Stovall's salary and check register paid by her and submitted to the board indicates that check number 1177 written on March 2, 2001, was actually approved and was an amount that Stovall was due. However, the check was written prior to the payroll ending period.

The District Attorney's Office acquired from the Bank of Holly Springs copies of the Holly Springs Tourism and Recreational Facilities Bureau bank account as well as copies of bank accounts of Stovall and/or her mother, Alice Allen. Also included in the District Attorney's acquisition was another bank account of Stovall's at First State Bank. Beside the analysis of the Tourism account, I analyzed the personal accounts acquired. All three bank accounts of Stovall and/or her mother indicated numerous instances of being overdrawn.

In addition, each account revealed withdrawals from an automated teller machine in Robinsonville, Mississippi. [Robinsonville is close to the casinos in Tunica County.]

Stovall received $15,844 in excess salary checks. Besides the one check mentioned previously, Hall and Crittle contend each of ten (10) different checks were forged by Stovall in the amount of $1,584. The four (4) checks written to Stovall's daughter totaled $24,663. Each of these checks indicate the payment to be for either "Sales" or "Contract Payment." There was no contract or agreement with Stovall's daughter. The remaining seventeen (17) checks written to Stovall indicated various reimbursements, conventions, or trade shows. The Tourism Board did not approve any of these payments.

A Marshall County grand jury indicted Sandra Stovall on four counts of forgery on July 27, 2001. All four counts charged that she forged John Crittle's name on Holly Springs Tourism and Recreational Facilities Bureau checks with herself as the payee. The dates and amounts of the checks were: March 5, 2001, $2,500; March 20, 2001, $5,732; April 1, 2001, $1,584; and March 30, 2001, $2,700. Since each count carried a maximum penalty of fifteen years in prison, Stovall faced up to sixty years of incarceration.

On September 20, 2001, Phil Bryant issued a demand on Sandra A. Stovall and Old Republic Surety Company for $125,798. This total represented $111,992 of payments made without authority, $9,443 interest, and $4,363 in recovery costs. Because the demand was not paid within thirty days, Bryant referred the matter to Attorney General Mike Moore on October 19, 2001. The insurance company paid $25,000, the maximum amount payable under Stovall's bond, directly to the Holly Springs Tourism and Recreational Facilities Bureau on January 13, 2003.

On May 30, 2002, based on a plea agreement worked out by District Attorney Jim Hood and attorney Kent Smith, Stovall pled guilty to all four counts. Prior to sentencing, the Holly Springs Tourism and Recreational Facilities Bureau and its members had opposed any plea bargain. Court records include the following May 28, 2002, statement signed by board chairman Mike Lynn.

The Holly Springs Tourism and Recreation Board does not support ANY plea bargain agreement between the State and Defendant.

Because of the enormity of the crime against the citizens of Holly Springs, the Board is vitally interested in full restitution of taxpayers' funds and justice under the law.

Court records also include a written statement by Mabel M. Hall noting that over a short period of only four months Stovall forged checks, falsified financial records, and used the ill-gotten gains for personal advantage. Hall asked the court to do everything within its means to ensure that Stovall was held accountable for her actions. Hall requested that the court ensure repayment of the missing public funds and that it impose appropriate punishment for the crime.

Sandra Stovall was sentenced to a term of ten years with eight years suspended, leaving two years to be served without privileges in a restitution center. In addition, Stovall was ordered to pay restitution of $111,992, interest at 1 percent per month from the date of the crimes, and the OSA's investigative cost of $4,363. All payments were to be made within five years of release from incarceration, and she was to serve five years' probation after her release. Other provisions of the sentence handed down by Circuit Court Judge Andrew Howorth included requirements that Stovall file within ninety days a sworn accounting of all expenditures of all stolen funds and her assets from January 2000, that she cooperate fully in recovery of the funds, and that she assign any recovery from any pending civil lawsuits up to the amount owed. This last provision came back to haunt Stovall and the bureau.

The transcript of the sentencing hearing includes the following exchanges among Judge Howorth, Stovall, and Assistant District Attorney Jim Hood:

THE COURT: All right. I'll ask her a few questions and then—and then, I'll allow you to do so also.

Q. All right. I want you to know that for the time being, I am going to take this recommendation [the district attorney's sentencing recommendation] under advisement. I need to ask you some questions. I want to understand a little bit more about the underlying crime, and I understand there may be some victims here that wish to speak in regard to any sentence imposed by this Court, and there may be—you may have family or friends that wish to speak in mitigation of the sentence, and I will allow you to do so before I impose sentence in this case.

Now, I want to ask you a little about this crime. According to the Department of Audit, the funds misappropriated directly attributable to this crime totaled $111,192. Do you have any reason to disagree with their calculation as to the amount of money that you personally misappropriated?

A. No sir.

Q. All right. Do you agree that that figure is accurate?

A. Yes sir.

Q. You don't know what the total is?

A. No sir.

Q. But you don't have any reason to disagree with it in that amount?

A. No, sir.

Q. All right. You are not telling the court that you know it to be less or that you know it to be more, are you?

A. No sir.

Q. Okay. Now, assuming the figure is correct, and I think we can assume that, can you tell us where the $111,992 is now?

A. Yes, sir.

Q. Okay, where is it?

A. It—it was gambled away.

Q. You have a gambling addiction or a gambling problem?

A. I had.

Q. Okay. Where did you gamble?

A. The casinos.

Q. In Tunica?

A. Yes, sir.

Q. Okay?

A. And since that time, I've been with Gamblers Anonymous out of Jackson.

Q. All your personal assets have been gambled away?

A. Yes, sir.

Q. You have no savings?

A. No, sir.

Q. No part of this money went anywhere other than the casinos?

A. That's correct, Your Honor.

Q. Okay. You didn't use this money to buy—buy something you still own?

A. No, sir.

Q. You didn't use any of this money to give or loan to someone else?

A. No, sir.

Q. Okay. All right. Do you understand that part of the recommendation of the District Attorney's Office in this case is that you provide records and an accounting of not only of where this money went but also of any personal assets that you have in a sworn form? Do you understand that as being part of their recommendation?

A. Yes, sir.

Q. If the Court imposes a sentence in that effect, will you have a problem complying with it?

A. No, sir.

Q. All right?

A. I don't have anything.

Q. I understand that you don't have anything, but we would like to—I would like to know that you can provide us with some information?

A. Yes, sir.

Q. Your bank records, you know, debit slips, whatever is reasonably requested of you to prove that all of the misappropriated money ended up in the gambling hall somewhere.

A. Yes, sir.

Q. Not only that, but that you will give us this statement in a sworn form; in other words, a statement that you sign under oath under penalty of perjury that everything in there is true and correct, including your own personal financial statement.

A. Yes, sir.

Q. You understand what that recommendation entails?

A. Yes, sir.

Q. And I, the Court orders that, you're telling the Court you can comply with that.

A. Yes, sir.

THE COURT: All right. Anything else you want to voir dire the witness?

MR. HOOD: Your Honor, I have two questions.

THE COURT: All right. The District Attorney is going to ask you a few questions.

VOIR DIRE BY MR. HOOD:

Q. Was there anyone else involved in this—in the theft?

A. No, sir.

Q. Anybody conspire to assist you in any way?

A. No, sir. Maybe to their—they might have not known that they were assisting me, but no, sir.

Q. Did you agree with anybody to take—take this money?

A. Oh, no, sir.

Q. Did you give it to anybody else?

A. No, sir.

Q. What about the $20,000 that was sent to your daughter in Atlanta, Georgia?

A. That's why I say they may not have known that—she thought she was setting up a computer system over at the—over at the tourism office and thought she was setting up an accounting system for me, but that money was given back to me, and she didn't use any of that money.

Q. You have an address in Atlanta, Georgia. Did you buy a house in Atlanta with any of those assets?

A. Oh, no, sir.

Q. Does your daughter have any of those assets?

A. No, sir.

MR. HOOD: That's all we have, Your Honor. Thank you.

EXAMINATION BY THE COURT:

Q. All right. You're telling us that this $20,000 that the District Attorney has referred to was sent to your daughter; you can document that it was returned to you.

A. Yes, sir.

Q. All right?

A. Yes, sir.

Q. All right. That would be an example of what—what the recommendation of the District Attorney is about part of your sentence is that you would be able to establish these things; that that money was sent away by you, came back to you. All right. You'll be able to do that; is that what you are telling the Court?

A. Yes, sir.

Q. All right.

During the sentencing hearing, Mike Lynn asked Judge Howorth whether the part of the sentence with respect to the assignment of any civil suit judgment was binding. The judge said that it was binding between the court and the defendant but not against any third-party payer. A civil suit against Stovall would be necessary to perfect a claim against a third-party payer such as an insurance company. The Holly Springs Tourism and Recreational Facilities Bureau subsequently attempted to perfect its claim to the proceeds from a civil action only to find that the claim had already been paid.

Stovall was in jail June 14, 2002, at the Marshall County Justice Complex when Jim Hood filed a motion to revoke her eight-year suspended sentence or conduct another sentencing hearing. The grounds for the motion were that Stovall had committed perjury. She was said to have perjured herself by agreeing to assign any recovery she might receive from a pending civil action, when, in fact, the case had been settled in March 2002 with Stovall receiving $74,888. Travelers Insurance Company had paid Stovall that amount on a workmen's compensation claim on March 4, 2002. Hood noted that the plea bargain was based on a recommendation of the state, which was contingent on Stovall assigning to the state any recovery from the civil action. Hood also contended that the recommendation of the lenient sentence was based on a fraudulent representation that Stovall would soon recover a large sum of money in the civil suit. According to the motion, "The defendant never mentioned to the state nor the court that this civil action had already been settled."

On November 1, 2002, Judge Howorth issued an order overruling the motion to revoke the suspended sentence. This ruling seems to be based on the technical facts in the case. It appears that, when the plea bargain was struck, the workmen's compensation civil case was pending, and Stovall was willing to assign any proceeds. However, that action was settled by a payment made directly to Stovall prior to her sentencing. Therefore, there was no civil action pending at the date of sentencing. Stovall claimed to have no money at the time of sentencing.

Mike Lynn, chairman of the board of the Holly Springs Tourism and Recreational Facilities Bureau, wrote to Judge Howorth on January 28, 2004, stating that no restitution had been received from garnishment of Stovall's pay although she had been in the work-release program for over a year. Lynn asked that the judge direct the proper authorities to release the funds to the bureau and to make future payments quarterly. Shortly after this request, approximately $2,000 of restitution was received from the restitution center.

Epilogue

Mississippi public officials continue their corrupt practices unabated, and unfortunately it affects the poorest of the Magnolia State's citizens. A January 3, 2005, *Clarion-Ledger* front-page headline read: "Alleged Holmes corruption fits disturbing trend." The article by investigative reporter Jerry Mitchell explained why.

Holmes County is one of the nation's poorest counties, a place where poverty seems plentiful.

So, why are there so many allegations of corruption in a place so little?

District Attorney James Powell confirmed last week that Tissie Brocks, who oversaw the Holmes County Economic Development Authority, allegedly stole at least $80,000 by forging the names of those who sign checks. "It's in that neighborhood or a little more," he said.

In April, Durant Mayor Eddie Logan was indicted on grand larceny and embezzlement charges for allegedly taking appliances and cabinets valued at about $3,000 from the former Roberts Cabinet Co., which has since gone bankrupt. The missing appliances and cabinets have been returned.

Less than a year before that, former city clerk Rosie Hogsett Mitchell, deputy city clerk McShelle Williams and utilities clerk Connie Larabel were each charged with embezzling city money. Following those charges, the city cut its police force in half.

Last January, Lexington city clerk Pamela Williams was arrested on three counts of embezzlement involving more than $500 each.

With more than a third of the population living in poverty, the county has struggled—and mostly failed—to attract corporations to locate there. Durant Electric closed long ago and so have textile plants, hundreds of jobs going to Mexico or Asia.

One ray of hope has come with the nearby Canton Nissan plant, providing much-needed jobs. Although the unemployment rate no longer hovers around 20 percent, it is still 14.4 percent—nearly triple the national rate.

Allegations of corruption have concerned Wilbur Redmond, a community leader with the local Freedom Democratic Party, but "I wouldn't say (Holmes County) is more corrupt. I'd just say that people in positions have allegedly abused their oath of office. It's happening in other counties too."

State Auditor Phil Bryant's office is investigating the case involving Brocks, and Powell said he expects to get that report soon. Once he receives it, he will move forward with the case. "To protect the integrity of this case, we will have no comment at this time," said Mike Bullock, a spokesman for Bryant.

Doug Aldridge with Holmes County Economic Development Authority also wouldn't comment.

Powell said he had no explanation for the rash of corruption cases in Holmes County. "Looks like everybody has gone on a stealing binge," he said.

He said one reason for the recent allegations is the authority's board members have met infrequently, "sometimes only once a year," he said.

Hope Smith, who heads up the Holmes County Bank in Lexington, also had no explanation. "It's all kind of mounting up," he said. "It's regrettable, but those things happen."

They recently have been happening a lot nationally too. Prosecution of corruption cases has risen by up to 15 percent in the past four years in federal court, and two governors have recently resigned in the wake of scandals. Add to that the growing list of executives who have been convicted or face charges relating to accounting improprieties that improperly inflated the value of their corporations.

In the past two years, Mississippi has seen a growing list of officials accused of stealing money from the public trust or from revered charities. Almost a year ago, the *Corporate Crime Reporter*, a legal publication based in Washington, D C., called Mississippi the most corrupt state, basing that title on public corruption convictions in U.S. District Courts between 1993 and 2002.

Mississippi had 215 convictions for a population of 2.9 million, a rate of 7.48 per 100,000 people. The rest of the top ten were North Dakota, Louisiana, Alaska, Illinois, Montana, South Dakota, Kentucky, Florida, and New York.

But those who did the report acknowledge the numbers may be skewed toward smaller states (all of the top seven, except Illinois, have populations of less than 4.5 million, and four of the top seven, the northwestern states plus Alaska, have populations of less than 1 million). The report's authors also acknowledge that the numbers fail to reflect how much total corruption there is since some corruption may go undetected.

In Mississippi, both U.S. attorney's offices have been aggressive in prosecuting public corruption in recent decades. Dick Johnson, chairman of Common Cause/Mississippi, said he thinks the apparent rise in corruption relates to a loss of values, Americans substituting selfishness for service. "Rather than becoming something, we're emphasizing getting more things," he said. "It's not so much what you have, it's that you have more than somebody else." The more comfortable our lives become as Americans, and "the more we can have, the more we value things," he said. "What we become as human beings gets lost."

Eddie Logan, who had been Durant's mayor for almost four years, was convicted of embezzlement and grand larceny February 15, 2005, and ordered removed from office. Logan was convicted for taking appliances and cabinets from a bankrupt cabinet company in February 2003. District Attorney James Powell said that the bank that held a lien on the property of Roberts Cabinet Co. auctioned off the property, and people who bid on the items arranged to pick them up the next day. Powell noted that the next day people saw the mayor loading a truck with about $1500 worth of equipment from the business. "The mayor went to the building, tore out the built-in cabinets owned by the City of Durant, took them home and used them," Powell said. Holmes County Circuit Court Judge Jannie Lewis sentenced Logan to three years in prison, but suspended all three years. Logan was also ordered to serve six months' community service and six months' probation.

Logan planned to appeal his removal from office and his conviction. He claimed that he had told Vice Mayor Howard Roberts and the city's board of aldermen of his plans to take the items. He also claimed to have told the board that he would return the property if it belonged to anyone. Logan later fired Roberts for reporting the theft to the OSA. Logan said, "I think as far as I'm concerned, the accusations were not substantiated. They didn't belong to anybody that could specifically identify them." He claimed there were no identifying tags of the items he took.

Logan changed his mind about appealing his removal from office, and he did not appear in Holmes County Circuit Court on February 18 to challenge his ouster. The former mayor said, "On advice of my attorney, it might have been a waste of time." However, Logan still planned to appeal his conviction, saying, "I got to. An appeal has been initiated." Logan, who said he planned to run for reelection in June, confirmed that the appeal had not yet been filed. The city's board of aldermen elected former Vice Mayor Howard to complete the remaining months of Logan's term.

Mr. Logan seemed to live in another world. Kosciusko's weekly newspaper, the *Star-Herald*, ran the following on May 13, 2004, shortly after Logan had been arrested by OSA agents and charged in the case.

The following is a letter from Durant Mayor Eddie Logan, who was charged with grand larceny and embezzlement two weeks ago. The letter, which is printed as it was submitted, was written in response to an independent auditor's findings and during the state auditor's investigation, but it was written before the charges were made. Logan was the city's fifth employee charged with embezzlement in a little more than a year.

By Eddie Logan
special to the Star Herald

To the Citizens of the City of Durant, I am submitting this writing for publication to inform you relative to concerns relates to this City. Prior to discussing various concerns relating to this City, allow me to quote Proverbs Chapter 3 Verse 5 & 6.5) Trust in the Lord with all thine Heart; and lean not to thine own understanding. 6) In all thy ways acknowledge him, and he shall direct thy paths.

Be assured that I ask the Board daily to direct by thinking, action, behavior in executing by duties as Mayor of this great City. Sure, I hold a Masters Degree from Fisk University, Nashville, Tennessee, and education degree is not a perquisite to be an effective administrator for municipality. However, asking for divine guidance in making sound choices and decisions is a perquisite. Making decisions for this City directly related to enhancing the quality of life for the residents of this City. Decisions made by me are based on needs. Needs are verified by research and analysis and prior to defining a conclusion.

I am committed to providing optional service for the Citizens of this City. On the basis of behavior exemplified by some of your Board of Alderpersons providing effective to you appears not to Mayor concerns. I will define some behavior exemplified by future date.

For example, some Board of Alderpersons have wasted time in communicating information to the State Auditor's Office relative to administrative decisions that I have, which for some unjustifiable reason they did not agree with. Be reminded that a make administrative decisions based on the needs of individuals that relates to services needed. Board of Alderpersons that have make call need to realize that calling the State Auditor's Office deter me from trying to provide efficient service for all Citizens of this City. Be reminded that the State Auditor's Office is the administrative office of this City.

Be reminded Board of Alderpersons that your in City Government is a legislative role, not an administrative. Some of you have tried to involve yourself (without my permission) in trying to involve yourself in the daily administrative aspect of City business. I have not requested and do not need your administrative assistance. To remind you in case you have forgotten your duties and responsibilities relative to your title of Board of Alderpersons, is defined: ordinace, law policy & procedures that relate to City Government.

Financial status

Rumors relating to the City has it that the City of Durant is broke and can not pay it's financial obligations. Allow me to set the record straight. Durant is not broke. Current financial obligations for the City are being paid. However, old outstanding financial obligations are being dealt with.

Projected income for the City of Durant is above what was collected last fiscal year: $130,000 + $31,000 + $50,000 + $20,000. The total above equals to two hundred thirty one thousand dollars ($231,000). The two hundred thirty one dollars are funds that we are currently collecting this fiscal year that we were not collecting last fiscal year. I will define the source of projected income at a later date. Concerns relative to former city employees that were accused of embezzling City funds in retrospect my thoughts are that this administration and Board of Alerepersons acted hastily in firing the accused employees. There is a term used in the legal arena, "You are innocent until proven guilty." It appears to me those accused employees should have been put on administrative leave without pay.

In Durant, theft continues unabated. On May 12, 2005, Phil Bryant announced the arrest and indictment of Durant Electrical Supervisor Robert Teague. According to the five-count indictment, during the period July through September 2004, Teague "willfully and feloniously converted to his own use" monies that came into his possession in violation of state law.

Barry Minkow perpetrated the famous ZZZZ Best Co. fraud in the 1980s. In this $1 billion scam, Minkow falsified financial statements and ran the stock price up from $12 to $80 per share. When he was twenty-one years old, Minkow was sentenced to twenty-five years in prison and ordered to pay $26 million in restitution. Today, the reformed thirty-eight-year-old ex-convict is pastor of the Community Bible Church in San Diego and heads the Fraud Discovery Institute. Minkow published a book, *Cleaning Up*, in January 2005 that detailed his misadventures with ZZZZ Best, a carpet cleaning company. Minkow, wearing an orange prison jumpsuit as a warning, now speaks to groups of executives about fraud.

The *CFO* (Chief Financial Officer) journal published an interview with Minkow in January 2005. Minkow made the following points that those entrusted with public monies and those who have stolen public monies should heed:

> (T)he best way to stop fraud is to talk people out of perpetrating it in the first place by doing two things: increasing the perception of detection and increasing the perception of prosecution.
>
> [The Sarbanes-Oxley federal law] hit a common denominator of corporate fraud—bypassing systems of internal controls. I would not have been able to perpetrate the ZZZZ Best fraud if I had not been able to bypass the system of internal controls. And you know who the heroes are now—the internal auditors . . .
>
> I don't care if anyone goes to jail. The number one thing white collar criminals need to do is give the money back to those hurt the most.
>
> [Asked when he would be satisfied that he had paid his debt to society, Minkow replied]: I won't be. Union bank had a $7 million loan [to ZZZZ Best], and I have a long way to go. But I haven't missed a payment in nine years. They've gotten over $100,000 this year alone.

It is hoped that this book will help increase the perception of detection and prosecution of embezzlement of public monies in Mississippi. It is also hoped that this book paints the personnel of the Office of the State Auditor as the heroes they truly are.

Sources

Preface

Clarion-Ledger (Jackson)—2-19-1999; 8-26, 9-19, 23, 11-18-2001; 2-4-2002;
12-24-2003
Enterprise-Journal (McComb)—6-14-2000
Meridian Star—5-22, 27, 7-31-2002
Southern Herald (Liberty)—5-20-2004
Starkville Daily News—5-31-2002
OSA Media Release 1-30, 3-6-2002
OSA Web Site

Introduction

W. Steve Albrecht, *Fraud Examination*, Thomson South-Western, Mason, OH
(2003)
David Jeremiah, *Searching for Heaven on Earth: How to Find What Really Matters in Life*, Integrity Publishers, Nashville (2004)
Bonita K. Peterson and Paul E. Zikmund, "10 Truths You Need to Know about
Fraud," *Strategic Finance* (May 2004)
Curtis Wilkie, *Dixie: A Personal Odyssey Through Events That Shaped the
Modern South*, Scribner, New York (2001)
Corporate Crime Reporter, "Public Corruption in the United States," January 16,
2004
The Mississippi Code
WhiteCollarCrimeFYI.com

Chapter 1. Chancery and Circuit Clerks

William M. (Mel) Williams, Greene County Chancery Clerk
Clarion-Ledger (Jackson)—8-5-2002; 8-18-2005
Greene County Herald—4-29-2004
Hattiesburg American—6-16-2004
Mississippi Press (Pascagoula)—8-5-2002
Sun Herald (Biloxi) 6-17-2004

Court Records: *State of Mississippi v. William M. Williams*
OSA Records
Darrell Chance, interviews (oral and written), September 2004 through summer 2005
Richard (Ricky) Earl Churchwell, George County Chancery Clerk
    Clarion-Ledger (Jackson)—9-4-2003
    Hattiesburg American—7-24-2002
    Sun Herald.com 7-24-2002; 5-15, 16-2003; 9-3, 4-2003
    Court Records: *State of Mississippi v. Ricky Earl Churchwell*
    OSA Media Release 7-23, 11-5-2002; 5-15-2003
    OSA Records
    Darrell Chance, interview 8-20-2004
Steve Duncan, Madison County Chancery Clerk
    Mississippi Office of the Attorney General Release 3-20-2002
    Clarion-Ledger (Jackson)—6-13-2002, 1-29-2003
    Madison County Herald—1-30-2003
    Madison County Journal—4-10, 5-2, 5-16-2002
    Sun Herald (Biloxi)—3-21-2002
    Court Records: *United States of America v. Stephen E. Duncan*
    OSA Media Release 1-28-2003
    OSA Records
    E-mail from Wallace Collins 9-7-2005
Larry Koon, Union County Chancery Clerk
    Clarion-Ledger (Jackson)—4-14-1999
    New Albany Gazette—2-3, 4-9, 6-30, 10-27, 12-22-1999
    LexisNexis AP 4-13, 6-29, 12-24-1999; 1-8-2002
    OSA Media Release 6-28-99, 9-18-2000
    Court Records: *State of Mississippi v. Larry Koon*
    OSA Web Site
Lynn Presley, Jackson County Chancery Clerk
    Clarion-Ledger (Jackson)—12-2-1998; 10-5-1999; 6-15-2001
    Mississippi Press—11-1-2000
    Sun Herald (Biloxi)—10-30, 11-21, 12-1, 4, 6-1998; 4-24, 5-18, 7-2,10, 10-5, 6, 9, 12-4-1999; 1-11-2000; 3-21, 22, 23, 31, 4-19-2001
    Court Records: *United States of America v. William Lynn Presley, Donald S. Hearn, Sr., and Donald S. Hearn, Jr.; William Presley v. State of Mississippi*
    Darrell Chance, interview 8-20-2004
    E-mail from Ben Norris 5-20-2005
    OSA Records
Lisa Jenkins, Tallahatchie County Deputy Circuit Court Clerk
    Charleston Sun-Sentinel—5-28-1998
    Court Records: *State of Mississippi v. Lisa C. Jenkins*
    OSA Records
    Mississippi Department of Public Safety Criminal Investigation Bureau Records
    E-mail from Walt Drane 4-22-2005

Linda Kay Olsen, Pontotoc County Deputy Circuit Court Clerk
Pontotoc Progress—3-18, 12-9-1998; 8-9-2000
Court Records: *State of Mississippi v. Linda Kay Olsen*
OSA Records
Gregory Jones, Supervisor of Finance, Harrison County Circuit Court
Clerk's Office
Clarion-Ledger (Jackson)—12-12-2002; 5-8-2003
Sun Herald (Biloxi)—9-29-2001; 12-11-2002; 5-13-2003
Court records: *State of Mississippi v. Gregory Eddie Jones*
OSA Records
OSA Media Release 5-5-2003

Chapter 2. Tax Assessors/Collectors

Evan Doss, Jr., Claiborne County Tax Assessor/Collector
Clarion-Ledger (Jackson)—11-4-1987; 12-29-1989; 11-23,12-23-1995; 5-14, 15,
6-29-1996; 2-17, 11-14-1997; 3-7-1998, 6-13-1998; 12-27-2002
Sun Herald (Biloxi)—12-27-2002
Court Records: *Mississippi Southern Bank v. Claiborne County, Mississippi,
Evan Doss, Jr., and Derek A. Henderson; United States of America v. Leola Dickey;
United States of America v. Evan Doss, Jr.; United States of America v. Evan
Doss Jr.; Evan Doss, Jr. Corp.*
Mississippi Attorney General Memorandum 2-25-2004
OSA Records
Mary Jones, Claiborne County Tax Assessor/Collector
Clarion-Ledger (Jackson)—5-28, 7-8-2004
Sun Herald (Biloxi)- 5-27-2004
Vicksburg Evening Post -10-5-2004
Court Records: *State of Mississippi vs. Mary Levon Jones*
OSA Records
Carla Chris Haley, Lincoln County Deputy Tax Collector
Daily Leader (Brookhaven)—2-6-2000
Court Records: *State of Mississippi v. Carla C. Haley*
OSA Records
OSA Web Site
Anna Addison Langston, Sunflower County Tax Assessor/Collector
Clarion-Ledger (Jackson)—9-18, 10-11, 16, 17- 2003; 11-2-2004; 2-26-2005
Enterprise-Tocsin (Indianola)—4-22-2004
Hattiesburg American—10-6-2003
Court Records: *State of Mississippi v. Anna Addison Langston*
OSA Media Release 6-6-2005
OSA Records
Stacy Montgomery, Lincoln County Deputy Tax Collector
Daily Leader (Brookhaven)—1-22, 2-3, 3-12, 21-2000

Court Records: *State of Mississippi v. Stacy Montgomery*
OSA Press Release 3-20, 4-1-2000
OSA Records

Stephanie Taylor-Beam, Itawamba County Deputy Tax Collector
Itawamba County Times 1-26-2000
Court Records: *State of Mississippi v. Stephanie Taylor-Beam*
OSA Media Release 5-1-2000
OSA Records

Chapter 3. Justice Court Clerks and Sheriffs' Employees

Cora Lou Thrash Carnley, Jackson County Sheriff's Department Bookkeeper
Mississippi Press (Pascagoula)—10-18-2001; 3-15-2003
Sun Herald (Biloxi)—10-18-2001; 1-22, 3-14, 15, 7-11-2003
Court Records: *State of Mississippi v. Cora Lou Thrash Carnley*
OSA Media Release 10-17-2001; 1-21-2003
OSA Records
E-mail from Jesse Bingham 5-18-05
Darrell Chance, interviews 2004–2005

Jennifer Green, Jasper County Deputy Justice Court Clerk
Jasper County News—1-28, 2-25, 4-29, 7-29-1998
Court Records: *State of Mississippi v. Jennifer Green*
OSA News Releases
OSA Records

Alberta Baker Longstreet, Leflore County Justice Court Clerk
Clarion-Ledger (Jackson)—12-17-2004
Greenwood Commonwealth—11-4-2003
Court Records: *State of Mississippi vs. Alberta Longstreet; United States v. Alberta
Baker Longstreet*
OSA Media Release 4-30, 5-4-2004
OSA Records
E-mail from Louise A. Stewart 5-2-2005
E-mail from Jesse Bingham 8-11-2005

Georgia Faye Moss, Rankin County Justice Court Clerk
Clarion-Ledger (Jackson)—9-19-2001
LexisNexis AP 8-9, 9-15-2001
OSA Web Site
OSA Media Release 8-9-2001
OSA Records
E-mail from Earl Smith 6-12-2005

Cassandra Price, Jefferson Davis County Justice Court Clerk
Prentiss Headlight—3-24, 31, 9-29-1999; 12-18 -2002
Court Records: *State of Mississippi v. Cassandra Price*
OSA Records

Shirley Ferrell, Belzoni Deputy City Clerk
  Prentiss Headlight—3-24, 31, 9-29-1999; 12-18-2002
  Court Records: *State of Mississippi v. Cassandra Price*
  OSA Records
Larry Niewoehner, Long Beach Municipal Court Clerk
  Sun Herald (Biloxi)—6-21, 28, 12-4-1998, 5-15-1999
  FBI Report
  OSA Records
Betty Sisco, Brookhaven Municipal Court Clerk
  Clarion-Ledger (Jackson)—1-17-1998
  Court Records: *State of Mississippi v. Betty Sisco*
  OSA Records
  E-mail from Walt Drane 4-25-2005
Beverly Taylor, Corinth Deputy City Clerk
  Daily Corinthian—2-10, 11, 12, 13, 14-1998
  Court Records: *State of Mississippi v. Beverly Jean Taylor*, U. S. Bankruptcy
  Court Records
  OSA Records

Chapter 5. Schools

Sharon Morgan, Columbus Municipal School District Bookkeeper
  Commercial Dispatch (Columbus)—2-26-1999
  Court Records: *State of Mississippi v. Sharon Morgan*
  Columbus Police Department Records
  OSA Media Release 9-30-2002
  OSA Records
Gerilyn Murphy, South Jones High School Bookkeeper
  Clarion-Ledger (Jackson)—2-7-2003; 1-13-2004
  Leader-Call (Laurel)—2-6-2003; 1-30-2004
  Court Records: *State of Mississippi v. Gerilyn E. Murphy*
  OSA Media Release—2-5-2003; 1-27-2004
  OSA Web Site
  OSA Records
Mary Nelson, Moss Point High School Bookkeeper
  Clarion-Ledger (Jackson)—11-22-2003; 8-6-2004
  Sun Herald (Biloxi)—11-21-2003
  gulflive.com—11-21-2003
  Court Records: *State of Mississippi v. Mary Nelson*
  OSA Media Release
  OSA Records
  E-mail from Earl Smith 7-11-2005

Bennie Tillman, Yazoo City Schools Athletic Director
   Clarion-Ledger (Jackson)—2-29, 2000
   Yazoo Herald—5-2-2002
   OSA Media Release 4-10-2000
   Court Records: *State of Mississippi v. Bennie Tillman*
   OSA Web Site
   OSA Records
   Materials faxed from Ardis Russell 6-17-2005
   E-mail from Earl Smith 6-22-2005
Scott Blouin, Pearl River Community College Remote Sensing Education and
Training Coordinator
   Hattiesburg American—12-2-2004
   Court Records: *State of Mississippi v. Scott M. Blouin and Janet M. Blouin; State*
   of Mississippi v. Janet M. Blouin; State of Mississippi v. Scott Blouin
   OSA Media Release
   OSA Records
James Hilton, Manager, Aquarium Admissions Office and Gift Shop, J. L. Scott
Marine Education Center and Aquarium, University of Southern Mississippi
   Mississippi Press (Pascagoula)—10-23-2003
   Sun Herald (Biloxi)—10-23-2003
   FBI Press Release 11-21-2003
   Court Records: *United States of America v. James Robert Hilton*
   OSA Records
   E-mail from Jesse Bingham 5-20-2005
   E-mail from Vijay Patel 4-21-2005
Lisa Lindsey, Mississippi State University Print Shop Clerk
   Starkville Daily News—8-20, 10-30, 11-3-2003
   Court Records: *State of Mississippi v. Lisa Lindsey*
   OSA Media Release 10-29-2003
   OSA Records
Danny Oswalt, Mississippi State University Housing Business Manager
   Clarion-Ledger (Jackson)—4-18-2002
   Starkville Daily News—7-2-2001
   Court Records: *State of Mississippi v. Danny Oswalt; State of Mississippi v.*
   William Shivers
   OSA Media Release 4-17-2002
   OSA Records
Greg Rector, University Emergency Physicians Practice Group Operations Manager,
University of Mississippi Medical Center
   Clarion-Ledger (Jackson)—2-9, 7-2-1999; 9-19-2001
   Court Records: *United States of America v. Gregory Neal Rector*
   United States Bankruptcy Court for Middle District of Tennessee (Rector,
   Gregory Neal—Debtor)
   OSA Records
   E-mail from Denver Smith 8-11-2005

Keith Blaylock, Director, Economic Development Partnership of Monroe County
Amory Advertiser—7-29-1998; 11-19-1999
Daily Journal Online—4-22-1999
LexisNexis AP 7-28, 8-6, 9-26-1998
Court Records: *State of Mississippi v. Keith Blaylock*
OSA Records

Fred J. Heindl, Executive Director, Mississippi Agribusiness Council
Clarion-Ledger (Jackson)—1-9, 10, 4-7, 5-22-2004; 3-31-2005
Hattiesburg American—1-11-2004
Court Records: *State of Mississippi v. Frederick J. Heindl; United States v. Glenn C. Patterson; United States v. Michael Walters; United States v. Jimmy R. Watt*
OSA Records
E-mail from Earl Smith 4-19-2005, 4-22-2005

Sandy Johnson, Director, Mississippi Firefighters Memorial Burn Association
Clarion-Ledger (Jackson)—9-7-2003; 1-8, 9-24, 26-2004; 5-17, 18, 25, 27, 6-3, 7, 13-2005
Delta Democrat Times (Greenville)—1-17, 19, 5-23, 9-9-2003; 1-9, 9-9-2004
Hattiesburg American—5-25-2005
Court Records: *State of Mississippi v. H. S. Sandy Johnson*
OSA Records

Deidre Ann Marshall, Bookkeeper/Accounting Audit Technician, Allied Enterprises of Harrison County, Mississippi Department of Rehabilitation Services
Sun Herald (Biloxi)—9-11-1999
Court Records: *State of Mississippi v. Deidre Ann Marshall*
AG Records
OSA Records
E-mail from Scott Womack 2-2-2005

Sandra Allan Stovall, Executive Director, Holly Springs Tourism and Recreational Facilities Bureau
Clarion-Ledger (Jackson)—9-28-2001
South Reporter (Holly Springs)—6-20-2002
Court Records: *State of Mississippi v. Sandra A. Stovall*
OSA Media Release 8-7-2001
OSA Records
Telephone interview with Mike Lynn 12-6-2004

Epilogue

Clarion-Ledger (Jackson)—1-3, 2-16, 18-2005
Hattiesburg American—2-16-2005
Star-Herald (Koscuisko)—5-13-2004
OSA Press Release 2-15-2005, 5-12-2005
CFO (January 2005)

Index